370.19342
D93m

124613

DATE DUE			

A Moderate Among Extremists

Dwight D. Eisenhower and the School Desegregation Crisis

James C. Duram

Nelson-Hall nh Chicago

In memory
of
Alfred H. Kelly,
who influenced some of us
far more than he ever knew.

LIBRARY OF CONGRESS CATALOGING IN PUBLICATION DATA

Duram, James C., 1939–
   A moderate among extremists.

   Bibliography: p.
   Includes index.
   1. School integration—United States.   2. Eisenhower,
Dwight D. (Dwight David), 1890–1969.   3. School
integration—Law and legislation—United States.
I. Title.
LC214.2.D87   370.19'342   81–542
ISBN 0–88229–394–X (cloth)   AACR2
ISBN 0–88229–788–0 (paper)

Contents

"So, let us remember that there are people who are ready to approach this thing with the moderation, but with the determination to make progress that the Supreme Court asked for.

"If ever there was a time when we must be patient without being complacent, when we must be understanding of other people's deep emotions, as well as our own, this is it.

"Extremists on neither side are going to help this situation, and we can only believe that the good sense, the common sense, of Americans will bring this thing along, and the length of time I am not even going to talk about; I don't know anything about the length of time it will take."

---

*Transcript of presidential press conference, 24 March 1956, Whitman File (Press Conference Series), Box 4, Dwight D. Eisenhower Presidential Library, Abilene, Kansas.

Preface

History is most easily written and enjoyed by those exposed to success stories with happy endings. Historians, though, are equally obligated to examine those aspects of the human experience which have resulted in controversy, frustration, confrontation, and bitterness. The general subject of this book, the Eisenhower administration's response to the crisis precipitated by the United States Supreme Court's decisions in the 1954 and 1955 school segregation cases, is in this category. It is a story of sadness, disappointment, and the failure of good intentions—one which reveals much about President Dwight D. Eisenhower's personality, the nature of his administration, and their interacting reaction to one of the most critical issues confronting Americans in this century.

Though the strong emotions have only partially subsided in the two and one-half decades since the decisions, sufficient time has elapsed and sources discovered to develop an accurate reconstruction and analytical perspective on the events and personalities involved. In his review essay, "Working on Ike," Elmo Richardson, the author of a significant monograph on the Eisenhower presidency, outlined what he regarded as the proper approach that historians should develop to that topic: "Extensive research into the barely worked quarry of official and personal archives will ultimately establish in full the nature and significance of the Eisenhower administration."[1] What follows is a study utilizing this approach. It is the product of some ten years of sporadic research conducted primarily in what is the most important of the "quarries" noted by Richardson, the Dwight D. Eisenhower Presidential Library in Abilene, Kansas.

It is the thesis of this work that Eisenhower's approach to the desegregation crisis which developed during his presidency was a consistent, though often ineffective and even frustrating one, which was the normal outgrowth of his cautious nature, his particular definition of effective leadership, and his belief in the limited scope of executive authority in federal-state relationships. This study, then, is neither an apologia nor a condemnation of his actions, but rather an attempt to present an in-context perspective on the causes and some of the effects of Eisenhower's behavior. The particular emphasis of the work is on the president's own perception of the problems generated by the Supreme Court's decisions in the 1954 and 1955 school segregation cases through examination of his often sharply contrasting public statements and private comments on the desegregation crisis. Hopefully, such an approach will enable us to develop understanding of the president's perception of the problems confronting him, their causes, and the ways he felt they could be overcome by his practice of moderation.

This historical reconstruction of a most crucial aspect of the Eisenhower administration's civil rights policies is something far different than it started out to be. It had its inception in the long-standing desire of this writer to do a book-length study of the significance of the school segregation cases. Because of several extended delays during the course of my research on that project caused by such things as a Fulbright professorship and additional postdoctoral studies in The Netherlands, the arrival of another heir, the development of new undergraduate history courses, and completion of a volume about Norman Thomas, I came to the realization that other scholars had made better use of their time than I had. Authors such as Albert P. Blaustein and Clarence Clyde Ferguson, Jr., Loren Miller, Jack Greenberg, and, most recently, Richard Kluger have produced a series of competent studies on all aspects of the segregation cases.[2] The first three chapters which describe the historical background of the school segregation issue in as nontechnical language as possible are, however, a tribute to at least the partial fulfillment of my original dream.

At about the same time that I was surrendering my original intention in the face of reality, a second and equally important realization came to mind. Though there were opinions floating around, several of which were highly emotional in tone and content, there had been little serious nonpartisan analysis of the Eisenhower administration's civil rights policies. Since I was already deeply immersed, perhaps "inundated" is a better word, in the voluminous materials on civil liberties in the collections of the Eisenhower Library, the transition from more purely constitutional to presidential history was less traumatic and more feasible than it might otherwise have been. In addition, the process whereby court decisions make their way into actual practice has long fascinated me. Perhaps for that reason and out of insecurity, then, I chose to stay in an area of history related to my field of expertise and original intentions.

All this aside, it is my hope that this study and subsequent ones utilizing the massive collection of source materials on the Eisenhower presidency will contribute to a more dispassionate assessment of the people and events of that era. Fortunately, there are signs, if one notes the recent spate of monographs and bibliographic essays on that topic, that such a reassessment is underway. Charles C. Alexander, Herbert S. Parmet, and Gary W. Reichard's recent works suggest that those involved in that reexamination of the Eisenhower presidency will avoid the extremes of emotion, "Schadenfreude," and political partisanship which have characterized the historiography of the cold war years in general and the Truman presidency in particular.[3] Only time will tell, of course, whether subsequent authors of more specialized aspects of the Eisenhower period will maintain the judicious, yet critical, approach reflected in the works of those authors cited above as they present more detailed pictures of both Dwight D. Eisenhower and the details of his administration.

There is still another important point which deserves mention in this preface. This study is written in a time regarded as the "post-idealistic" period by Americans who have examined the entire question of racial equality in America. Its subject centers on a person, events, and actions of an earlier, more optimistic time when neither the problems nor the solutions offered for them seemed as complex and as ineffective as many of them do today.

Much—possibly far too much—is still being written about the school segregation cases. Far too little beyond the generalizations which satisfy political expediency, our omnipresent demand for stereotypes, or our tendency to simplify complex human events has been written about the personalities and events which shaped the Eisenhower administration's response to the school segregation issue. A large number of scholars, for example, have cited and bemoaned the seeming unwillingness of the Eisenhower administration to vigorously enforce the segregation decisions because of the exposed position in which they left the Supreme Court and the federal district courts. Writing in 1976, for example, Archibald Cox, the distinguished legal scholar, typified this charge when he asserted: "For half a decade after *Brown* there was no significant executive or legislative support for school desegregation, and progress was halting under judicial decree."[4] It is my hope that the following study will provide a valid frame of reference in which to assess the validity of such charges, one which accurately portrays the problem Eisenhower and the members of his administration confronted.

Finally, a few remarks about the organization of this work are in order. It is divided into four parts of greatly varying length. The first part, chapters 1–3, is a reconstruction of some of the salient features of the historical evolution of the desegregation issue which culminated in the school segregation cases of 1954 and 1955. The second part, chapters 4–10, examines President Eisenhower's reaction to the desegregation crisis during his two terms. It is an in-depth study of his pre-1954 beliefs, his response to the 1954 and 1955 decisions, his behavior during the rising tide of defiance to court-ordered desegregation which culminated in the Little Rock crisis in the autumn of 1957, and his efforts on behalf of civil rights legislation from 1956–1960. The third part of this work, chapters 11–13, is an extended case study of the impact of the president's moderate approach to the desegregation issue on his administration's proposals for federal aid to education. Emphasis in this part of the study is on the complicating effect the school segregation issue had on other aspects of administrative policy. The last part of the work, chapter 14, is an attempt to present some conclusions about the historical significance of Eisenhower's reaction to the school segregation crisis, with particular attention to what that reaction says about the validity of the earlier and more recent views of his presidency.

Acknowledgments

No book is ever really the product of a single individual. I would like to acknowledge the financial assistance given by the Wichita State University Faculty Research Fund and Dean Lloyd M. Benningfield, its understanding chairman. To my close friend David Haight and to numerous other members of the superbly competent archival staff of the Dwight D. Eisenhower Presidential Library go my sincere thanks for their assistance in providing the massive amounts of materials on which this study is primarily based. One cannot help but develop a fondness for people one has worked with so well over such a long period of time. The same must be said for the assistance given me by Russell E. Dybdahl, Thoburn Taggart, Jr., Dale R. Schrag, Kenneth C. Knight, and other members of the Wichita State University Ablah Library Reference Department as well as numerous persons connected with the Columbia University Oral History Collection, the Library of Congress, and the United States Supreme Court Library.

Especially important was the encouragement and criticism I received from John Rydjord, Phillip D. Thomas, William E. Unrau, Donald M. Douglas, James Gray, George W. Collins, John E. Dreifort, and the rest of my colleagues in the Department of History at Wichita State University. The intellectually stimulating atmosphere which they have preserved in this time of crisis in the humanities is wondrous to behold. Most importantly, my wife, Eleanor, deserves special thanks for her research assistance, patience, advice, and the care shown in her typing of this manuscript. All of these things she accomplished in addition to the increased family responsibilities which she assumed to free me for work on this study.

Chapter 1

The Long Prelude

The battle against segregated education in the United States can best be understood as a part, perhaps the most important part, of the continuing struggle of the black man to achieve full equality and a just share of the American dream. Essential to an understanding of that struggle is an awareness of the impact of the slave experience upon American blacks and, more significantly, upon the whites who dominated the society in which they both lived. Although the Civil War resolved the argument about the nature of the Union, it did not specify or define the status of the newly freed slaves. The majority of whites after 1865 long remained convinced that the black man, though no longer a slave, was still an inferior being.

Many of the economic, social, and political manifestations of this assumption surfaced in a vehement debate about the status of the black freedmen that developed in the post–Civil War years. One of the principal aspects of this debate was a discussion of what should be the nature and goals of education for blacks.[1] The belief in black inferiority held by so many white Americans provided a powerful rationale for those persons advocating separate schools for the two races.

1

Another important factor influencing this debate was the belief of nineteenth-century Americans that education provided a means of upward social mobility.[2] In the immediate postwar period, both the advocates and detractors of full citizenship for the freedmen sensed the power of education as a means of social change. This awareness proved, in the long run, to be a major motivating force behind the creation of potent legal arguments by the forces favoring and opposing desegregation of public schools. As Carl N. Degler has noted:

> Individuals expect the schools to assure them of an improving livelihood, while society as a whole expects the schools to solve difficult and recalcitrant problems like segregation and racism. Indeed, the heated and sometimes violent conflicts over the nature and purpose of schools, which have punctuated the life of many American communities in the last few years, must be viewed as a measure of the exaggerated value Americans attach to education and the common school.[3]

It was perhaps inevitable that the question of segregated education would become a significant legal conflict. Most of the significant social issues in American history have been translated into judicial conflicts. The nature of our judicial process, with its emphasis on finality of decision and our traditional faith in its viability as a means of conflict resolution, encouraged the victims of segregation to challenge the constitutionality of separate schools in the courts. The result has been the creation of a massive amount of case law and legal precedents which reflect the complexity and longevity of the constitutional debate about this issue in America.

Roberts: The Creation of a Convenient Precedent

The initial legal attack on segregated education occurred before the Civil War in the classic *Roberts* v. *City of Boston* case, decided in 1849.[4] The case provides an early foretaste of the bitter frustration blacks experienced for so long in their struggle to destroy the legal basis of separate schools in the United States. The legal arguments presented by both sides in the case and the Supreme Court of Massachusetts' decision were reargued again and again in subsequent cases. The *Roberts* decision thus became one of the major precedents cited in support of segregated education in the post–Civil War period.

The basic questions raised in the case about the legal status of separate schools have proven to be of such long-range importance that an examination of them is in order.

In 1849, the father of five-year-old Sarah Roberts, a black, brought suit against the Boston School Committee on the grounds that its use of a separate, dilapidated school for black children violated the equality for all persons guaranteed by the Massachusetts Constitution. As a further argument against school segregation, Roberts cited a legislative act of 1845 forbidding exclusion of any child from the public school system. The *Roberts* case was argued by Charles Sumner, a distinguished attorney and orator who was soon to emerge as a leading spokesman of the antislavery cause.

Sumner based his principal argument on the grounds that all persons were equal before the law and that Massachusetts law failed to create or recognize racial distinctions. He further maintained that a separate school for black children was inconvenient because of the distance it was located from their homes. He concluded his argument with the statement that segregation "tends to create a feeling of degradation in the blacks, and of prejudice and uncharitableness in the whites."[5]

The similarity between the last argument used by Sumner in the *Roberts* case and the Supreme Court's conclusion in its *Brown* decision of 1954 that segregation is "inherently unequal" is striking.

Massachusetts Chief Justice Lemuel Shaw, in deciding against Roberts, held that the only question before the court was whether or not the requirement for separate schools for black children was a violation of the equality before the law to which they were entitled. Shaw held that the Boston School Committee had been vested by the state in an appropriate use of its police power with the rights to distribute and classify schoolchildren, and that the good of both black and white children was best obtained by separate educational facilities. Emphasizing that prejudice was neither created nor destroyed by law, Shaw held that the Boston School Committee in practicing segregation was not violating the legal guarantees of equality possessed by all citizens of Massachusetts.

Although the segregated school in Boston was eventually abolished by state legislation in 1855 in the midst of the abolitionist fervor that swept Massachusetts, the *Roberts* decision put forth what a number of scholars regard as the first judicial rationale of the "separate but equal" doctrine, which, with the Supreme Court's acceptance of it in *Plessy* v. *Ferguson* in 1896, became the legal basis of segregated education in America until the *Brown* decision of 1954.[6] The *Roberts* case was commonly cited as a justification for the constitutionality of separate schools in both state and federal cases from 1849 onward. Its prominent place in the briefs presented by the states in the five cases argued under the *Brown* title in 1953 reiterates the continued faith that segregationists placed in its validity as a sound precedent.[7]

Reconstruction: The Continuation of Segregation

The North's victory in the Civil War and the subsequent ten-year domination of Congress by the Radical Republicans did not result in first-class citizenship for the newly freed blacks. What began with the high hopes in 1867 of a number of idealist-reformers as a comprehensive political and social program to raise the status of the black man to one of equality in American life ended in 1876 with the removal of federal troops from the South and the emergence of white-dominated "redeemer" governments. A major policy of these governments was the institution of socioeconomic and legal practices that would perpetuate second-class citizenship and racial inequality for blacks.

How did the Radical hopes for a reconstructed South with the black as a full political participant come to such a disappointing, bitter end? Though dominant in the federal government from 1866 until the mid-1870s, the Radical wing of the Republican party, armed with the Fourteenth and Fifteenth Amendments which were specially designed as "black protection" amendments and the sweeping powers of the Civil Rights Acts that were passed to enforce them, nevertheless proved unable to create the necessary socioeconomic revolution the creation of black equality would have required.[8]

The causes of this failure were complex. Most important was the Radical failure to support black political power in the South with economic power. This failure combined with southern intransigence to frustrate Radical plans for a strong Republican party in the South. The tragic power of history was never more evident than in the South's refusal to accept the changes resulting from the Civil War. The use of terror, force, and economic coercion to topple the reconstructed Republican state governments is an example of the extent to which many southerners were willing to go to defend their traditional social beliefs.

The division among the Radicals themselves regarding motives, tactics, and goals was another factor in the failure. The continuing congressional opposition of Republican and Democratic conservatives also worked to limit the Radical attempts to build black political power. The same Congress that passed the Fourteenth Amendment segregated the schools in the District of Columbia.

The rapid acceleration of industrialization, with all of its confusing manifestations, soon pushed the aspirations and problems of Reconstruction into the background. The need for national unity and economic integration had a corrosive effect on the ideals of many of the Radicals. Enterprising Yankees came to look upon the South as a fertile market and an area for industrial expansion. Political leaders in the Republican party, the decisive ones, soon became aware of the political implications of this new industrialism. It could not subsist on the politics of "the bloody shirt." The disputed election of 1876 and the deal that followed it recognized belatedly the death of Radical Reconstruction. The long-standing belief of whites in both sections in black inferiority was soon reinforced by the newer notions of Anglo-Saxon racial purity and superiority which resulted from the impact of Social Darwinism in the United States. The winning of the West with its powerful distracting effect also played a role that cannot be ignored in the waning of national interest in Reconstruction.[9]

The collapse of Reconstruction was, then, the result of an interaction of complex forces whose impact was felt in many areas of American life. Just as its causes were complex, so were its results. One of these results, however, was certain: the collapse worked to perpetuate black inequality. It removed the protective shield of the federal government from the freedmen, thus leaving them without the political, economic, social, and soon, by decisions of the federal courts, the legal protections which were supposed to be theirs by virtue of the Fourteenth and Fifteenth Amendments.[10]

There is a certain degree of ironic truth in the charges of some modern historians, such as C. Vann Woodward, Kenneth M. Stampp, John Hope Franklin, and numerous black militants, that the national reconciliation after the Civil War was purchased at the price of the black people's continued inequality.[11] Such a view, however, should be kept in its proper perspective. The failure of Reconstruction was part of a massive shift in national goals and values which individuals were unable to resist. The prevalent prejudices of the period were so strong that Radical Reconstruction never stood a chance for success. Thaddeus Stevens, Charles Sumner, and the other idealists among the Radicals were ahead of their time.

It is with this background in mind that we turn to an examination of the important factors contributing to the development of segregated schools in the Reconstruction period. Looking first at the congressional treatment of school segregation, we see that, as Richard Bardolph has stated: "Contemporary scholarship relating to the Civil War Amendments leans to the view that the Fourteenth Amendment was probably not intended by its framers to prevent the segregation of Negroes in public schools."[12] As stated previously, the Thirty-ninth Congress created both the Fourteenth Amendment to guarantee equal rights for blacks and the segregation of the schools in the District of Columbia.

The question of the "intent of the framers" of the Fourteenth Amendment was, as were so many of the aspects presented in this background chapter, to be the subject for heated arguments in the school segregation cases in the 1950s. So intense was the debate on the history of the Fourteenth Amendment and so different were the conclusions of the contending sides that the Supreme Court turned away from history and relied instead on the findings of sociologists and social psychologists as the basis of its May 1954 segregation decision. As Albert P. Blaustein and Clarence Clyde Ferguson, Jr., concluded in their excellent study of the segregation cases: "The nine men were on safe ground when they pinned the 'inconclusive' label on the intent of the Congressmen who framed and voted on the Fourteenth Amendment."[13] Some members of the Thirty-ninth Congress did assume that the Fourteenth Amendment proscribed segregated schools, while others did not. Alfred H. Kelly's research indicates that subsequent attempts of the Radical Republicans and other friends of the black people to legislate against school segregation also sharply divided the Congress and came to naught.[14]

As Radical Reconstruction waned in the face of the numerous forces cited above, the "redeemer" governments in the South, after some initial overt pretense at including blacks in politics, moved to perpetuate white supremacy by placing a variety of legal restrictions on the black freedman.[15] Restrictions on mixed marriages (also frowned upon in a number of western and northern states), unequal punishments for the same crimes, exclusion from jury service, and other discriminations against "persons of color" all constituted parts of a legal configuration which operated to keep the races separate and the black person unequal. It should not seem surprising that the southern states utilized separate schools for whites and blacks as a basic means of perpetuating this pattern.[16] The pattern of permanent separate schools was fully developed in all of the southern and many of the other states by the end of Radical Reconstruction in 1876.

Segregated public schools were not, of course, an original creation of the white "redeemer" governments which emerged with the downfall of Radical Reconstruction in the South. As Bardolph reminds us:

> State constitutional and statutory support of segregation in the public schools—whether by failure to include black children of the state, or by authorizing or requiring separate schools—were commonplace before 1865. Even under Radical Reconstruction, southern states were permitted to separate the races in schools. . . .[17]

Of the thirty-seven states in the Union at the time of the Fourteenth Amendment's passage, nine either established or continued to operate already-segregated school systems. These were: Indiana, Pennsylvania, New York, New Jersey, Illinois, Ohio, Kansas, Nevada, and Oregon. Two northern states—Connecticut and Michigan—outlawed segregation in their public schools at the time of the ratification of the Fourteenth Amendment. Nine other states maintained nonsegregated schools at the time of ratification.[18]

However, the pattern of separate schools that had fully developed in all of the southern and border states by the end of Reconstruction proved to be an important part of a total attempt at social separation of the races in a far more rigid sense than any known outside of the South. Though the provisions creating the separate school were written into the state constitutions or into the general laws of the state and though the extent and structure of the systems of public education varied from state to state, all repeated or paraphrased the expression found in chapter 13, section 35, of the *Mississippi Laws* of 1878 that "white and colored pupils shall not be taught in the same school-house, but in separate school-houses."[19] The pattern of race relations that came to characterize the emerging South after 1876 had at its heart a segregation designed to perpetuate the inferior socioeconomic and political status of the black person.[20] In this atmosphere, school segregation became a potent weapon in the hands of white supremacists, one which they regarded as fundamental for the preservation of the southern way of life.

Segregated education in the Reconstruction era and the decade that followed did not escape legal challenge. In a number of decisions, both state and federal courts faced the question of the legality of segregated education and in nearly all cases sustained it.[21] Many of these legal challenges occurred in northern or border states, and all denied that the practice of segregation of the races in the public schools was a denial of either the privileges-and-immunities clause and/or the equal protection clause of the Fourteenth Amendment. In this period, the legal doctrine enunciated by Chief Justice Shaw of the Supreme Court of Massachusetts in the earlier *Roberts* case came to be the pattern-setting precedent in most of these cases.[22]

State-enforced segregation was upheld successfully in Ohio, Indiana, California, New York, West Virginia, and Missouri. The supposed civil rights guarantees of the Fourteenth

Amendment were no match for the preferences of the judges for the segregation justified by reliance on the state police power in the *Roberts* precedent. As Harry S. Ashmore has noted: "It was perhaps symptomatic of the declining popular interest in the Negro cause that none of this litigation reached the United States Supreme Court."[23] It is also highly probable that those involved in the state cases were already aware of the Supreme Court's growing reticence to defend the civil rights of blacks. The Court in *Hall* v. *DeCuir,* an 1878 decision, made a reference to segregated schools as an example of the types of classifications which states could make for their citizens.[24]

The most well known and frequently cited state case of this type was *Ward* v. *Flood,* an 1874 decision of the California Supreme Court.[25] In this case, the parents of a black child in San Francisco tried, through the use of a writ of mandamus, to force her admittance to a white public school that was nearer to their home than the black school. The state court denied the request after rejecting the petitioner's argument that the refusal of the school principal to admit their child was a violation of the privileges-and-immunities and equal protection clauses of the Fourteenth Amendment. The California Supreme Court relied on the restrictive definition of the rights of natural citizenship which the United States Supreme Court had attributed to the privileges-and-immunities clause of the Fourteenth Amendment in its 1873 decision in the *Slaughterhouse* cases. It did this by holding that the privilege of public school attendance is not a right related to national citizenship. It rejected the equal protection arguments of the petitioner on the grounds that separate schools did not discriminate more heavily against one group than the other since both were excluded from each other's schools.[26]

In another decision often cited as a precedent by the advocates of segregated schools, the New York Court of Appeals in *People* v. *Gallagher* in 1883 upheld that state's 1864 school law which permitted segregated schools if school officials decided they were in the best interest of education in their respective districts.[27] In this case, the parents of the black child involved did not argue that she was being deprived of an equal education, but rather that she was not receiving it "at the precise place which would be most gratifying to her feelings."[28] Their attempt to use a writ of mandamus to force her admission to a white public school in Brooklyn was denied by the New York Court of Appeals on the grounds that the privileges-and-immunities and equal protection clauses of the Fourteenth Amendment had not been violated because:

> The right of the individual, as affected by the question in hand, is to secure equal advantages in obtaining an education at public expense, and where that privilege is afforded him by the school authorities, he cannot justly claim that his educational privileges have been abridged, although such privileges are not accorded him at the precise place where he most desires to receive them.[29]

Once again, the *Roberts* case was cited as a precedent justifying school segregation.

As the preceding cases illustrate, the state courts found little difficulty in narrowly construing the privileges-and-immunities and equal protection clauses of the Fourteenth Amendment so as to exclude the practice of segregated education from the list of restrictions which the amendment placed upon the states. As Loren Miller has emphasized in his fine study *The Petitioners: The Story of the Supreme Court of the United States and the Negro,* it is amazing that blacks continued to seek legal redress from the evils of segregation in the courts in view of the courts' long record of frustrating their attempts.[30] But it is important to remember that courts often reflect the trends, values, and prejudices of the society of which they are a part.

Nowhere was this more true in American constitutional development than in the years between the Civil War and the

First World War.[31] Racial equality and other egalitarian sentiments in American culture were subordinated to the demands of the emerging industrial order.[32] The Fourteenth Amendment, originally intended to protect blacks' freedom, was transformed through judicial interpretation into a protector of corporate property. It would be a long time before the civil rights of blacks would receive a sympathetic hearing before the Court on the grounds of Fourteenth Amendment guarantees.

1883–1896: The Trend Continues

The period from the end of Reconstruction to the First World War was marked by the hardening of the "color line" in American society. With the death of Radical Republicanism and the passing of Reconstruction, the Fourteenth and Fifteenth Amendments underwent a transformation through judicial interpretation in the federal courts which virtually destroyed their use as "black protection" amendments.[33]

Actually, the judicial modification of the Fourteenth Amendment took place on two levels. On the one hand, its scope with regard to black rights was construed very narrowly. On the other hand, its scope as a protector of business rights was greatly broadened through the ruling that corporations were artificial persons before the law whose rights were protected by a substantive interpretation of the Fourteenth Amendment's due process clause.[34]

The courts, in what proved to be one of the genuine ironies of American constitutional development, thus created a situation through selective inclusion and exclusion whereby the same amendment was used to circumscribe the rights of blacks at the same time it was used to expand those of corporations.[35] The causes of this dualistic judicial response were firmly rooted in the rapid industrialization of America that occurred from 1865 to 1914.

As Robert G. McCloskey's study of Supreme Court Justice

Stephen J. Field illustrates, the impact of capitalistic industrial materialism wrought striking changes in the American judicial mind regarding the relationship between property and individual civil rights in the post–Civil War decade. He stated:

> The disparities in Field's decisions are instructive because they reflect a shift in value premises which is characteristic not only of Field but of his age. . . . Evidently, the property right is the transcendent value; political ambition ranks next when it is relevant; and the cause of human or civil rights is subordinate to these higher considerations.[36]

This phase of our American constitutional development illustrates how closely trends of judicial decision making have been related to the predominant socioeconomic values in American society. Without an awareness of this fact, it is impossible to grasp the complexities at work in the historical evolution of the case precedents leading to the Supreme Court's school desegregation decision of 1954.

The most important of the two phases of Fourteenth Amendment development for those studying the legal background of segregated education is the judicial limitation of the scope of individual civil rights protected by that amendment. In a series of decisions beginning in the late 1870s and continuing through 1896, the United States Supreme Court effectively gutted the major clauses of the Fourteenth Amendment. C. Vann Woodward, in assessing this process, asserted that: "The court, like the liberals, was engaged in a bit of reconciliation—reconciliation between federal and state jurisdiction, as well as between North and South, reconciliation also achieved at the Negro's expense."[37]

After the Court narrowly defined the privileges-and-immunities clause in the 1873 *Slaughterhouse* cases, it enunciated a series of decisions restricting the use of the equal protection and due process clauses as protectors of black civil rights. The culmination of this trend occurred in the Court's decision in the 1883 *Civil Rights* cases when it held that the Fourteenth and Fifteenth amendments were only applicable to state-enforced segregation. Privately enforced segregation was ruled beyond the scope of the two amendments.[38]

Though not specifically related to school segregation, the Court in the *Civil Rights* cases surrendered to the growing tendency in both the South and the North to permit blatant segregation and discrimination against black Americans in nearly every aspect of life. The area of state-enforced segregation prohibited by the amendment was so narrowly construed as to be virtually meaningless. The subversion of the earlier intentions of the Radicals and other idealists who hoped to provide black Americans with a legal shield against discrimination was apparent in the *Civil Rights* cases.

Twelve years after the *Civil Rights* cases, the Supreme Court completed its attack on the civil rights guarantees of the Fourteenth Amendment in *Plessy* v. *Ferguson*. In that decision the Court held that segregated facilities in interstate railroad transportation were not in violation of the equal protection and due process clauses of the Fourteenth Amendment as long as the facilities were "substantially equal."[39] The long-time existence of segregated education was one of the major examples the Court's majority cited to justify its decision that laws requiring separation of the races did not fall within the practices forbidden by either the general interpretation of the Thirteenth Amendment or the equal protection clause of the Fourteenth Amendment. As Justice Henry B. Brown stated:

> Laws permitting, and even requiring, their separation in places where they are liable to be brought into contact do not necessarily imply the inferiority of either race to the other, and have been generally, if not universally, recognized as within the competency of the state legislatures in the exercise of their police power. The most common instance of this is connected with the establishment of separate schools

for white and colored children, which have been held to be a valid exercise of the legislative power even by courts of states where the political rights of the colored race have been longest and most earnestly enforced.[40]

The rise of the now famous "separate but equal" doctrine after the *Plessy* case as a justification for segregation in state-controlled and regulated facilities was to have sweeping and long-lasting effects in the field of public education. Although the Supreme Court justified the "separate but equal" doctrine of *Plessy* in part with the use of an obiter dictum which noted the existence of segregated schools, it did not rule directly on the constitutionality of such schools in that decision. The association of segregated schools with the "separate but equal" doctrine which arose in that case proved, however, to be a lasting one. Subsequent Supreme Court decisions upholding separate schools all cited the *Plessy* precedent and ignored the fact that the reference to segregated schools in the case was in an obiter dictum and not a specific point at issue in the case. As Harry S. Ashmore has noted: ". . . in the famous *Plessy* v. *Ferguson* case, the Court dragged Justice Shaw's precedent [in the *Roberts* case] into federal jurisprudence by a side door."[41] The demands of the times conspired with predominant judicial sympathies to obscure the highly questionable justification of segregated schools through the application of the *Plessy* precedent. The existence of segregated schools was used to justify the "separate but equal" precedent which in turn was used to justify segregated schools.

One justice objected strongly to the "separate but equal" doctrine enunciated by the Court's majority in the *Plessy* case. In an eloquent, renowned dissent, Justice John Marshall Harlan asserted that the doctrine was, in reality, a mask for the subordination of the black person. In words that foreshadowed the 1954 decision in the segregation cases, he asserted:

Our Constitution is color-blind, and neither knows nor tolerates classes among citizens. In respect of civil rights, all citizens are equal before the law. The humblest is the peer of the most powerful. The law regards man as man, and takes no account of his surroundings or of his color when his civil rights as guaranteed by the supreme law of the land are involved.[42]

Justice Harlan's plea, however, fell on deaf ears and the Court's dispensation in *Plessy* became the law of the land for fifty years.

1897–1930: The Plessy Doctrine Reigns Supreme

The application of the "separate but equal" doctrine, enunciated in the *Plessy* decision as a justification for separate schools, was not seriously challenged in the courts until the "graduate school" cases in the 1930s.

Why this judicial inaction on the part of blacks? Ashmore, in his seminal work, *The Negro and the Schools,* noted that despite the inequalities in southern schools and the movement toward increased segregation in the North, chances for judicial attack on the "separate but equal" doctrine were minimal because: "Many Southern Negroes apparently felt that legal action would endanger the delicate balance of their relationship with the dominant whites, while the Northern Negro leadership saw no hope of relief under the doctrine of *Plessy*."[43]

These feelings, the long series of federal court decisions which had narrowed the scope of the Fourteenth Amendment, and the general mood of white Americans all played a role in destroying the confidence of black Americans in the efficacy of legal action. Another important factor which helps to explain black inaction against segregated education in the years after *Plessy* was the U.S. Supreme Court's acceptance of "substantial equality" in place of "literal equality" of segregated facilities in its application of the "separate but equal" doctrine.

Only three cases which dealt with black education reached the Supreme Court between 1896 and 1930. None of these involved a direct challenge of the constitutionality of segregated schools. Each did, however, result in a discouraging decision for blacks.[44] Moreover, each reiterated the Supreme Court's acceptance of the applicability of the *Plessy* precedent to separate schools despite its failure to so rule in that opinion.

In the first case—*Cumming* v. *Richmond County Board of Education,* decided in 1899—the Court heard an application for relief from a group of black parents who called for the closing of two white high schools after a Georgia school board had closed the only black high school in the county.[45] The petitioners based their claim on the argument that their rights to equal protection of the laws were violated by the board's decision to close the black school.

In ruling that the relief required by the blacks was improper and the issue of racially separate schools was not before the Court, Justice Harlan noted:

> The education of people in schools maintained by state taxation is a matter belonging to the respective states, and any interference on the part of the Federal authority with the management of such schools cannot be justified except in the case of a clear and unmistakable disregard of rights secured by the supreme law of the land. We have here no such case to be determined.[46]

Here, the court illustrated how its recent narrow interpretation of the Fourteenth Amendment's equal protection clause could be combined with an acceptance of a broad view of the state police power to justify inequalities in education for blacks. As Kelly has observed, the *Cumming* case symbolized the Court's acceptance, by implication, of separate schools for whites and blacks.[47]

In 1908, the Supreme Court decided in *Berea College* v.

Kentucky that Kentucky could force a private college chartered by the state to enforce segregation of its student body against the will of its students and its administration.[48] Although the decision was based on technical grounds related to the state's right to exercise its police power over a private institution by forcing it to obey a charter written for it by the state legislature, the case clearly illustrated the Court's willingness to leave the question of segregated education up to the states.

The impact of the *Cumming* and *Berea* decisions upon the state courts was significant. They gave credence to the belief that the "separate but equal" doctrine was a constitutionally respectable one in the field of public education despite the lack of a specific ruling by the Supreme Court on its constitutionality. The rapidity with which *Plessy* became firm case precedent and judicial doctrine in the field of education is indicative of its usefulness to a society which was in the process of rationalizing the wisdom of segregation.

Gong Lum v. *Rice* in 1927 was the third and final case dealing with segregated education that reached the Supreme Court in the three decades after *Plessy*.[49] In it, the Court upheld the state of Mississippi's right to classify a Chinese child, Martha Lum, as "colored" and thus require her to attend a black school. The Court, in its opinion, referred to its previous ruling in the *Cumming* case that public school education was a matter of state concern and that the issue of separate schools and the classification of students had long been accepted as being within the power of the state legislature to decide without the interference of federal courts.[50]

The net effect of the Supreme Court's actions regarding segregated schools in the three decades after the *Plessy* decision was one of reinforcement of the idea that they were constitutionally respectable. As Loren Miller put it in his book, *The Petitioners: The Story of the Supreme Court of the United States and the Negro:*

The practical result was that lower federal and state courts fashioned a separate-but-equal formula for schools out of the Plessy, Cummings, [*sic*] and Berea cases, and in time the fiction grew that the Supreme Court had considered and determined that issue with finality, whereas the truth was that it had only skirted around the question and had spoken only by evasions and indirection.[51]

The *Plessy* doctrine stood supreme.

The inability to make progress against segregated education in the federal courts was accompanied by a corresponding lack of success on the part of blacks in the state courts. Taking their cue from federal court rulings that the practice of separate schools was a justifiable use of the state police power and acceptable under the equal protection clause of the Fourteenth Amendment, the state courts had little difficulty in beating back legal challenges to segregated education. Research by Richard Bardolph has revealed that

In the seven decades from 1865 to January 1, 1935, cases challenging the validity of school segregation reached state courts of last resort thirty-seven times, and in each instance the courts upheld the separate school. There were, in addition, some twenty-nine cases in which Negro plaintiffs managed to prevent segregation in states where there were no laws on the subject; but nowhere was the legal principle of school segregation successfully opposed. In twenty-eight suits, blacks initiated court action to compel the provision of more genuinely equal facilities in the separate schools, and in only nine of these instances were they wholly or in part successful.[52]

The results of such a failure were readily apparent. Bardolph also noted:

In 1938 nearly half the states still either required (as did all the southern states) or expressly permitted segregation in the schools. In 1935–1936, when the gap had in fact narrowed, current expenditures per pupil in daily attendance in ten southern states were $17.04 for Negroes, compared with nearly three times that amount for whites, $49.30. . . . These figures reflected lower salaries for teachers in Negro schools, substantially larger classes than those in white schools, less transportation, shorter school terms, and inferior physical facilities.[53]

The results of the "separate but equal" doctrine in education were truly tragic. The unwillingness of the federal and state courts to interfere with established practices and the predominant racial attitudes of the white society are readily apparent. Only when the courts were faced with evidence that the public mood was changing did the judges begin to re-examine the implications of the *Plessy* doctrine.

Chapter 2

The NAACP Goes to Court

The National Association for the Advancement of Colored People, the organization that was to become the prime mover in the attack on segregation, was established in 1910 by a small group of black and white liberals who were appalled at the increasing growth of violence against blacks throughout the country.[1] William English Walling, writing in a 1908 issue of the *Independent* about the Springfield, Illinois, race riot of that year, expressed the kind of concern which led to the founding of the association when he stated:

> Either the spirit of Lincoln and Lovejoy must be revived and we must come to treat the Negro on a plane of absolute political and social equality, or Vardaman and Tillman will soon have transferred the race war to the North. . . . Yet who realizes the seriousness of the situation, and what large and powerful body of citizens is ready to come to their aid![2]

The NAACP was created by Walling and those like him who felt that black people needed an organization to protect their rights.

Very early in its existence, W. E. B. Du Bois, one of the association's founders, announced the goals of the NAACP in an editorial in its official publication, the *Crisis*. These goals included:

(1) the abolition of enforced segregation;
(2) equal educational opportunities for Negroes and whites;
(3) enfranchisement of the Negro;
(4) enforcement of the Fourteenth and Fifteenth amendments.[3]

Despite limited financial resources, struggles over leadership, and disagreements as to the best means to achieve its stated goals, the association did manage to develop major campaigns on behalf of antilynching legislation and black voting rights during its early years.[4] However, events soon conspired to cause the NAACP to become increasingly confident that its legal activities could be used as a means of overcoming segregation.

The origins of the increasing legal orientation of the association can be traced to a number of striking successes in court cases during its first decade of existence on behalf of black rights. By 1919, the association had seen a number of its local branches successfully fight off attempts of northern states to introduce segregated schools. Perhaps the best example of such action could be seen in the successful legal fight of the Ypsilanti, Michigan, branch to block the creation of a separate black high school in 1915.[5] The attempt of the Kansas legislature to broaden its school segregation laws to permit second-class as well as first-class cities to maintain racially segregated schools was defeated in 1919 at least in part because of massive NAACP pressure on the state legislature and the threat of lawsuits.[6] Agitation was initiated and court action threatened in the Deep South by NAACP branches in the same period over the issue of unequal appropriations for black and white schools.[7] These and similar local actions added to the confidence of the fledgling association that the resort to court action or the threat of it could, in many instances, bring redress of wrongs caused by segregation.

Even more important as a cause of growing NAACP confidence in the use of legal action was its success in a number of cases decided by the U.S. Supreme Court. Beginning in 1915 when the court in *Guinn* v. *United States* struck down the "grandfather clause" which had been used to disenfranchise blacks and in 1917 when the Court struck down residential segregation ordinances in *Buchanan* v. *Warley,* NAACP attorneys scored what proved to be an impressive string of victories against the legal foundations of segregation in American life.[8] Thus, very early in its existence, the NAACP was drawn by success toward the evolution of what was to become its most important activity, a comprehensive legal attack on segregation in the United States.

This legal activism, it should not be forgotten, was initiated somewhat sporadically at first and continued to be only one aspect of the NAACP's efforts to secure equality for blacks. Undoubtedly, the early leaders of the NAACP regarded legal action as a defensive weapon, one which could be used to protect blacks from some of the worse effects of segregation. The realization of the potential of court action as an offensive weapon to be used as the basis of a comprehensive attack on segregation did not develop until a later time, after the NAACP had developed a clear-cut set of integrationist objectives.

As the result of its early experiences, the NAACP legal staff, ably led by the brilliant Moorfield Storey, had by 1919 developed a number of criteria and principles that became the foundation of the legal strategy that was to bring the association numerous triumphs in its legal battle against segregation.[9] Charles F. Kellogg, the leading historian of the early history of the NAACP, aptly summarized these principles:

> Two criteria determined whether or not the Association would enter a case. It must involve, first, discrimination based upon color and, second, some fundamental right of citizenship. Moorfield Storey had firmly impressed upon the

NAACP that out-of-state counsel was at a serious disadvantage and that as far as possible local attorneys should handle local cases until they reached the federal courts. Storey himself would not argue any case before the United States Supreme Court which he felt he would not be able to maintain, and twice he refused to argue cases which he was convinced lacked the proper legal basis for making a successful appeal. The adoption of this policy had become well established by 1919 and accounts for the astounding number of victories in later years in the United States Supreme Court. . . .

Another legal policy laid down was that of making local branches financially responsible so far as possible for litigation instituted by them with the advice and approval of the national legal committee. The Association tried to concern itself only with cases involving people with staying power, able to follow through and to take advantage of the rights won for them at law in spite of ostracism and other social pressures.[10]

These principles were the pragmatic result of the association's early experiences in the courts. The policy proved to be a firm foundation a decade later when the NAACP decided that the time was ripe for a legal attack on segregated education. The habits of patience and deliberate action developed in the early cases proved decisive in the long run.

It was, perhaps, inevitable that the success of its legal attack on so many other facets of segregation would result eventually in one on segregated education. The NAACP almost from its inception was interested in the question. It had initially concentrated its efforts on a campaign to secure equal opportunities for blacks in the public schools of the South by insisting upon fair distribution of educational funds.[11] As part of this early attempt, the NAACP became one of the first organizations in this century to advocate federal aid to education. Its executive board, after considerable debate, decided in 1914 that the most effective means of marshalling broad public support for such a program would be through the demand that such aid be made available to all Americans regardless of race.[12] The type of legislation desired by the NAACP did not become a reality until fifty years later because of its implications for segregated education, the South's control of congressional committees, and the general indifference of most Americans toward such aid. The frustration of this approach to the improvement of black education after two decades of effort was one of the factors leading the NAACP to shift to a legal attack on the inequalities of segregated education in the 1930s.

Why, given the strong success of the NAACP's legal attack on segregation in other areas of American life, did it take so long to mount such an attack on segregated education? Disagreement in the NAACP leadership about how best to approach the problem was certainly a significant aspect of the delay. The association's awareness of the formidable legal edifice constructed in defense of segregation was certainly another factor. The very breadth of the NAACP's activities in the first two decades of its existence and its relatively limited funds were also inhibiting factors. Faced with these realities, Walter White, who emerged as the leader of the NAACP in the mid-1920s, concentrated on directing the energies of the association to activities which promised more immediate returns.[13] Campaigns against lynching, opposition to government appointments for men with racist biases, and the defense of individual blacks on an ad hoc basis formed the heart of the association's activities in the twenties. Such activities reinforced the already well-established defense-mindedness in the association and prevented the development of an activistic, coordinated antisegregation strategy based on a clearly integrationist program.[14]

The Importance of Atmosphere

The Great Depression ushered in a period of striking change which greatly altered the social, political, economic, and judicial context in which the NAACP was forced to operate. The Depression and the subsequent New Deal, in the words of Jack Greenberg, "coincided with and created a climate conducive to new legal and social relationships."[15] Before proceeding to a discussion of how the NAACF developed its attack on segregated education, a discussion of these striking changes is necessary. Hopefully, it will increase our understanding of the relationship between social change and constitutional development that culminated in the school segregation decision.

At the heart of these changes was a "second revolution" in the status of the black Americans, one that would take them far beyond the second-class citizenship which the destruction of slavery and the following Reconstruction period had bestowed upon them. Alfred H. Kelly, while emphasizing the ongoing nature of this revolution, characterized it as one which "was to inaugurate the progressive destruction of the racial caste system in the United States and to commence at the same time the genuine integration of the Negro into the social, economic and political fabric of American life."[16] The "second revolution" in the status of the black people proved to be one which would fulfill the dreams that remained after the frustrations of the earlier one.

While there is a need for a more comprehensive study of the specific details of this "second revolution," a number of its essential features are evident. It originated in the development of what Kelly described as "numerically important and hence politically significant" black communities in the big cities of the North. These large concentrations of blacks were the result of successive waves of migration from the states of the Old South by people in search of a better life.[17] Despite the tremendous economic and social discrimination experienced by members of these northern black communities, the persons living in them did have the right to vote. Black leaders soon utilized this voting power in the urban political machines.[18]

The onset of the Depression and the coming of the New Deal gave what had been up to that time highly localized pockets of black political power an access to national politics. The black voter became an important component of the New Deal political coalition forged by Franklin D. Roosevelt in the early 1930s. Thus, as Kelly noted, "For the first time since Reconstruction, the Negro had a recognized position in a winning political combination of national scope."[19] The resulting tie between a sense of political power and the long-cherished dream of first-class citizenship which developed in the thirties was a natural one. Access to political power created confidence among many American black leaders that the time was ripe for an expanded attack on segregation.[20]

Lest this discussion suffer from idealistic oversimplification, however, it must be pointed out that the New Deal, though it had brought blacks back to national political importance, also worked in many ways to inhibit a more rapid movement toward first-class citizenship for them. One such negative aspect of the New Deal was its intense preoccupation with the economic problems caused by the Great Depression. Distressed urban blacks benefited greatly from such New Deal programs as direct relief, CCC, WPA, and PWA projects. Preoccupation with the struggle for survival greatly inhibited the development of an élan for desegregation among blacks in the early thirties.[21] The very nature of the New Deal coalition also prevented it from becoming an effective vehicle for desegregation. Roosevelt's coalition within the Democratic party consisted of an uneasy combination of urban political machines—of which blacks were a crucial component—and white southern conservative Democrats who maintained themselves in power through patently segregationist politics in the South. The dominance of the congressional wing of the party by such southerners necessitated Roosevelt's reliance upon them and prevented him from expressing public sympathy for the aspirations of blacks.[22] The price of national political power for blacks was such that it prevented the clear-cut opportunity for a direct political attack on segregation in the thirties. Frustration in this realm worked to encourage black leaders to consider nonpolitical alternatives.

The coming of the Second World War also worked to increase the political power and economic opportunities for American blacks. One historian aptly described this process in the following terms:

> It created an unprecedentedly large demand for Negro labor in the great cities of the North. This not only produced a new wave of migration from the South which increased the voting power of the Northern urban community; it also forced the Negro into jobs, pay ratings, union memberships, and the life never open to him before.[23]

Despite the ugly race riots in Detroit in 1943, it was readily apparent during the war years that increasing numbers of white Americans were becoming sympathetic to the aspirations of black Americans for first-class citizenship.[24] The U.S. government's war propaganda against Hitler's "master racism" reinforced these feelings. Manifestations of this sympathy could be seen in such things as presidential orders requiring employment of blacks in the federal bureaucracy, creation of a Civil Rights Division in the U.S. attorney general's office in 1939, "no discrimination" clauses in war contracts, creation of the Fair Employment Practices Commission in 1941, exemption from the poll tax for black servicemen, and the La Follette Civil Liberties Committee investigation against lynchings.[25]

And what of the implications of these changes for the black people's long struggle for true equality? As Kelly stated:

> It was inevitable that the Negro's new nationalized political power, his enhanced economic position, and the vast im-

provement in ideological climate in the country presently would spill over into the courts, to produce a new series of decisions reflecting the altered position of the Negro in America.[26]

The restructuring of the U.S. Supreme Court which occurred in the decade after 1937 also had a positive effect in the creation of a more sympathetic atmosphere for black civil rights cases. President Roosevelt's appointment of loyal Democratic partisans—like Hugo L. Black and Stanley F. Reed, who understood the implications of the blacks' important role in the Democratic coalition—and liberal academicians—like William O. Douglas and Felix Frankfurter, who were strongly oriented to civil rights for reasons of principle—enhanced the possibilities for a legal attack on segregation. This pattern of appointing politically aware, intellectually liberal men continued during the postwar years.[27] Although the postwar appointments to the Court were for the most part more conservative than those of FDR, all of the men appointed—Republicans and Democrats—possessed an awareness of the changing status of blacks.

Increasing awareness of the problems faced by minority groups caused President Harry S Truman in 1945 to appoint a large number of distinguished black and white Americans to his newly created President's Committee on Civil Rights. *To Secure These Rights,* the report the committee published in 1947, was a comprehensive document which urged sweeping action to secure equal rights for all Americans. The report concluded:

> In any event we believe that not even the most mathematically precise equality of segregated institutions can properly be considered equality under the law. No argument or rationalization can alter this basic fact: a law which forbids a group of American citizens to associate with other citizens in the ordinary course of daily living creates inequality by imposing a caste system on the minority groups.[28]

Perhaps unwittingly, the report underscored the rationale the NAACP would use in its final assault on segregated education. Such were the essentials in the situation that faced the association in the 1930s and 1940s, the critical period when it initiated its campaign against separate schools in the United States.

The Attack on Segregation: The Origins of the NAACP Legal Strategy

The NAACP's decision to mount a legal attack on segregation had its inception in the depths of the Great Depression. In 1930, the directors of the American Fund for Public Service, that remarkable fund created by the wealthy Charles Garland to support reform causes, pledged $100,000 toward the creation of a joint effort with the NAACP to develop a coordinated legal attack on segregation.[29] Prior to the formalization of plans, the directors of the American Fund for Public Service had a memorandum prepared which proposed a sweeping attack on segregated education.[30] It suggested the use of taxpayers' suits to force literal enforcement of the "separate but equal" doctrine in education. The initial strategy called for the granting of $2,000 each to support the filing of such suits in seven southern states. It was anticipated that such suits would:

(a) make the cost of the dual school system so prohibitive as to speed the abolishment of segregated schools;

(b) serve as examples and give courage to Negroes to bring similar actions;

(c) cases will likely be appealed by city authorities, thus causing higher court decisions to cover wider territory;

(d) focus as nothing else will public attention north and south upon the vicious discrimination in the apportionment of public schools funds so far as Negroes are concerned, in certain of these states.[31]

The responsibility for implementation of such a plan was placed in the hands of Nathan R. Margold, a prominent member of the New York Bar, capable civil rights attorney, and former U.S. assistant attorney general.

Despite the fact that the initial amount which the American Fund for Public Service had pledged shrunk because of the Depression, Margold, as a first step toward implementing the memorandum, prepared a comprehensive study of the legal and historical aspects of discrimination against blacks in America.[32] He became convinced that the plan proposed in the original memorandum would prove inadequate. Instead, he urged an all-out attack on the constitutionality of segregation itself based on the precedent in the 1886 *Yick Wo* v. *Hopkins* decision, which had emphasized that the Fourteenth Amendment forbid unreasonable classifications of citizens by the states.[33] He justified this plan of action in the following manner:

> It would be a great mistake to fritter away our limited funds on sporadic attempts to force the making of equal divisions of school funds in the few instances where such attempts might be expected to succeed. . . .
>
> On the other hand if we boldly challenge the constitutional validity of segregation if and when accompanied irremediably by discrimination, we can strike directly at the most prolific sources of discrimination.
>
> We can transform into an authoritative adjudication the principle of law, now only theoretically inferable from *Yick Wo* v. *Hopkins,* that segregation coupled with discrimination resulting from administrative action permitted but not required by state statute, is just as much a denial of equal protection of the laws as is segregation coupled with discrimination required by express statutory enactment. And the threat of using the adjudication as a means of destroying segregation itself, would always exert a very real and powerful force at least to compel enormous improvement in the Negro schools through voluntary official action.[34]

Significantly, both the original memorandum of the American Fund for Public Service and Margold's own proposal called for a legal offensive against segregated education. The difference between the two plans was one of degree and conceptualization. The former emphasized a longer, more sporadic, and limited approach while Margold's proposal called for an immediate, head-on confrontation which would have had sweeping implications.

The NAACP leadership, convinced of the wisdom of a more cautious legal program and aware that segregated education was well entrenched in tradition and practice, did not begin to seriously implement Margold's call for a direct attack on the constitutionality of public school segregation until 1950. Nevertheless, the early studies by the American Fund for Public Service and Margold did play an important role in formulating legal strategy developed by the NAACP for its attack on segregated education. As Jack Greenberg has stated, "Their scholarly, thorough, and thoughtful approach underscored the need for a program which would employ the highest skills, build precedent, and treat each case in a context of jurisprudential development."[35] In 1933, Margold, convinced that he had found the best means of attacking segregated education, resigned as director of the campaign and accepted an appointment as solicitor general of the Interior Department.

The following year, the American Fund for Public Service, its resources tremendously diminished by the Depression, finally gave the NAACP one-tenth ($10,000) of the amount it had originally pledged. The executive board of the NAACP named Charles H. Houston, vice dean of Howard University Law School, as Margold's replacement and announced a reorganized campaign with a major emphasis on the elimination of educational inequalities for blacks. Houston's intellectual brilliance and superb legal education made him an ideal choice. His career at Howard had been marked by his efforts to train lawyers who would defend black civil rights. He lost no time in recruiting a dedicated core of brilliant, young black attorneys for the legal department of the NAACP.[36] Houston's appointment was accompanied with the announcement that: "It should be made clear that the campaign is a carefully planned one to secure decisions, rulings and public opinion on the broad principle instead of being devoted to merely miscellaneous cases.[37] The earlier calls for the creation of a comprehensive legal strategy were about to be translated into reality.

Houston initiated the NAACP's attack with suits against segregated graduate-professional schools. On the surface, it seemed like a very modest approach. It was, however, one based on shrewd reasoning and it led to significant results. He was convinced that the obvious inequality of opportunities and facilities for blacks in graduate-professional education could be easily proven. Moreover, the duplication of segregated higher educational facilities would be so expensive that it would generate economic pressure for desegregation. He also felt that judges would be more sympathetically inclined toward cases at the graduate-professional level because of the greatly reduced chances for violence in such cases. Finally, regardless of whether blacks were admitted to existing graduate-professional schools or to substantially "separate but equal" ones created for them, there would be an increase in opportunities for blacks and a growing pool of black leadership.[38]

Houston's approach called for both patience and persistence. It was designed to expose the inequities in education permitted by the laxity in enforcement of the "separate but equal" doctrine. It was also opportunistic. It hoped to take advantage of increasing judicial good will toward blacks to press for a more demanding definition of the term "substantial equality" than that used in the past to avoid fulfilling the demands of the *Plessy* doctrine for equal facilities for both races. The previously discussed changes in the political and economic status of blacks resulting from the New Deal worked to create an atmosphere conducive to this modification of the interpretation of the *Plessy* doctrine.

Chapter 3

To the Threshold of *Brown*

The first application of Charles H. Houston's strategy which resulted in a victory occurred in *Pearson* v. *Murray,* a case decided by the Maryland Court of Appeals in 1935.[1] Because of the relatively small number of black students desiring legal education in Maryland and five other border and southern states, they were provided with out-of-state tuition grants to be used in states whose law schools were not segregated. In 1935, the Maryland legislature created a Commission on Higher Education of Negroes and appropriated $10,000 annually for it to disburse among qualified blacks who desired graduate-professional training. Each student was to receive a tuition scholarship of $200 to be used at an out-of-state institution.

The Murray Case

Donald Murray, a black resident of Maryland and Amherst College graduate, initiated a writ of mandamus action against the University of Maryland Law School when it refused his admission on the grounds of his race. Thurgood Marshall, the NAACP attorney who argued Murray's case, based his client's request for admission to the University of Maryland Law School on the grounds that the $200 out-of-state tuition scholarship was inadequate and that the lack of facilities for the legal education of blacks in Maryland constituted a denial of the equal protection clause of the Fourteenth Amendment. Marshall supplemented this argument by noting the inhibiting effects that an out-of-state legal education would have on a person who sought to practice law in Maryland. He emphasized the harm that would result from Murray's lack of contact with future colleagues and Maryland legal practices. On appeal, the Maryland Court of Appeals upheld Marshall's contention that the out-of-state scholarship provision was woefully inadequate and ordered Murray admitted to the University of Maryland Law School.

Though the decision was a significant one, it was obviously limited in its scope and applicability. Nothing in the decision actually challenged the constitutionality of segregated education. The decision, as the editor of the *Yale Law Journal* observed in 1936, failed to even settle the question of whether out-of-state tuition scholarships to blacks were constitutional or not because "the scholarship provision on which the respondents relied was palpably inadequate, and the court expressly refused to decide whether 'with aid in any amount it is sufficient to send the negroes outside the state for like education.' "[2] The NAACP, however, had its foot in the door. The matter of "substantial equality" and its relation to the Fourteenth Amendment's equal protection rights that arose in *Pearson* v. *Murray* and subsequent cases became the subject of increasing judicial scrutiny. The association's insistence upon more rigid enforcement of "substantial equality" proved to be the most effective weapon in its antisegregation arsenal for two decades after the *Murray* decision. Its success was dependent on judicial receptivity to the idea that a movement away from the traditional loose interpretation of the *Plessy* precedent was overdue.

The Gaines Case

The answer to the question left unanswered in the *Murray* case—whether or not more equitable out-of-state scholarships for blacks than that struck down in the Maryland case were constitutional—was not long in coming. In 1938, the U.S. Supreme Court struck down such a plan in *Missouri ex rel. Gaines* v. *Canada.*[3] The basis of the Missouri out-of-state tuition plan was a 1929 statute that stated:

> Pending the full development of the Lincoln university (the state supported college for negroes), the board of curators shall have the authority to arrange for the attendance of negro residents of the state of Missouri at the university of any adjacent state to take any course or to study any subjects provided for at the state university of Missouri, and which are not taught at the Lincoln university and to pay the reasonable tuition fees for such attendance; *provided* that whenever the board of curators deem it advisable they shall have the power to open any necessary school or department.[4]

The Missouri law gave the state an escape valve in the event that its out-of-state tuition plan was blocked: it could still practice segregation under the *Plessy* doctrine by creating the necessary programs at Lincoln University. The Missouri law illustrates the point that the obstacles placed in the path of those developing the legal attack on segregation were indeed formidable.

The Missouri case began in 1936 when Lloyd Gaines, a qualified black university graduate, was refused admission to the University of Missouri's segregated law school. Claiming that this constituted a denial of the Fourteenth Amendment's equal protection clause, Gaines' attorney sought a writ of mandamus to compel the Board of Curators of the university to admit him. The Missouri Supreme Court denied the writ on the grounds that the out-of-state provisions established "substantial equality" when adequate instruction was not available at the state-supported university for blacks. The case was then taken on appeal to the United States Supreme Court.[5]

In their arguments before the Supreme Court, the NAACP attorneys reiterated the objections to out-of-state tuition plans for blacks that they had raised initially in the *Murray* case. They maintained that the student would have less opportunity to study Missouri law and practice in an out-of-state institution, and that such an education would not have the prestige incidental to a Missouri law school education among his clients.[6] The State of Missouri, on the other hand, repeated its earlier position that the out-of-state tuition plan was an equitable, sensible solution to the difficult problem created by the small number of blacks in the state who sought graduate-professional education.

The Court's majority rejected the state's arguments and decided the case on even more comprehensive grounds than those presented by the NAACP lawyers. Chief Justice Charles Evans Hughes, in holding that the Missouri scholarship provision failed to satisfy the state's obligation to blacks under the equal protection clause of the Fourteenth Amendment, noted: "By the operation of the laws of Missouri a privilege has been created for white law students which is denied to Negroes by reason of their race."[7] Missouri, Hughes asserted, could not foist off the responsibility of providing educational equality within its borders on another sovereign government. He thereupon ordered Gaines admitted to the University of Missouri Law School.

The Supreme Court majority's broad approach avoided perpetuating the uncertainty that would have arisen from a decision based on the narrow question of the financial inadequacy of the out-of-state grants which had been left undetermined by the earlier *Murray* decision. Not even Gaines' mysterious disappearance shortly after the decision could change the fact that his case had created an important precedent, one with far-reaching implications. The *Gaines* decision, like the *Murray* case before it, failed to directly challenge the validity of the "separate but equal" doctrine. In both cases, the Court upheld the right of a black to be admitted to a state-supported white law school when no "separate but equal" black institution existed in the state. The most immediate threat to segregation lay in the implications of the practical consequences of the two cases. As Alfred H. Kelly has explained:

Careful observers soon concluded, however, that the South's entire system of segregated educational institutions was in serious trouble. Separate facilities for Negroes throughout the South—in buildings, libraries, trained teacher personnel, and academic standards—were notoriously unequal to those for whites. This fact might ultimately lead to a judicial conclusion that equality and segregation were intrinsically incompatible with one another.[8]

One such "careful observer," the editor of the NAACP's *Crisis,* left no doubt as to his view of the implications of the *Gaines* case. Writing in the 10 January 1939 issue, he stated:

The great importance of the decision lies in the basis it provides for an attack on the whole structure of public education as it is now set up in states having separate school systems. The inequitable distribution of federal funds for education, the pitiable elementary schools, the lack of high schools, and the wide variation of salaries for teachers can now be brought into court with brighter chances of victory.[9]

The carefully developed legal strategy of the association had born its first fruits. The time for agonizing reappraisal of the South's educational system was fast approaching.

Southern awareness of the implications of the law school decisions was evidenced in a number of attempts to comply with the Supreme Court's ruling in *Gaines* that graduate-professional training for blacks must be provided within each state. Missouri, for example, quickly set up separate law and journalism schools for blacks. Kentucky established an improvised engineering school.[10] Moreover, between 1940 and 1950 a number of southern school boards took action to overcome the inequalities existing between black and white elementary and secondary schools in the hope that they could head off anticipated NAACP suits questioning the constitutionality of segregated schools at those levels.[11] The southern reaction to the more demanding definition of the "separate but equal" doctrine enunciated in the *Gaines* decision made it abundantly clear that the South was determined to go to great lengths to perpetuate segregated education.

Faced with this intransigence and increased demands for legal action against segregation in other areas of American life, the NAACP in 1939 reorganized its legal department into the NAACP Legal Defense and Education Fund, a technically separate corporation.[12] It was hoped that the divorce of legal activities from the more generalized propaganda and legislative activities of the association would lead to a more effective use of its limited resources. In 1940, Thurgood Marshall, one of Houston's former students at the Howard University Law School and a member of the legal staff since the mid-1930s, was named general counsel of the Legal Defense Fund. Marshall, as a friend of his noted, brought to the organization "a wonderfully keen and incisive mind, a sharp sense of legal strategy and political realities, and an ebullient spirit tempered both by a mordant sense of humor and a deep dedication to the Negro cause."[13] As Marshall and a whole corps of his competent associates were to prove, Houston's earlier educational and recruiting efforts at the Howard University Law School and his adoption of an indirect attack on the constitutionality of educational segregation would soon lead to more effective results.

The reorganization of the association's legal staff not withstanding, the period from 1938 to 1948 saw an abatement in the attack on segregated education which Houston had initiated in the mid-thirties. As Marshall explained:

> This campaign moved along slowly for three reasons: (1) There was a lack of full support from the Negro community in general; (2) few Negroes were interested enough to ask to be plaintiffs; and (3) there was a lack of sufficient money to finance the cases.[14]

The reduction of graduate-professional school enrollments during World War II also helped to explain this situation. Despite these obstacles, the NAACP continued its campaign against segregated education during the war years by carrying out a concentrated effort for the equalization of black teachers' salaries in the South. The association's attorneys argued more than forty cases in which such salary discrepancies were at issue. All were settled in the lower courts, and most resulted in substantial gains for the black teachers involved.[15] Such suits fit very well into the overall NAACP strategy of making segregation too expensive under a more literal interpretation of the "separate but equal" doctrine and the development of increased economic power in the black community.

The salary equalization cases were overshadowed during the war years by a series of victories for blacks in cases argued by the association's attorneys and those of other civil rights groups before the U.S. Supreme Court. The cases covered a broad range of civil rights for blacks. Included were decisions which permitted black organizations to picket places which discriminated, cases forbidding states to discriminate in jury selection, restrictions on conviction of blacks based on forced confessions, the abolition of "white only" primary elections, and restrictions against racial discriminations in labor union membership.[16] All of these decisions created legal precedents which could be used in later attacks on segregation. More importantly, the destruction of the rationale for segregation which occurred in these cases had the effect of isolating the "separate but equal" precedent which buttressed segregated education. The victories were also important in another sense. They greatly encouraged NAACP lawyers because they symbolized the growing sympathy which the victims of segregation received from the justices of the Roosevelt Supreme Court.

The Later Higher Education Cases (1945–1950):
The Erosion of the Plessy Doctrine

The postwar expansion of American higher education provided the NAACP with the opportunity to renew its deliberate attack on discrimination in graduate-professional education. Having obtained the destruction of out-of-state tuition programs for blacks in the prewar higher education cases, the NAACP turned its attention in the postwar period to the inadequacy of "separate but equal" facilities for graduate-professional education within the states. The same assumptions which had led to the prewar concentration on selected higher educational institutions in the South lie behind the association's postwar program. Two of these assumptions were paramount. First, there was the belief that the small number of blacks seeking graduate-professional training would not arouse southern sensitivity about race as much as an attack on elementary and secondary education, where greater numbers were involved, would. As Marshall wryly explained:

> Those racial supremacy boys somehow think that little kids of six or seven are going to get funny ideas about sex and marriage just from going to school together, but for some equally funny reason youngsters in law school aren't supposed to feel that way. We didn't get it but we decided that if that was what the South believed, then the best thing for the moment was to go along.[17]

Second, that it was extremely difficult if not impossible for economic reasons to make segregated black facilities for higher education even approximately equal to those of whites.[18] Such was the thinking as the NAACP legal staff sought to use the *Gaines* precedent as the basis to further weaken the *Plessy* doctrine.

The continued success of the NAACP strategy was evident in the Supreme Court's decision in *Sipuel* v. *Board of Regents of the University of Oklahoma* in 1948.[19] The case had its origins when Ada Lois Sipuel, an otherwise qualified black woman, was denied admission to the University of Oklahoma Law School solely on grounds of her color. Sipuel applied for a writ of mandamus in an Oklahoma district court to force the Oklahoma Board of Regents to admit her. That court and eventually the Oklahoma Supreme Court decided that Sipuel had no right to attend an all-white school under the equal protection clause of the Fourteenth Amendment, and that the proper remedy for her complaint, given the *Plessy* precedent, would be to request the creation of an all-black law school, something which she had not requested.[20] Finding this suggestion unacceptable, she then appealed, with NAACP support, to the U.S. Supreme Court.

On 12 January 1948, the U.S. Supreme Court handed down a unanimous per curiam opinion, which reversed the opinion of the Oklahoma Supreme Court. It stated:

> The petitioner is entitled to secure legal education afforded by a state institution. To this time, it has been denied her although during the same period many white applicants have been afforded legal education by the State. The State must provide it for her in conformity with the equal protection clause of the Fourteenth Amendment and provide it as soon as it does for applicants of any other group.[21]

The extended subsequent litigation in both the Oklahoma courts and the U.S. Supreme Court and the actions of the Oklahoma legislature which finally resulted in the petitioner's admission to the University of Oklahoma Law School need not detain us here.[22] The Supreme Court's decision in the *Sipuel* case was an amplification of the doctrine it had expounded in the *Gaines* case. Not only was the state held responsible for the education of all of its citizens who qualified for graduate-professional education, but it was obligated to provide the facilities as promptly for the members of one race as it was for the applicants of any other race. Once again, as in the prewar graduate-professional education cases, the Court carefully avoided passing judgment on the validity of separate school facilities.

However, two decisions of the Supreme Court in 1950 suggested, as Alfred H. Kelly has noted, "that the court's attitude toward equal educational facilities for Negroes in higher educcation would speedily make segregation on this level a practical impossibility."[23] The Court in *Sweatt* v. *Painter* dealt with the question of whether a state-supported separate black law school in Texas conformed to the requirements for "substantially equal" facilities under the *Plessy* doctrine. The case had its beginnings in 1946 when Heman Marion Sweatt, a black student, was denied admission to the segregated University of Texas Law School in accordance with state law. Sweatt, with NAACP support, then sought admission by a writ of mandamus. The initial trial of his petition in a Texas district court led to a ruling that the state's refusal to admit Sweatt to the law school was unconstitutional and that it would have to furnish him with "substantially equal" facilities for his legal education. However, instead of admitting Sweatt immediately, the court gave the state six months to establish a "separate but equal" means of providing him with a legal education.[24] The State of Texas hurriedly established a makeshift law school for blacks initially in Houston and later in Austin and informed Sweatt that:

> Dean Chas. T. McCormick of the University of Texas Law School will serve as Dean . . . and the courses and instructors

will be identical with those available at the University of Texas Law School. . . . A library is being installed and full use of the State Library . . . is available for research prior to the delivery of a complete law library now on order.[25]

Sweatt, upon the advice of his NAACP attorneys, refused to attend the makeshift law school on the grounds that it could not provide him with the quality of legal education offered at the University of Texas. Sensing a serious threat to its segregated system of higher education, the State of Texas then built a $2 million educational building to house a black law school and other graduate programs. Sweatt again refused to attend the new law school on the grounds that it would not match the quality of legal education available to him at the University of Texas.

Encouraged by the sympathy shown Sweatt by the students and faculty at the University of Texas, where a poll indicated that 76 percent of the faculty favored the admission of blacks to the existing graduate school, the NAACP attorneys again brought the case back to the Texas courts.[26] Hopeful of making a leap from the strategy of requiring the enforcement of "separate but equal" to a direct attack on segregation, they introduced a new argument at this point. They contended that the *Plessy* precedent was erroneous because segregated education itself violated the U.S. Constitution. In addition to their charge that the separate black law school was flagrantly unequal, their brief asserted that

the Constitution and laws of Texas requiring segregation of white and Negro students [are] in direct violation of the Fourteenth Amendment to the United States Constitution. Insofar as the Constitution and laws of Texas . . . prohibit Relator from attending [the] University of Texas because of his race and color such constitutional and statutory provisions of the State of Texas as applied to Relator are in direct violation of the Fourteenth Amendment to the Constitution of the United States.[27]

The NAACP attorneys presented massive amounts of comprehensive social scientific evidence to support their contention that such segregation was harmful.

Their arguments cited the vast physical differences between the superb University of Texas Law School and the school being built for Sweatt. They condemned the inferior library, the number and quality of its faculty, and the lack of "honors and incentives" available at the new school. They also used expert testimony by the deans of the University of Chicago and University of Pennsylvania law schools that the success of the "case method" approach, which was at the heart of modern legal education, was dependent upon the interaction of a law student with his fellows. Sweatt would have no such opportunity if he studied by himself or if he were segregated with a few other blacks. Robert Redfield, chairman of the anthropology department at the University of Chicago, testified that segregated education

> prevents the student from the full, effective and economical coming to understand the nature and capacity of the group from which he is segregated. My comment therefore applies to both whites and Negroes, and one of the objectives of education is the full and sympathetic understanding of the principal groups in the system in which the individual is to function as a citizen. . . .[28]

Dean Charles Thompson of the Howard University Graduate School testified that "separate but equal" schools in Texas had created grossly inferior black graduate education there and in the South as a whole. Donald Murray, the first black to enter the University of Maryland Law School, testified in refutation of the arguments that integration was both harmful and impossible.[29] The sociological emphasis of the preceding arguments is obvious. The NAACP attorneys in the *Sweatt* case urged the Texas court to review the *Plessy* doctrine from a broadened perspective, one that would substitute actual social conditions for long-accepted legal precedent.

Despite these powerful arguments, the Texas court adhered to the *Plessy* precedent and held that the new law school for blacks furnished "substantial equality." Sweatt promptly appealed the decision to the U.S. Supreme Court. In a unanimous decision which disregarded the NAACP's call for the overthrow of the *Plessy* doctrine, Chief Justice Fred M. Vinson held that the black law school failed to furnish an equal legal education. He cited its shortcomings in library, faculty, buildings, and prestige and concluded: "It is difficult to believe that one who had a free choice between these law schools would consider the question close."[30] Sweatt's exclusion was overruled on the grounds that it violated the equal protection clause of the Fourteenth Amendment.

The Supreme Court had effectively destroyed the hope of those who felt that separate graduate-professional schools would pass the test of "substantial equality" traditionally associated with the *Plessy* doctrine. The fact that Sweatt flunked out shortly after his admission to the University of Texas Law School did nothing to alter the precedent that his case had created. Though the Court had studiously avoided facing it, the NAACP had managed to bring the question of the "inherent inequality" of segregation before it for the first time. It had also drawn the legal noose even tighter around the "separate but equal" doctrine.

The Supreme Court announced its decision in another important case dealing with segregated graduate-professional education on the same day as its decision in the *Sweatt* case. In *McLaurin* v. *Oklahoma State Regents,* the Court faced the question of the constitutionality of segregated facilities within a graduate school.[31] The case originated when G. W. McLaurin, a black, with NAACP assistance, won admission to the University of Oklahoma Graduate School after extensive litigation.[32] After his admission, the state forced him to sit at special desks apart from the white students in his classrooms, to use a special desk in the library, and to eat apart from his fellow students in the cafeteria.[33] McLaurin, with Thurgood Marshall as his counsel, sued the Oklahoma State Board of Regents in a federal district court on the grounds that such segregation denied him equal protection of the laws. In Marshall's argument before the district court, he emphasized that "[McLaurin's] required isolation from all other students, solely because of the accident of birth . . . creates a mental discomfiture, which makes concentration and study difficult, if not impossible."[34] The district court denied his claim and held that such segregation was permissible under the *Plessy* doctrine. McLaurin then appealed to the U.S. Supreme Court.

Once again, Chief Justice Vinson, speaking for a unanimous Court, declared that the type of segregation to which McLaurin was subjected was unconstitutional. As he stated:

> We hold that under these circumstances the Fourteenth Amendment precludes differences in treatment by the state based upon race. Appellant having been admitted to a state-supported graduate school, must receive the same treatment at the hands of the state as students of other races.[35]

Again, as in the *Sweatt* case, the Supreme Court carefully avoided the NAACP's call for a reexamination of the *Plessy* precedent in light of contemporary knowledge.

The *Sweatt* and *McLaurin* cases represented the culmination of the NAACP's campaign against segregated graduate-professional education. They constituted the "outer limits," so to speak, of what the association could achieve through the advocacy of a literal application of the *Plessy* doctrine. The cases were thus important because they brought the NAACP to a crossroads. It was time to develop and apply a new strategy, one that would directly attack the constitutionality of segregation.

In 1948, the editor of the *Michigan Law Review* had assessed the *Sipuel* decision in the following terms:

The court in a brief per curiam opinion, however, ignored the fundamental question of the validity of segregation and based its decision solely on the *Gaines* case. . . . Thus again the Supreme Court has left the fundamental question unanswered. If this attitude is to be continued, it is apparent that it will be very difficult to present a case which will decide the issue, since the states which compel segregation are the very states least likely to provide facilities which will meet the equality test. Thus the Supreme Court will always be able to avoid the fundamental question by finding that the facilities provided colored students are not in fact adequate or equal.[36]

Though unwittingly, the editor had pinpointed both the strengths and weaknesses of the NAACP strategy in the higher education cases. While the *Sipuel* decision, and the *Sweatt* and *McLaurin* ones that followed it, saw the Court develop an even more rigid definition of the "substantial equality" aspect of the *Plessy* doctrine, it did nothing to challenge its basic constitutionality.

There are those, of course, who maintained that the precedents established in the *Sweatt* and *McLaurin* cases could conceivably be used to question segregated education on all levels. Clifford S. Green, writing in the October 1950 issue of the *Temple University Law Quarterly,* argued:

While it is true that the *Sweatt* and *McLaurin* cases involved segregation on the professional and graduate level, it would seem that the same criteria for equality would be applicable to state-supported schools on all levels. Freedom to associate and exchange views is as important an element in the education of a child in elementary school as it is in the education of a law student.[37]

The later graduate-professional education decisions of the Supreme Court obviously blurred the former sharp distinction which it had maintained between violations of the *Plessy* doctrine on the grounds that they denied true equality and the idea that segregation was "inherently unequal."

Thurgood Marshall and the NAACP legal staff were faced with a crucial decision in 1950. On the one hand, they were certain that they could use the *Sweatt* and *McLaurin* precedents to destroy racial segregation in graduate-professional education throughout the South.[38] The decisions did in fact eventually result in voluntary or relatively rapid court-ordered desegregation of graduate-professional facilities in all of the states except Alabama, Georgia, Mississippi, Florida, and South Carolina. The NAACP had managed to raise grave judicial doubts about the wisdom of the *Plessy* doctrine. This was apparent in the line of cases which began with *Pearson* v. *Murray* and extended through the *Sweatt* and *McLaurin* decisions. For these reasons, the judicial atmosphere seemed ripe for an expansion of the attack to include segregated public elementary and secondary education.[39]

Yet on the other hand, the Court had technically done nothing to destroy the old *Plessy* "separate but equal" rule. As a matter of fact, its opinions in both the *Sweatt* and *McLaurin* cases had been based on the conclusion that the facilities offered blacks were unequal because they had failed to measure up to the requirements of the *Plessy* doctrine. The Court had purposely ignored the NAACP's attempts to get a direct ruling on the constitutionality of segregation in the *Sweatt* and *McLaurin* cases. Thurgood Marshall, as Kelly has stated, realized that

> the legal gap between the Sweatt and McLaurin cases on the one hand and an outright destruction of the Plessy precedent appeared to be appallingly wide, and he and his colleagues were not at all sure they could cross it. Might it not be well to "go along" with the Southern procedure, at least in part? At this stage of the game, Marshall later told the author, if the school boards in key Southern states had shown a general

disposition to accept any kind of gradualist program combining more adequate schools with some primary and secondary desegregation, the Association might well have agreed to cooperate, at least for a time.[40]

The NAACP legal staff was aware of the possibility that the continuing massive efforts of southern public school boards to carry out crash building programs for black schools, to equalize salaries for black teachers, and to apportion educational funds more equally between white and black students all worked to bring them more closely into compliance with the Supreme Court's more demanding definition of "substantial equality."[41]

Any frontal attack on public school segregation would thus conceivably be vulnerable on both legal and pragmatic grounds. What would happen to the sympathetic judicial atmosphere which the NAACP had worked so hard to cultivate if the judges sensed the threat of massive violence and social disorder as a possible result of a desegregation decision for the South's public schools? What types of judicially acceptable evidence could be mustered to support the argument that segregation was "inherently unequal" and thus in violation of the Fourteenth Amendment's equal protection clause? Would the Court follow the NAACP as it attempted to bridge the gap between the use of the *Plessy* doctrine for its own purposes and an outright destruction of it? If not, would the Court permit the extension of the same criteria for equality which it approved in the graduate-professional education cases to the public elementary and secondary schools? Would the social scientific evidence introduced without much success in previous cases be any more acceptable to judges if the NAACP used it to support a direct attack on the constitutionality of segregation?

These and similar questions created consternation among the NAACP leadership in the early fifties. As Marshall and his staff pondered and hesitated, events were working to force a major change in their legal strategy, one that would lead directly to the *Brown* decision of 1954.

The crisis precipitated by that decision and the subsequent attempts to implement it would soon provide Dwight D. Eisenhower, the first Republican chief executive in twenty years, with the most persistent and critical domestic challenge of his eight-year presidency. His response to that challenge is the subject of the rest of this work.

Chapter 4

The Shaping of the Moderate Mind

What follows is an attempt to reconstruct in historical context the principles, attitudes, and experiences that shaped President Dwight D. Eisenhower's cautious, moderate approach to the school segregation issue prior to the crisis precipitated by the Supreme Court's decisions in the school segregation cases in 1954 and 1955. Utilizing the contrast between the always restrained public utterances and his candid private opinions which the president stated during his two terms in office as a framework, this and the following chapters present a close-up view of his attempt to develop a policy consistent with his beliefs and the country's needs in the face of significant opposition.

Such an approach seems worthwhile for at least two reasons: first, such a perspective is crucial because it explains much about the initial attempts of the president to translate the assumptions which governed him into tangible policies dealing with the school segregation issues. This, in turn, provides a basis to judge the continuity and consistency of his reaction to the subsequent phases of that crisis which are treated in the rest of this volume. Second, the guiding principles and the moderate position which he adopted have become the subject of renewed study by those involved in the rapidly developing reassessment—still in its infancy—of the Eisenhower era. Ultimately, those involved in such a reassessment will have to confront the question of whether or not the president's moderation stemmed from a much more realistic perception of the complex implications which surrounded desegregation than that held by many of those who initially criticized or condemned his response.

As a point of departure, it is important to realize that President Eisenhower's beliefs about civil liberties and race relations must be understood in the context of his general philosophy. Fundamental to this philosophy was his belief in the necessity of avoiding extremes. Eisenhower liked to refer to his general approach as the "middle way." Writing to an old friend in July 1954, he presented a succinct characterization of his position:

> Frankly, I think that the critical problem of our time is to find and stay on the path that marks the way of logic between conflicting arguments advanced by extremists on both sides of almost every economic, political and international problem that arises.[1]

Eisenhower was utterly convinced of the superiority of this approach. Not surprisingly, it became the basis of his approach to the desegregation question, even though it ultimately brought him much criticism from both opponents and defenders of segregation.

As to the style of leadership which would best befit the implementation of his "middle way," the president also held firm convictions:

> Clearly, there are different ways to try to be a leader. In my view, a fair, direct and reasonable dealing with men, a reasonable recognition that views may diverge, a constant seeking for a high and strong ground on which to work to-

gether, is the best way to lead our country in the difficult times ahead of us.[2]

The president envisioned true leadership as that of the "honest broker" concept.

Coupled with these were his beliefs in the importance of limited government and an accompanying skepticism about the uses of law for the solution of fundamental human problems.[3] Underlying these beliefs was a personal habit of caution which seemed during his presidential years to always dominate his response to crisis. Taken together, such principles and traits pointed to moderation in the exercise of presidential powers. Expectedly, that is precisely the position which the president tried to define and assume for himself during the desegregation crisis—a situation, or perhaps more accurately, a series of situations dominated by persons who either rejected or seriously challenged Eisenhower's approach.

Federal Versus State Powers: The Blurred Border

Sensitized by the advanced status of the NAACP's legal attack and the resultant media and public attention to the desegregation question, Eisenhower was forced to publicly articulate and define his attitudes toward that issue from the very beginning of his administration. An examination of the public and private remarks which the president made prior to the May 1954 *Brown* decision presents a clear picture of the basic attitudes and assumptions he carried with him into what proved to be the major domestic crisis his administration confronted. As the following indicates, the president's basic assumptions about the segregation issue were already well formulated prior to the *Brown* decision, that he was already, during 1953 and early 1954, fully aware of the complexities involved in the issue and already convinced of the need for caution.

President Eisenhower publicly stated one of the basic principles which governed his approach to the desegregation crisis in his 14 March 1953 press conference. When asked by Alice Dunnigan of the Associated Negro Press about the apparent contradiction between his announced policy of eliminating segregation in the U.S. Army and the existence of segregated schools on military posts in Virginia, Oklahoma, and Texas,[4] the president made the first of what proved to be many statements on this subject. After admitting that he was not familiar with the situation and promising that he would have Presidential Press Secretary James C. Hagerty look into it for him, he said:

> I will say this—I repeat it, I have said it again and again: wherever federal funds are expended for anything, I do not see how any American can justify—legally, or logically, or morally—a discrimination in the expenditure of those funds as among our citizens. All are taxed to provide those funds.
>
> If there is any benefit to be derived from them, I think it means all share, regardless of such inconsequential factors as race and religion.[5]

The chasm between the president's statement of principle and its implementation, given his narrow conception of the scope of federal powers, proved, however, to be a difficult one to bridge. Moreover, despite his subsequent strong support for the implementation of desegregation in the District of Columbia's public schools and facilities, those who believed in the broad application of federal power in the civil liberties realm were to become increasingly disenchanted with both the president's narrow perception of the scope of those liberties and the reticence he exercised in applying them.

There was, of course, no question that Eisenhower moved with dispatch in the narrowly defined area where he felt federal power and responsibility were complete. His completion of the desegregation of the armed forces, his resurrection and use of the so-called Lost Laws forbidding segregated facilities in the District of Columbia, as well as his support for desegregation of its public school system were vigorous.[6]

Though sweeping in their effects and certainly the cause of much controversy, actions in these areas were completely consonant with his limited conception of the scope of executive power and federal law.

However, many of the most complex aspects of the desegregation problem began at that point where there was an interaction of state and federal authority, or appeared in the realm which custom and usage had reserved to the states under their police powers. Here were areas to which the president felt the powers and responsibilities of the federal government did not extend, and strong presidential leadership for desegregation in those areas proved difficult to muster.

The promise that the president made in the previously cited press conference produced two responses within his administration which underscored the complexity of the school desegregation issue. First, with regard to his promise that he would look into the matter of segregated schools on bases, his press secretary asked for and got a memorandum from Secretary of the Army Robert T. Stevens.[7] In it, Stevens explained that there were two kinds of schools operating on army posts where segregation was practiced. The one operated by the army under Section 6 of Public Law 874 at Fort Benning, Georgia, was run on a segregated basis at the request of local authorities. That school, Stevens noted, was to be completely integrated in the fall of 1954. The second type, the kind which Alice Dunnigan had noted, was that operated by state authorities on military reservations under the provisions of Section 3 of Public Law 874. The secretary emphasized that in order to provide integrated schools, the federal government would have to duplicate existing school facilities. Continuing, he pointed out that as the result of discussions between Truman administration officials and the NAACP, steps had been taken to "have army commanders survey the problem to determine whether suitable arrangements can be made with local authorities for integrated schooling."[8]

Emphasizing that the situation was not yet clarified, Stevens cautioned that he could see two problems arising if the army built such duplicate facilities:

a. By declaring that existing facilities are not "suitable" and building new ones for no reason other than to eliminate segregation, the federal government could be attacked in the press and Congress, particularly by the Southern States' representatives, for needlessly spending public funds.

b. Even though the federal government can build new facilities and can provide the students, the government has no way of compelling nor can it counter a possible move of the state involved to refuse to grant teaching certificates to the instructors required to operate such schools. Since in a majority of cases high schools are operated off post, this could well lead to the state school system refusing to accept into its segregated high school (over which the Army, of course, has *no* control) those graduates of our integrated schools.[9]

The complex intermixture of state and federal responsibility involved in the education of military dependents was such that it defied easy application of the president's "desegregation wherever federal funds are involved" principle. Growing awareness of this certainly reinforced his narrow conception of the scope of federal powers.

Evidence that the president's statement had a confusing impact within his own administration appeared in a memorandum from Roger W. Jones, assistant director for legislative reference of the Bureau of the Budget, to Bernard M. Shanley, acting special counsel to the president.[10] Jones reminded Shanley that Public Law 874, which authorized payment to school districts "impacted" by large numbers of federal employees, was about to expire in June. Jones noted that the Federal Security Agency's proposed extension would continue its present policy of allowing segregation if demanded by state law for regular state and local schools. A problem arose, according to Jones, because: "The report of the President's press conference of March 19, suggests that he might favor measures to end segregation in all those cases where the schools are on Government property."[11] Jones then asked for advice on the question raised in order to complete Bureau of the Budget action on the draft bill amending Public Law 874. He also appended a postscript noting that Public Law 815 on school construction raised the same issue and that a rapid answer was necessary because the president had instructed Secretary of Health, Education, and Welfare Oveta Culp Hobby to send both bills to Congress before the Easter recess.

On 25 March 1953, President Eisenhower sent a memorandum to the secretary of defense summarizing the information he had received from the secretary of the army and the Bureau of the Budget on the question of segregated schools on army posts.[12] In it, he noted that the school operated by the army would be integrated by the fall of 1953, but that there were "complicating factors" present where states ran schools on federally owned property and that if army commanders could not bring about integration agreements, "other arrangements in these instances will be considered."[13] The president, aware of the cost of building separate schools, did not describe what the other arrangements might be.

In practice, the dividing line between state and federal powers proved far more difficult to distinguish than the president had previously realized. Eisenhower's 25 March memorandum signifies his discovery of that fact. What had appeared initially to him to be a sound and conceivably limiting rule of thumb contained the elements of much controversy.

Whose Brief?

The Supreme Court's 8 June 1953 invitation to U.S. Attorney General Herbert Brownell to file a brief and/or submit arguments in the pending school segregation cases guaranteed that the president would continue to devote great amounts of attention to the desegregation issue. Attempts to influence the president's thinking on that topic came from many sources.

One of the most persistent was that of the conservative southern Democratic politicians who had supported him, though with varying degrees of openness, in his 1952 presidential campaign. On 16 July 1953, Governor Allan Shivers wrote to the president regarding the Court's invitation to Brownell and stated: "The United States is not a party to this lawsuit except insofar as Truman and former Attorney General McGranery intervened."[14] Shivers then proceeded to warn the president about the dangers of administration involvement.

> I see in this unusual Supreme Court invitation an attempt to embarrass you and your Attorney General. There is nothing more local than the public school system....
>
> I assume that the invitation to your Attorney General by the Supreme Court will be accepted. I trust that he will see the implications involved and advise the Court that this local problem should be decided on the local and state level.[15]

Though the president's response to Shivers (actually drafted by Attorney General Brownell) merely advised the Texas governor that the study of the law pursuant to the Supreme Court's invitation was not yet completed, Shivers' message and others like it from his political allies in the South became the justification for caution on the part of the president. They worked to reinforce his desire to use federal power sparingly.

A clear expression of what the president regarded as the proper approach appeared in his 24 July 1953 diary notes on his conversation with Governor James F. Byrnes of South Carolina.[16] Eisenhower noted that Byrnes was fearful that a Court decision might abolish segregation and that such a decision would cause a number of states to immediately cease support for public schools, a consequence which the president's subsequent private statements indicate that he came to fear very much. Byrnes further warned that if the administration took a strong antisegregation stand in hopes of capturing the black vote, it would defeat forever the possibility of developing a viable Republican party in the South.[17]

Eisenhower's response to Byrnes was revealing. After assuring Byrnes that his response to the school segregation cases would not be formed by political expediency, the president proceeded to state his fundamental beliefs about the desegregation issue. He insisted that the South Carolina governor was

> well aware of my belief that improvement in race relations is one of those things that will be healthy and sound only if it starts locally. I do not believe that prejudice, even palpably unjustified prejudices, will succumb to compulsion. Consequently, I believe that Federal law imposed upon our states in such a way as to bring about a conflict of the police power of the states and of the nation, would set back the cause of progress in race relations for a long, long time.[18]

Thus, very early in his administration, Eisenhower stated the guiding principles behind his moderate approach to the race question. His oft-criticized approach was based on a rejection of compulsion in favor of gradual progress at the local level. These beliefs were certainly influenced and reinforced by his southern friends like Shivers and Byrnes who emphasized the dangers in the desegregation question. Unfortunately, the differing perceptions of what the president and his southern friends meant by leaving the desegregation question to be settled at the local level did not become obvious to him until much later. That, however, is not sufficient reason to charge the president with neglect or cowardice.

Another aspect of the president's beliefs that had an important effect on shaping his reaction to the desegregation issue appeared in his discussion of the brief which Attorney General Brownell prepared for the segregation cases. In a "Memorandum for the Record," written on 19 August 1953, Eisenhower drew a sharp distinction between the function of the

Court and the executive branch, and expressed uneasiness about the Court's behavior in the pending segregation cases.

> It seems to me that the rendering of "opinion" by the Attorney General on this kind of question would constitute an invasion of the duties, responsibilities and authority of the Supreme Court. As I understand it, the Courts were established by the Constitution to interpret the laws, the responsibility of the Executive Department is to execute them.[19]

The president was sufficiently moved by his concern that he telephoned Attorney General Brownell about it. He did this, he explained,

> because it seems to me that in this instance the Supreme Court has been guided by some motive that is not strictly functional. The Court cannot possibly abdicate; consequently, it cannot delegate its responsibility and it would be futile for the Attorney General to attempt to sit as a Court and read a conclusion as to the true meaning of the Fourteenth Amendment.[20]

The president concluded his memorandum by conceding that regardless of the conclusion about the questions he had raised, the attorney general would present a complete "resume of fact and historical record" about the Fourteenth Amendment.

Further evidence of Eisenhower's emphasis on the limited scope of federal responsibilities in the desegregation area appeared in his 5 November 1953 telephone call to Attorney General Brownell.[21] During their conversation, the president mentioned that he could see why the attorney general could not duck involvement in the issue in the District of Columbia, but that he questioned how the attorney general could be expected to speak out on the issue of state-enforced segregation.[22]

It is obvious, then, that the president felt the Supreme Court's call for advisory opinions had exceeded the proper nature of its judicial function by blurring the relationship between the executive and legislative branches. The president's knowledge of both constitutional history and legal procedure was, of course, limited, based more on theory than practical experience. The Justice Department had filed briefs in many cases heard by the Court in the past. The Truman administration had already intervened in the segregation cases with a strong brief arguing against the constitutionality of segregation, and it was not unheard of for the Court in significant and controversial cases to request or permit amicus curae briefs.

It appears that Eisenhower's strong beliefs in the separation of powers, his limited understanding of the judicial process, the influence of his southern friends, and his growing awareness about the highly explosive nature of the segregation question combined to push him toward a position of executive neutrality, one which separated his administration from accountability for the actions of the Court. His assertion that the Court was governed by some not strictly judicial motive, reflecting Governor Shivers' warning, indicates that the president's view of the judicial process was a narrow one which emphasized procedure over substance. He suspected the justices had violated some canon of neutrality. One thing is certain: the president was never enthusiastic about the Supreme Court's invitation for Attorney General Brownell's involvement in the case.[23]

As stated previously, the president was highly disturbed at Governor Byrnes' prediction that a desegregation decision would lead to the closing of the public schools of several southern states. In a telephone conversation with Attorney General Brownell on 16 November 1953, the president asked him what would happen if the states abandoned public education.[24] Brownell observed that Byrnes was coming to the White House for dinner the following evening and assured the president that he would try to convince the governor that "under our doctrine it would be a period of years and he wouldn't have to 'declare war' so to speak."[25] Eisenhower then expressed his fear that such a controversy would make education a function of the federal government. Brownell responded that he felt the states would work out the problem in ten to twelve years and that it might be helpful if Governor Shivers talked with Byrnes, since the Texan felt that things had worked out successfully in his own state.

There is no record of the president's response to his attorney general's advice. However, it is apparent that the president was less certain than Attorney General Brownell of the wisdom of the administration's involvement in the desegregation cases and certainly more pessimistic about their outcome. The president's more recently acquired fear that the South might close its schools rather than desegregate them increased the possibility that a federal takeover of education, something he had long abhorred, might result.[26] His desire to avoid such a consequence certainly pushed him away from willing involvement in the desegregation question.

Yet, ironically, he could not escape it. The Court's invitation to submit a brief in the school segregation cases had seen to that. Evidence of how closely his words and actions were being weighed by those involved in the case came in the reactions to his 18 November 1953 press conference. When a reporter asked the president whether he planned to confer with the attorney general prior to the Justice Department's filing its brief on the school segregation question, he answered: "Indeed I do. We confer regularly. And this subject comes up along with others, constantly."[27] Despite the president's previously cited private reservations, his offhand public remark was taken by many as an admission that he was personally involved in the shaping of the details of the Justice Department's brief, that it would represent his personal opinions on the desegregation issue.

Letters from and to the South

Consequently, two southern governors, James F. Byrnes of South Carolina and Robert F. Kennon of Louisiana, wrote letters to the president seeking to convince him of the wisdom of their position on the pending school segregation cases, thus influencing the substance of the Justice Department's brief. Governor Byrnes included in his letter some pages from the brief which the attorney for South Carolina's school trustees, John W. Davis, had prepared and proceeded to summarize its contents. In what amounted to a lecture in southern-style constitutional history, Byrnes asserted:

> In the brief our counsel will argue that the United States Supreme Court and every other court, federal and state, that has ever considered this question has held that the 14th Amendment did not prohibit a state from enacting a law requiring separation of races in public schools provided equal facilities were furnished all students. The question now is whether you will ask the Supreme Court to reverse its decisions and declare that the 14th Amendment now means something the Court has heretofore said it did not mean.
>
> The Court has no right to legislate.... The excerpts I enclose [for] you contain a discussion of the right of a state in the exercise of its police powers to make distinctions between people, provided such distinctions are not arbitrary and unreasonable. I hope your consideration will cause you to conclude that this is the proper position for you to take.[28]

Byrnes closed, not surprisingly, by reminding the president that South Carolina's position was consonant with one that he had taken consistently, "that the states should have the right to control matters that are purely local."[29]

Governor Kennon's letter took a somewhat different tack. He began by pointing out that the states had exercised the right of operating their own schools since the beginning of public education and that the Supreme Court had sustained that right in cases extending back for three-fourths of a century.[30] He then emphasized the great progress the South had made in public education for both races including salary equalization for black and white teachers and the construction of modern high schools for black pupils.

Turning to the possibility of Court-ordered desegregation, Kennon predicted dire results:

> A federal edict contrary to the established order and customs could well disrupt many local systems, particularly in the rural areas. Such a disruption would interrupt the present orderly improvement and do great damage to the fine racial relationships that have existed—and improved—over the years.[31]

Kennon emphasized his belief that every American deserved fair treatment regardless of race, color, or religion but that the solution to the school problem would be found at the state and local levels. He further insisted that the funds were simply not available to effect the changes in buildings, teachers, and transportation which a federal edict would involve. Like Byrnes, the Louisiana governor concluded his plea by appealing to the president's deep sense of commitment to the preservation of state and local government:

> However, the controlling consideration is not money or even segregation. It is one of preserving our dual system of federal and state government. I trust that the guiding principle of states rights, local self-government and community responsibility will be given the prime consideration it deserves, and that the position of the Department of Justice will be towards sustaining the fundamental American conception of state sovereignty.[32]

Despite their somewhat differing approaches, both Byrnes and Kennon made the same point: the school segregation question would be best solved at the local and state levels with the preservation of the "separate but equal" doctrine. The letters presented clear articulations of what proved to be the basic parts of the southern states' position during the entire desegregation crisis. This merger of constitutional and practical objections to desegregation would be heard again and again.

Assistant U.S. Attorney General J. Lee Rankin's letter—which, with the concurrence of Robert Shanley of the president's staff, went to Byrnes and Kennon under the president's signature—was a concise, noncommittal reply. It emphasized that the president had spent considerable time studying the case, that he was aware of the serious questions it raised, and that he had forwarded the governers' respective letters to the attorney general. The president could do little else at that time, given the pending nature of the school segregation cases.[33]

The strong assertions of state sovereignty and calls for judicial restraint in the letters from southern politicians certainly reinforced the president's desire to seek a moderate solution to the desegregation crisis. This was very apparent in the personal letter Eisenhower wrote, with Attorney General Brownell's concurrence, to Governor Byrnes, dated 1 December 1953.[34] It should be kept in mind that the president was aware by this time that the Justice Department's brief took a stand against segregated schools.

The president began by emphasizing that he had put much thought and study into the school segregation cases. He expressed hope that solutions could be found

> which would progressively work toward the goals established by abstract principle, but which would not, at the same time, cause such disruption and mental anguish among great portions of our population that progress would actually be reversed.[35]

No better characterization of the president's approach to the desegregation question can be found than in his speeches and writings. His problems would come when he sought the middle ground, which he needed to implement such an approach.

Continuing, the president complimented Byrnes for his study and knowledge of the segregation problem and assured the governor that he was sympathetic to the South's problems. As he put it:

> I recognize that there are very serious problems that you have to face—regardless of the exact character of the Court decisions in the pending cases. By this I mean that the task of establishing "equal but separate" facilities will involve, I am told, extraordinary expenditures throughout all the Southern states. Incidentally, I sometimes wonder just what officials of government would be charged with the responsibility for determining when facilities were exactly equal.[36]

The president's remarks reveal that he anticipated serious difficulties in the event of a Court decision requiring the southern states to adhere to a more rigorous definition of the "separate but equal" doctrine. Moreover, he was already concerned lest the Court present his administration with the unenviable task of enforcing such a decision. His remarks were consistent with his general wish that the desegregation question be resolved outside the federal judicial process.

He then hastened to add, however, that he was not actually involved in preparing the administration's brief because:

> In the study of the case, it became clear to me that the questions asked of the Attorney General by the Supreme Court demanded answers that could be determined only by lawyers and historians. Consequently, I have been compelled to turn over to the Attorney General and his associates full responsibility in the matter. He and I agreed that his brief would reflect the conviction of the Department of Justice as to the *legal aspects* of the case, including, of course, the legislative history of the enactment of the 14th Amendment. In rendering an opinion as to this phase of the case, it is clear that the Attorney General has to act according to his own conviction and understanding.[37]

Eisenhower's reason for disassociating himself from the preparation of the brief was a valid one. He was not a lawyer. At this point, he appeared to be acknowledging the existence of differences between his personal views and the conclusions of the Justice Department's brief.

The president assured Byrnes that no political considerations of any kind would be given any weight whatsoever in the Justice Department's brief and that "no matter what the *legal* conclusions might be, the principle of local operation and authority would be emphasized to the maximum degree consistent with his legal opinions."[38] The president's devotion to the principle of local resolution of the school desegregation issue was complete and consistent. Although it did not prevent his attorney general from presenting a brief rationalizing judicial activism, it is not surprising that the emphasis on local responsibility ultimately became the basis of the administration's 1955 brief on how to implement the desegregation decision.

The president concluded his letter to Byrnes with an attempt to prepare the governor for the Justice Department's forthcoming brief, which supported desegregation. As he put it:

> Two or three Court decisions of recent years have, as you know, tended to becloud the original decision of "equal but separate" facilities. One of these decisions, I am told, even held that a Negro in graduate school attending exactly the same classes as whites, but separated from them by some kind of railing, was held to be the victim of discrimination and could not be so separated from the white students. This and other decisions had all, of course, to be considered by the Attorney General and his staff. But I am sure that you have no doubt as to the complete integrity and broad capacity of the Attorney General—even if in this case I suspect you may question his legal wisdom.[39]

Though the version of the letter cited above was revised prior to its being sent by the Department of Justice, the original is valuable for what it reveals about the agonizing position in which the president found himself.

Summation

By late 1953, Eisenhower was caught between his desires for a moderate approach built upon state and local responsibility and gradualism and his own Justice Department's brief, which supported a judicial attack on discrimination. Though helpless to stop it, the president was convinced that the latter approach would lead to bitterness, confusion, and frustration. The situation by March 1954 was such that he was left with few options beyond the exercise of caution and moderation.

Evidence that even the president's moderate approach would not let him avoid controversy was soon forthcoming. Although he reiterated his promise to push hard for desegregation within what he felt were clearly defined areas of federal power in remarks to an NAACP conference on 10 March 1954,[40] the rush of events seemed to threaten the safety of that approach. During Eisenhower's 24 March press conference, Ethel Paynter, a reporter for Black Defender Publications, raised the following question:

> Since you have said that you are in favor of using Federal authority, where it is proper to do so, in the program of ending racial discrimination, will you urge the Congress to act favorably on S. 262, the bill to prohibit segregation in interstate travel?[41]

Here, the reporter touched upon an area—interstate travel —clearly within the realm of federal commerce power where the consequences of an attack on segregated facilities by the federal government at that time could have explosive consequences in the South. Eisenhower responded that he had not heard of the bill and that he would have to consult his attorney general about the sources of federal authority in that area.[42]

The president's response indicates that he was not fully aware of the breadth and implications of the attack on segregation that had already developed by 1954. More significantly, though, the interstate travel question, like the segregated federal facilities question discussed previously, reminded the president again that even his concept of the limited scope of federal powers could not assure his administration's uninvolvement in the larger desegregation controversy. Thus, he found another incentive for caution.

The events that occurred after the initial *Brown* decision in May 1954 only served to reiterate what his philosophy and experience had already combined to tell him: that there were strong reasons to gravely doubt the wisdom of the attempt to resolve the desegregation crisis by rapid actions involving judicial and legislative fiat. This belief proved to be a powerful brake on any temptation the president had to take strong action. At the same time, it must be remembered that his critics have charged that his failure to provide strong leadership in that crisis contributed greatly to its complexity and its longevity.[43] Whether one accepts that stern judgment or not, there is little doubt that the attitudes the president developed early on in the desegregation controversy stayed with him throughout and that they explain much of what he did and did not do.

Chapter 5

The NAACP and the Case for Immediate Desegregation

The year following the Supreme Court's May 1954 decision in the school segregation cases was a time of waiting for many Americans. The Court's decision to delay implementation until it had heard arguments from interested parties on how desegregation could best be accomplished made such a reaction inevitable. The extensive editorial discussions of the historical significance of the case and the way it should be implemented, which appeared in the first few days after the decision, soon gave way before what the editors regarded as more pressing events. The Court, after all, had decided a principle, but it had studiously avoided suggesting how it would be translated into reality.

For the protagonists in the school cases, however, the time was one of intense labor. The NAACP moved to develop both a program and a brief that would convince the Court of the wisdom of immediate desegregation of the public schools. The southern states—those that were parties to the suit and many of the others who were affected by the decision—considered means of evasion and developed briefs which called for extended delays in the process of school integration. The Eisenhower administration, caught because of political realities between the two major protagonists even though it officially favored school desegregation, labored to develop a nonpartisan stance and a brief that would permit gradual desegregation, the apparent preference of most Americans.

This chapter is an examination of the positions on implementation developed by the principals involved in the school cases, and the attitudes which shaped them. It begins with a characterization of the initial response of the nation's press to the decision. It then portrays the types of input that shaped the positions on implementation taken by the NAACP. The emphasis throughout is on the examination of the interrelationships between the legal position taken by that group and its perception of the situation in which it found itself at the time of the decision.

Press Reactions: North and South

The Supreme Court's May 1954 ruling that segregated schools were unconstitutional drew overwhelming praise in the editorial columns of major American newspapers outside the South. Seventeen of the nineteen big-city dailies examined endorsed the decision, and the other two expressed the necessity to end segregation though they questioned the need for Supreme Court action to accomplish it.[1]

A number of significant common themes emerge from an examination of these editorials. They present a convenient summation of the way the school segregation decision was explained to the American public outside the South in 1954.

All of the editors were convinced that the decision marked a great turning point in American history. While only the more observant noted that it had been preceded by a whole series of decisions which had restricted the scope of the *Plessy* precedent, most saw that it marked the end of the "separate but equal" doctrine. Most summarized or quoted Chief Justice Earl Warren's assertion that segregated schools were unconstitutional per se and thus in violation of the equal protection clause of the Fourteenth Amendment. Emphasis in the editorials, however, was not on the technical-legal aspects of the decision but rather on its implications. Many of the editors pointed out that the decision was unanimous despite the diverse backgrounds of the justices. They regarded this as a sign that it was time for the United States to redeem its integrity by destroying second-class citizenship.

The editors hailed the decision for two reasons. First, they were convinced that it would increase respect for America in the eyes of the world and thus provide us with a crucial victory in the cold war contest for the loyalties of the non-white peoples of the world. The editor of the *San Francisco Chronicle* typified this reaction when he wrote:

> Great as the impact of the antisegregation holding will be upon the States of the South in their struggle to make the physical and intellectual adjustment which it requires, still greater, we believe, will be its impact in South America, Africa and Asia to this country's lasting honor and benefit. We Americans, familiar with the process of social revolution by law, have been largely prepared for the Court's decision; to the vast majority of the peoples of the world who have colored skins, it will come as a blinding flash of light and hope. Yesterday's act of the Supreme Court presents a new picture of America and puts this Nation in a new posture of justice.[2]

The second theme the editors developed was their strong support of the Court's gradualistic approach to the implementation of desegregation. As the editor of the *New York Journal American* observed:

> The Court further displayed its high good sense in putting off until the Fall term the formulation of the mechanics by which this great change is to be made and by inviting the Attorneys General of the States concerned to appear as "friends of the Court" on this matter.

> A principle of this importance must be worked out slowly, carefully and reasonably. Impatience will only do it damage, and we think Negro leaders would agree with us on this point.[3]

The editors were aware that the problems of adjustment in the South would be formidable, but they were confident that the Court would permit the necessary time so they could be worked out. They assumed that the majority of white southerners would attempt to work in good faith for the implementation of the decision. The northern editors were confident that desegregation could be achieved without violence or disorder.

The response of the southern press contrasted sharply with that of the rest of the country. It was marked by a lack of enthusiasm for the decision and a preoccupation with the immediate effects of it in the South.

The small-town and rural southern newspapers surveyed by the *Cleveland Plain Dealer* and the large-city papers surveyed by the *Washington Star* agreed that the decision had created a crisis of major proportions for the South. Apparently, many of the editors of the smaller papers had anticipated the decision against segregation. Most of them deplored it. A number emphasized its conspiratorial implications. Jack Rider, editor of the Kinston, North Carolina, *Lenoir County News,* typified this view when he said:

> Some few here view the decision as an extension of the indemnity heaped upon the South at the end of the Civil War, and as a further effort to hamper the industrial competition that the South is developing for the Northeast.[4]

Still others fell back on traditional southern state sovereignty arguments and urged defiance. Editor May D. Cain of the *Summit* (Mississippi) *Sun* predicted that the Court decision "will be absolutely (and properly) disregarded. If Gov. White does not assert himself as the governor of a sovereign state . . . there will be those who campaign for governor next year."[5]

Another group expressed concern about the enormous problems which the decision created for the South. R. C. Rivers, Jr., editor of the Boone, North Carolina, *Watauga Democrat,* aptly summarized this view when he stated, "No one can tell the outcome of so drastic a change in the pattern of society."[6]

A final group, however, expressed faith that the problem could be worked out. Curtis H. Mullen of the Canton, Mississippi, *Madison County Herald* wrote that "the majority realize a change is in the making. They do not like it but will not object violently provided the change can be orderly and gradual."[7]

Nearly all of the larger southern newspapers called for a calm approach to the local problems created by the school segregation decision. While most expressed open disapproval, the editors expressed confidence that a great deal of time would elapse before integration of the schools would actually take place. One of the most succinct expressions of this mood appeared in the *Columbia* (South Carolina) *State and Record*: "This is a time for calm deliberation. We should think the Supreme Court would be practical in the application of its ruling. . . . It could well allow years to elapse before invoking its decree."[8]

A number, like the *Texarkana* (Arkansas) *Gazette,* urged a deliberate policy of evasion:

> It has been our feeling that the welfare of the Negroes and the whites would have been served best by a delay of several years. . . . Let those of us who are not able to make an immediate adjustment figure out a course of action which will suit us and follow that course with quiet determination. . . .[9]

The *Jackson* (Mississippi) *Clarion-Ledger* went even further when it concluded that:

It may confront these (Southern) States with the sole alternative of abolishing the public school systems and voting appropriations for the individual children instead of for the schools, to educate the children in private schools.[10]

The emphasis in the editorials on the possibilities of long delays, evasion, and defiance sheds light on the type of assumptions underlying southern attitudes on implementation of the school segregation decision.

A comparison of the response of the southern press and the previously cited northern press presents an example of the differing perceptions in each locale of what was at stake in the school cases. The northern editors viewed the decision as a step toward fundamental justice and felt its implementation was inevitable. The southern editors regarded it as a threat to the South's way of life and felt that it should be resisted. Close examination of the calls of the editors of both sections for a gradual period of implementation reveals a striking contrast in the expressed motives of the two groups. While the northern editors assumed that the end result of such a process would be integration, many of their southern counterparts felt that it could be translated into evasion or at least extensive delays. Sooner or later, the incongruities symbolized by the two definitions would come into conflict.

The NAACP in the Interim:
The Call for Immediate Desegregation

Joy over its victory in the school segregation decision did not cause the NAACP leadership to lose its sense of political realism. In the editorial in the June–July 1954 issue of the *Crisis*, the editor hailed the decision as a turning point in American race relations but hastened to warn his readers that one battle did not make a war. He expressed particular concern about the dangers of overconfidence:

We are at that point in our fight against segregation where unintelligent optimism and childish faith in a court decision can blind us to the fact that legal abolition of segregation is not the final solution for the social cancer of racism.[11]

The editor held no illusions about the gap between legal principles and social realities.

Turning to the various critics of the decision, the editor first dealt with those who condemned the NAACP as an extremist organization which, by opposing white southern segregationists, threatened to precipitate violence in the South. He emphasized that:

> The Association has always worked within the law without appeals to violence; actually its goal is enforcement of basic constitutional law, because we want America to maintain her spiritual solvency by practicing her democratic principles.[12]

The resentment against being categorized in the same group with segregationists underscores the strong sense of moral virtue the association attached to its cause. It helps to explain the bitterness created among members of the association when President Eisenhower attempted to develop a stance aloof from it and its southern adversaries in the months after the May 1954 decision.

Even more dangerous, according to the editor, were those who argued against immediate integration on the grounds that a peaceful changeover would take decades. In characterizing them, he stated:

> They are the fellows who are inviting *local Negro leaders* to sit around the conference table to work out amicable solutions which will be "fair to both races." What this group wants is continued segregation. And they are stressing the achievements of southern Negroes in the segregated South.[13]

The NAACP thus warned its members to beware of those who would feign cooperation as a technique for maintaining segregation. In so doing, it characterized what proved to be one of the favorite techniques used in the South by the opponents of integration.

The editor concluded with a discussion of what blacks could do to facilitate integration. Emphasizing that black reactions would be the crucial elements in determining both the character and the speed of southern school integration, he reiterated two guiding principles:

> First, the NAACP is absolutely opposed to any compromise of principle in the integration of white and Negro pupils in the public schools of the South. . . . Secondly, the NAACP is aware of the administrative problems involved in the changeover, but we are not going to coddle school boards and superintendents who may attempt to use these problems as an excuse for unnecessary delay or to avoid desegregation.[14]

The NAACP leadership was convinced that the time for integration was "now!" It viewed delay as both unnecessary and dangerous.

The association lost no time in moving to take advantage of the May 1954 decision. During the weekend following it, NAACP representatives from seventeen border and southern states met in Atlanta and formulated a declaration calling for early implementation of the decision. The declaration asserted:

> We stand ready to work with other law-abiding citizens who are anxious to translate this decision into a program of action to eradicate racial segregation in public education as speedily as possible.
>
> We are instructing all of our branches in every affected area to petition their local school boards to abolish segregation without delay and to assist these agencies in working out ways and means of implementing the Court's ruling.[15]

The national office hired three education specialists to help achieve rapid implementation at the local level. The three were directed to "facilitate, wherever possible, peaceful desegregation without legal action" through coordination of efforts of local NAACP branches and community organizations as well as professional advice to local school boards.[16] Its actions suggest that it realized the importance of cooperation with different groups in the local communities for successful integration efforts. It was readily apparent from its initial response that the NAACP supported immediate implementation of the decision wherever possible.

The association expressed pleasure at what it regarded as substantial progress toward voluntary desegregation, which occurred when the new school year began in September 1954. As its legal department reported:

> Local communities in eight states, including Arkansas, opened their school doors to Negro and white children alike for the first time. Washington desegregated its schools as did Baltimore. St. Louis and Kansas City and a score of other cities in Missouri initiated desegregation programs. Twelve counties in West Virginia completely integrated their schools and seventeen others partially desegregated. Compliance with the Court's ruling also proceeded in Delaware and in the permissive states of Arizona, New Mexico and Kansas.[17]

However, such integration, occurring as it did for the most part outside of the Deep South, was certainly the cause of concern as well as pleasure to the NAACP. Southern inaction left no doubt that the overwhelming number of that region's school boards had decided to do nothing until the Supreme Court made its implementation ruling. This stance convinced the association's leadership that it would have to mount heavy legal pressure and that the U.S. Supreme Court would have to maintain close supervision of the desegregation process in the South.

The NAACP also admitted that the integration of some schools had led to "demonstrations of defiance." It described a number of these, including the well-publicized incidents in the public schools of Baltimore and Washington, D.C. Noting that these instances had been investigated by social scientists serving on a NAACP volunteer committee, the legal department concluded:

According to their findings, these outbursts were adult-instigated and involved purely local matters; they in no way invalidated the NAACP contention that the public schools can be desegregated without delay provided there is intelligent, steadfast leadership in the community.[18]

The association refused to accept the argument that either disruption or the threat of violence should delay desegregation.

The NAACP lawyers used the time between the May 1954 decision and the implementation decision of May 1955 to build pressure for school desegregation through three types of activities. First, because of the absence of a mandate on implementation in the initial school segregation decision, the legal staff was called upon to coordinate the efforts of the local branches as they worked for rapid desegregation. Such a program placed a heavy burden on the limited number of attorneys available to the association, and yet it proved to be an important part of its desegregation efforts. Wherever possible, extensive use was made of local attorneys.

A second aspect of their work involved the continued attempts to test legal techniques and theories that were designed to broaden and protect the segregation decision. A New Jersey case raised the question of whether or not a school board was required to maintain maximum integration. NAACP lawyers argued cases in Delaware and Ohio to determine whether a local school board could order "resegregation" after it had enrolled blacks on a nondiscriminating basis. In a Tennessee case, the association won protection of the job rights of a black teacher who was fired because school administrators anticipated that he would be teaching white students because of impending integration.[19] The NAACP thus moved even before the implementation decision to plug some of the potential loopholes available to those seeking to evade desegregation.

The third aspect of the legal staff's work was its preparation of the implementation brief for the petitioners in the school segregation cases. The method used was the one that the NAACP had previously developed for the preparation of its 1953 rearguments in the school cases. In June,

> a group of lawyers, educators, sociologists and psychologists was assembled for a series of conferences. Specific research assignments were given staff members and consultants. These research memoranda were evaluated and revised by the entire group. Finally, this material was compressed into the brief which was filed in November.[20]

The NAACP sought to forge an overwhelming argument for rapid implementation from the same combination of legal and social scientific evidence that had carried its cause to victory in the May 1954 decision.

The NAACP filed its implementation brief on 15 November 1954. Its central premises were twofold: first, that individuals who have been denied rights are entitled to immediate relief in the courts; and second, that the burden of proof about the necessity for delays in school desegregation rested on the states. Applying these assumptions, the association called for the implementation of the decision as soon as "administrative and mechanical procedures can be completed."[21]

The association justified its position with a combination of case precedents and social scientific evidence. Citing as examples the Supreme Court decisions in *Youngstown Sheet & Tube Co.* v. *Sawyer*—the steel seizure case of 1952—and *Ex Parte Endo*—a Japanese-American civil liberties case of 1944 —its brief contended that: "Aggrieved parties showing denial of constitutional rights on analogous situations have received immediate relief despite arguments for delay more persuasive than any available here."[22] In an obvious attempt to rebut the argument that a gradual decree would bring about a more effective adjustment, the brief cited Harry S. Ashmore's recently published volume, *The Negro and the Schools,* and Kenneth B. Clark's article, "Desegregation: An Appraisal of Evidence," in the July 1953 issue of the *Journal of Social Issues.*[23] The major thrust of the evidence presented on this point was that gradual implementation had proven no more effective than immediate desegregation. The first part of the brief thus gave clear proof that the NAACP regarded rapid implementation as a crucial part of its continuing integration program. The association hoped that such an approach would undercut the forces opposed to the decision before they could become better organized.

The second part of the brief presented the NAACP's recommendations in the event that the Court decided to permit an "effective gradual adjustment from segregated school systems to systems not based on color distinctions."[24] It urged the Court to forego detailed desegregation decrees and to, instead, remand the cases to the lower federal courts with "specific directions to complete desegregation by a day certain."[25] The NAACP hoped that such a Supreme Court-imposed deadline would forestall unnecessary delays in the desegregation process. It was willing to admit the difficulty that would confront the Supreme Court in the event it attempted to direct the desegregation process. The NAACP reasoned, however, that the creation of a Court-imposed deadline would preclude the possibilities for long delays which it feared would develop if the less sympathetic lower federal courts oversaw the desegregation process on an ad hoc basis.

The NAACP concluded its brief by questioning the good faith of its opponents and recommending a specific deadline for implementation. It warned the Court to be especially cautious about the motives of the exponents of gradual integration:

> Much of the opposition to forthwith desegregation does not truly rest on any theory that it is better to accomplish it gradually. In considerable part, if indeed not in the main, such opposition stems from a desire that desegregation be not undertaken at all.[26]

Such an approach was designed to impugn the arguments for delay presented by the association's opponents. It was an attempt to destroy the attractiveness of what the Supreme Court justices might be tempted to regard as the most moderate, reasonable position in the controversy.

Reminding the Court that the petitioners were seeking "effective protection for adjudicated constitutional rights which are personal and present," the brief urged the Court to take decisive action: "Wherefore, we respectfully submit that this Court should direct the issuance of decrees in each of the cases requiring desegregation by no later than September of 1955."[27] Nothing is more indicative of the NAACP's position than the immediacy of the deadline date that it urged for complete desegregation.

As events were to prove, many Americans came to regard the NAACP's demand for immediate implementation as unrealistic and even radical. The widely publicized gradualist brief presented by the Eisenhower administration worked to reinforce this feeling. So also did the southern states' briefs, which emphasized the massive problems involved in adjustment. They had the effect of giving respectability to the group that the NAACP warned against in its brief: those who urged gradual implementation but actually opposed any desegregation. For these reasons, the NAACP's brief seemed the most rigid, unreasonable, and abrasive of those that the involved parties presented to the Court. It should not be forgotten, however, that it was a perfectly consistent position in light of the association's experience and previous successes. It was an attempt to rapidly consolidate its victory in the 1954 decision.

One other aspect of the implementation debate deserves

treatment at this time. During the subsequent oral arguments, attorneys for the NAACP and the southern states disagreed sharply over whether or not the Supreme Court should regard the five school segregation cases as class action suits under section 23.3(3) of the *Federal Rules of Civil Procedure*. Attorneys for the southern states, working to minimize the extent of the segregation decision, insisted that the question of "the extent of class" was not before the Court. This legal maneuver, of course, symbolized the desperation of the southern attorneys. If the Supreme Court accepted this position, its implementation decision could conceivably be limited to the specific cases and, more critically, to the specific individuals involved in the five cases before the Court. School desegregation could then be delayed interminably while the question was fought out in individual suits on a district-to-district basis before a number of hostile judges. Such extensive litigation, given the limited manpower and financial resources of the NAACP, would take years to accomplish.

On 6 May 1955 in response to an invitation from the Court, the NAACP filed a memorandum brief on the question. The NAACP reminded the Court that the five school cases had been regarded as class actions in the lower courts and in its own May 1954 decision. As the brief stated:

> The foregoing considerations also establish that the class which the individual plaintiffs brought on behalf of themselves and others similarly situated is precisely defined as to its racial, educational, residential and familial characteristics, as to the declarative and injunctive relief sought, and as to the nature of the right asserted. Defendants have had their day in Court and there is no equitable consideration which would justify any further litigation with the members of the class who were not individuals named.[28]

Its strong defense of the class-action principle underscored the crucial role that the concept played in the association's legal strategy. It was imperative that the Court extend the applicability of its decision to all of the victims of segregated education. Such a position contrasted sharply with the southern parties to the suits' perception of how desegregation should be implemented.

Chapter 6

The South and the Case for Delay

The response of southern political, educational, and community leaders to the May 1954 decision ranged from expressions of confidence that desegregation could be accomplished peacefully to calls for defiance. While the overwhelming majority of those quoted disagreed with the opinion, it was obvious that the Supreme Court's request for additional arguments on implementation greatly tempered their reactions by encouraging them to adopt a "wait and see" attitude. In so doing, it misled many Americans into believing that the opposition to school desegregation was far less formidable and widespread among white southerners than it actually was.

Moderate opinion was typified by the remarks of Harold Fleming, a spokesman for the Southern Regional Council, an interracial group dedicated to improving race relations in the South. Fleming expressed confidence that the manner in which the Court had rendered its decision would help the South to adjust. He felt that the unanimity of the decision would speed adjustment by giving "responsible Southern leadership a chance to work this thing out in a climate that can be relatively free of dissension and dispute as to what is the law of the land."[1] He regarded the Court's call for additional arguments on implementation as an "extension of time for negotiation, exploration and sound methods of thinking it through."[2] He was confident that white and black people in the South could sit down together at the school and community levels and work out acceptable integration programs.

In contrast to the NAACP leadership, Fleming was convinced that gradual implementation would work to undercut the growth of extremist opposition to school integration. As he put it:

> Indeed, if the demagogues can be curbed in any efforts to present the court decision as an immediate blow to so-called Southern traditions, it is very hopeful that the court's action can be properly presented to the South as actually an invitation and a challenge to join in the making of a sound adjustment program and not to be "obstructionists."[3]

Many moderates, like Fleming, felt it was imperative that the South be given time to desegregate its schools. They sincerely believed that this approach was the vehicle for progress. Their motives contrasted sharply with many other southerners who also called for a gradualistic approach to desegregation. The moderates added considerable respectability to the advocates of that approach to implementation.

The response of southern political leaders contrasted sharply with that of Fleming. Prior to the 1954 school decision, two states—Georgia and South Carolina—had passed legislation which empowered them to abolish their public school systems and establish private segregated schools in the event of court-ordered desegregation. The Virginia legislature, earlier in 1954, had hotly debated, but eventually voted down, three separate proposals to modify that state's public school systems in the event that the Court ruled against segregation. In so doing, it had adopted a "wait and see" attitude. Though some governors, like Allan Shivers of Texas and Frank G.

Clement of Tennessee, declared that their states' public schools would be preserved despite the desegregation decision, school officials in these states emphasized the need for years of delay to prepare the people for integration. Other governors, state school officials, and politicians in the South emphasized that they were studying the decision and awaiting the Court's position on implementation before deciding on a course of action. Many expressed the hope that the Court would create an implementation process that would take several years.[4]

The remarks of Georgia Attorney General Eugene Cook and Alabama State Education Superintendent W. J. Terry exemplified the evasive intent of many southern officials. Both insisted that they would not be bound by any desegregation orders of the Supreme Court since their respective states were not party to the litigation and hence not affected by its decision. They further contended that blacks would have to file suits against each of the school boards in their states to gain an extension of the ruling.[5]

The most striking expression of defiance on the state level came from Governor Herman Talmadge of Georgia. Immediately after the decision, he announced that he was calling the State Commission on Education at once "to map a program to insure continued and permanent segregation of the races."[6] Talmadge then urged Georgians to approve a state constitutional amendment in the upcoming fall election that would abolish the state's public schools. In words that would soon become a familiar part of the segregationist attack on the school decision, he asserted:

> The court has thrown down the gauntlet before those who believe the Constitution means what it says when it reserves to the individual States the right to regulate their own internal affairs. Georgians accept the challenge and will not tolerate the mixing of the races in the public schools or any of its public tax-supported institutions. The fact that the high tri-

bunal has seen fit to proclaim its views on sociology as well as law will not make any difference.[7]

Talmadge's remarks, though echoed by a few state legislators, contrasted sharply with the cautious public remarks of most state politicians in the South in the year after the segregation decision.

A number of journalists observed that school desegregation quickly became a usable issue for political candidates in the South. W. D. Workman, Jr., writing in the *Charlotte* (North Carolina) *Observer,* for example, noted that all of the candidates for governor and lieutenant governor in the 1954 South Carolina campaign proposed means of preserving segregated schools. All emphasized that they supported the wishes of the majority of their constituents that separate schools be maintained.[8]

The rapidity with which the school decision became an issue in southern state politics is indicative of the intense feelings it aroused in the South. The haste of many southern politicians to "get right" with their constituents on the issue suggests as much fear on their part as it does opportunism. The segregation decision did, after all, challenge one of the pillars of southern society. Though the Supreme Court's call for additional arguments softened the blow, its declaration that segregation was inherently unconstitutional had ominous implications for the white South. It is impossible to escape the conclusion that there was a symbiotic relationship between the reaction of southern politicians and what they sensed to be the true feelings of their constituents. It is difficult to determine whether southern politicians took advantage of the school segregation issue or were entrapped by it. Certainly, some willingly exploited the decision ruthlessly; others only because they had no choice.[9] Both groups were trapped by the long shadow of the South's tragic past.

The reaction of the South's congressional leaders to the school decision was similar to that of its state politicians. The bulk of the southern congressmen expressed disappointment and disagreement with the decision, but only a few urged defiance and directly condemned the Court. Again, as on the state level, the initial southern congressional response was greatly tempered by the call for additional arguments on implementation by the Court.

Philip Dodd of the Chicago Tribune Press Service summarized the salient features of the southern congressional response that emerged in the week immediately following the decision:

1. The decision will set back racial relations in the south fifty years, with harshness replacing the average southerner's benevolent attitude toward the Negro.
2. Violence can result from forcing white and Negro children to attend the same school, particularly in rural areas.
3. The Negroes will be the big losers—Negro teachers who will be unable to get jobs in integrated schools and Negro children who will be shunned by their white playmates.
4. Southern states will suffer great financial loss, having spent hundreds of millions of dollars on duplicate school facilities under the 1896 "separate but equal" doctrine overthrown by the high court Monday.
5. Further court decrees upsetting traditional social patterns are feared . . . which the southerners have been able to block in Congress.
6. The declining era of the Dixie demagog [*sic*] will be prolonged because southern officeholders will have to become more rabid on the racial question to protect their political positions.[10]

As the preceding summary indicates, southern congressional leaders found numerous practical reasons to rationalize their opposition to the decision besides a belief in white supremacy.

Two senators, Richard B. Russell of Georgia and James O. Eastland of Mississippi, openly attacked the Supreme Court and urged that its powers be checked. Senator Russell, up for reelection amidst the rumors that Governor Talmadge was considering challenging him, charged in the Senate that the Court was the "pliant tool" of the Executive Department and insisted that: "Ways must be found to check the tendency of the court to disregard the Constitution and the precedents of able and unbiased judges. . . ."[11] Senator Russell, incensed at the Court's decision, proceeded to lecture it on what he considered "proper" constitutional doctrine.

Eastland, in a Senate speech on 27 May 1954, presented an even more extreme denunciation of the school decision and the Supreme Court. He charged that the Court was trying to use its segregation decision to take "absolute control of the country."[12] Asserting that the South would keep its schools segregated despite "northern meddlers," he characterized the Court's decision as a "reckless disregard of official oath and public duty." Eastland announced that he would soon introduce a constitutional amendment to check the Court's interference with states' rights, one that would say, "there shall be no interference with or limitation upon the power of any state to regulate health, morals, education, marriage and good order in the states."[13]

Turning to an explanation of the ruling against segregation, the Mississippi senator charged that the Court was "indoctrinated and brainwashed by Leftwing pressure groups." As evidence, he accused five justices of violating judicial propriety, a charge he attempted to prove through the dubious technique of guilt by association. Justice Hugo L. Black had received an award at an interracial banquet of the Southern Conference for Human Welfare, which Eastland characterized as a "notorious Communist-front organization." Justice Sherman Minton had spoken at the same meeting. Justice William O. Douglas was characterized as "virtually a protégé" of the CIO, which had helped finance the fight against segregation. Moreover, the senator continued, Douglas had once advocated the American recognition of Red China. Eastland completed his attempts at character assassination by noting that Justices Stanley F. Reed and Felix Frankfurter "broke all precedents" by testifying as character witnesses for Alger Hiss, the former State Department official who was convicted of perjury for denying that he had Communist associations. As a finishing touch, he condemned the Court ruling because it had "usurped the legislative powers of the Congress and of the legislatures of the separate states."[14] The decision, according to Eastland, proved that the Supreme Court was un-American, radical, and probably dominated by subversives.

The Russell and Eastland speeches are significant. The two senators openly expressed the reaction of hard-core segregationists to the school decision. Though surrounded by the more moderate or tentative statements of their colleagues and dismissed as the thoughts of "hotheads" and "political posturers" by the northern press, the Russell-Eastland stance did represent the feelings of a large number of white southerners who were unalterably opposed to integration. This group was sincerely convinced that the survival of racial separation was absolutely crucial and that the decision threatened the South's entire way of life. Talk of gradual desegregation or long delays did nothing to lessen the opposition of this group. Again, the tragic consequences that have stemmed from the South's inability to escape its own history are evident.

The Russell-Eastland position set the pattern for the vehement attack on the Supreme Court that was to become one of the standard tools of the more extreme opponents of the school segregation decision. The portrayal of the Court as an alien, subversive force that threatened traditional states' rights and the American way of life proved to be an effective means of obscuring the crucial question about the wisdom of segregation which the Court had raised in its May 1954 decision. The Court's subsequent sweeping liberal decisions in the areas of criminal law, legislative apportionment, and freedom of association provided additional "evidence" to support the Russell-Eastland charge.[15] This response was, in reality, an admission of fear about the ultimate implications of the decision. Many white southerners, overcome by such fears, would soon adopt the two senators' "Alice in Wonderland"-like assumptions about the Court as their own.

One significant conclusion is apparent in the initial response of the South to the May 1954 decision. Despite their calls for calm and moderation, the political leaders in the Deep South were looking for an out, some way to preserve segregated schools.[16] Remarks like those of Virginia Governor Thomas B. Stanley, who called for the creation of "a plan which will be acceptable to our citizens and in keeping with the edict of the court," summarized the dilemma in which southern leaders found themselves.[17] Given the fact that the wishes of their constituents and the demands of the segregation decision were diametrically opposed, these leaders had little choice except to seek means of getting around the Court's opinion. Plans to accomplish this went into effect immediately. The governors of the other southern states created study commissions or conferred with legislative committees about the best means to preserve their segregated schools.[18]

The cold reality of the South's opposition to desegregation was clearly expressed in the briefs on implementation presented by Virginia, South Carolina, and the amicus briefs of Florida, Texas, and other southern states whose separate school systems were threatened. The contrast between the major assumptions and recommendations in these briefs and those of Kansas, Delaware, and the District of Columbia—the other respondents in the school cases—brings this point into even clearer focus. For this reason, an examination of the major arguments presented in their implementation briefs is in order.

The Kansas, Delaware and
District of Columbia Briefs on Implementation

The Kansas response on implementation came in two briefs, one from the Topeka Board of Education and the other from the state's attorney general. The general theme of both was that Kansas was making rapid progress toward desegregation and that no major implementation problems had arisen. The brief filed on 27 September 1954 by Peter F. Caldwell for the Topeka Board of Education was simply a progress report on integration in the public schools under its control. It described the board's three-step plan, which would lead to full integration by September 1955. The board emphasized that it was in the process of terminating segregation "as rapidly as is practical with full public cooperation and acceptance by both White and Negro teachers and parents." It stated that since its actions were "in good faith" there was no need for the Supreme Court to appoint a special master to formulate specific decrees regarding the particular steps needed to terminate segregation in the Topeka schools.[19] The Topeka Board of Education insisted that there was no need for further Supreme Court action.

The brief submitted on 16 November 1954 by Harold R. Fatzer, Kansas Attorney General, summarized the rapid progress toward desegregation in the first-class cities that had permitted segregation.[20] Such extensive progress toward desegregation had been made in Kansas, according to the attorney general, that all the Supreme Court had to do was "reverse the judgment of the District Court and remand the case to such Court with directions to enter judgment with the opinion herein and to retain jurisdiction thereof until said judgment be complied with."[21] No recommendation for a decree was made. The attorney general assumed that the district court would decide the time needed for desegregation.

It is obvious from the wording of the attorney general's brief that the recommendation that the case be remanded was motivated by the assumption that the transition to desegregated schools in Kansas was occurring rapidly and with little difficulty. Nothing in the brief suggested or rationalized the need for delay in school integration. The recommendation for district court supervision was merely for convenience. Segregated schools, long permitted in cities of the first-class but never mandatory in Kansas, were not regarded by most Kansans as fundamental pillars of their society.

Delaware Attorney General H. Albert Young filed that state's brief on implementation on 15 November 1954. The brief opened with a long discussion of the operation of the Delaware school system up to the time of the school segregation decision. It continued with a summation of the results of desegregation to date. It emphasized that real progress had been made but that many Delaware citizens opposed desegregation.[22] In light of this situation, Delaware urged the Supreme Court to do two things: first, "permit a gradual adjustment from segregated public education to a system without race distinctions"; and second, "remand the case to the lower courts for formulation of decree for the admittance of plaintiffs to public schools without regard to race as soon as practical within a time limit to be set by this Court."[23] The Delaware brief thus argued the necessity for a period of transition to complete the integration process it had already begun. It did, however, urge the U.S. Supreme Court to set a time limit in which such desegregation should be accomplished. The tone of its brief reflected confidence that such a process would lead to full desegregation, and that its citizens would be brought into compliance.

Milton D. Korman, the corporation counsel for the District of Columbia, filed its implementation brief on 15 November 1954.[24] The brief began with a summary of the progress toward integration in the District's schools and stated that the process would be completed by 1 September 1955. It justified the Court's right to grant a short transition period with reference to the same cases cited in the District's 1953 reargument brief. It noted the broad variety of opinion on the District of Columbia Board of Education regarding the timing of desegregation as a justification for the requested delay in implementation. The brief stated:

> Unless, therefore, the Court disagrees with the first premise, i.e., that the unconstitutionality of segregated schools does not require an immediate transition to an integrated system, it is submitted that no directive of compliance with the decision of May 17th is necessary, because the time schedule which the respondents have put into operation for the accomplishment of complete integration . . . is as short as can reasonably be done to establish in orderly fashion a school system that complies.[25]

The emphasis in the brief was on the shortness of the period required for the completion of full integration.

The major emphasis in the Kansas, Delaware, and District of Columbia briefs was on rapid compliance with the May 1954 decision. While all assumed that some time for a transition to a desegregated school system was reasonable, none used this position to rationalize a long delay in the implementation process. All emphasized that the "periods of transition" they requested would be used to complete school integration programs already well underway.

The three briefs, like the United States government's, took a position between the NAACP's call for immediate desegregation and the southern states' arguments for extended delays. Though certainly closer in intent and spirit to the position of the NAACP than that of the southern states, Kansas, Delaware, and the District of Columbia, by supporting the Supreme Court's power to permit short periods of transition, added to the pressure on the Court to adopt a gradual, flexible approach to implementation. The substantial progress which they had made toward integration added plausibility to their position.

The Virginia and South Carolina
Briefs on Implementation

The implementation briefs of two southern states, Virginia and South Carolina, were filed on 15 November 1954. The brief presented by Virginia Attorney General J. Lindsay Almond, Jr., typified the position of the southern state governments on the school desegregation issue.[26] An examination of its contents underscores the unique assumptions about implementation which the South held.

The first part of the Virginia brief emphasized the Court's power to permit gradual adjustment of existing conditions. It justified this position through a quite different application of equity law than that which the NAACP used to demand immediate restoration of rights denied the victims of segregation.

In defense of this position, the Virginia brief cited the Supreme Court's order for further argument on the question of implementation. It asserted that the five school segregation cases, as actions in equity, came under the well-recognized rule that the Court may create, withhold, delay, or condition any remedy that it finds appropriate. As a further example, it cited the extended periods of time permitted in various antitrust cases to implement Court decrees. The brief insisted, moreover, that there were compelling legal and historical reasons why this aspect of equity law should be applied in the implementation decision:

> In earlier school cases, when equality of facilities was at issue, time was customarily permitted for equalization. Those cases concerned enforcement of the same right as that of the appellants, and the fact of present right does not encompass the right to immediate remedy. The power to permit gradual adjustment clearly exists.[27]

Just as the NAACP brief had pointed out that the court possessed clear-cut precedents permitting immediate relief, so the Virginia brief pointed out that it had clear-cut precedents to opt for gradual implementation.

Having established the Supreme Court's legal power to permit gradual adjustment by defining the segregation cases as equity law, Virginia then developed a rationale for the application of such an approach to its own public schools. The brief placed particular emphasis on the time needed to create varying plans for different localities. It noted that the percentage of blacks varied from zero to 77 percent in Virginia communities and that this situation was further complicated by the differing levels of public health, educational attainment, and areas of residence among blacks and whites. Obviously, the creation of an integration plan which considered all of these variables would be a challenging task. Consequently, the brief warned: "Time is needed for the preparation of such a plan; without such a plan, Virginia's schools may be closed."[28] The brief thus made it explicitly clear that the Court would have to grant an indefinite period for implementation or risk having the public schools closed in defiance. In effect, Virginia told the Court that it had no choice.

The brief reinforced this warning by reminding the Court that the major obstacle to desegregation in Virginia would be the difficulty in creating a favorable community attitude toward it. The obvious antagonism toward desegregation "already evident in Prince Edward County and other parts of Virginia" would not be easily overcome. It stated:

> An integrated system will require more than time. It will require a complete change in the feelings of the people. Only if time that the Court may properly permit is given to devise a workable plan can public education continue to serve its object and purpose.[29]

The authors of the Virginia brief, as did the authors of the brief from the state of South Carolina and the amicus briefs submitted by the other southern states, insisted that the amount of time needed for such an adjustment could not be determined by the Supreme Court. Nowhere was this position more evident than in Virginia's specific recommendations about the nature of the decree which the Supreme Court should issue.

Virginia asserted that the Court had "no evidence of record on which a final decree could be based."[30] This was so, because

> the evidence of record relates primarily to the effect of segregation; the final decree must generally be based on evidence as to the effect of integration. None is now before the Court; without it a final decree would be based purely on conjecture.[31]

The question of integration, if one accepted this line of reasoning, was separate and distinct from segregation. Though the Court had outlawed the latter, it could not automatically claim knowledge of how to impose the former. The Court, according to Virginia, simply had no evidence upon which it could formulate a final decree because racial integration was nonexistent in the Virginia schools.

Moreover, the Court, according to the Virginia brief, had never framed specific decrees in any of the previous school cases which it had decided. It also had refused the task in numerous other cases. The Virginians capped their evidence on this point with a reference to the Court's behavior in the case at hand: "The mere fact that the Court seeks now a statement of the issues to be determined by a final decree points up the impossibility of its present preparation."[32] The brief interpreted the Court's calls for reargument as an admission of its own inadequacy. And the appointment of a master to gather information and advise the Court about the nature of a decree would not be worthwhile, asserted Virginia. It dismissed such an approach as "a cumbersome and impractical method of obtaining evidence for framing the decree." The use of a master would, it alleged, fail because of his lack of familiarity of local conditions.

Virginia's sharp criticism suggests that it feared that the Court's contemplated use of this approach would provide it with the type of detailed evidence necessary to formulate a specific decree. Such a stand was part of the state's effort to give the Supreme Court a massive inferiority complex on the subject of implementation.

The Virginia brief thus concluded that nothing the Supreme Court could do would make up for its lack of information. Who then should direct the implementation process? The advice in the brief was not unexpected:

> The proper solution is reversal and remand to the Court below for further proceedings in accordance with very general instructions to enforce the decision of this Court while permitting the preservation of the local school system. In this regard, the Court below should be permitted to allow such time as is reasonably necessary consistent with the preservation of the school system and local community attitudes.[33]

To the Virginians, the possibility of rapid implementation on a fixed time schedule was out of the question. Critics asserted that their recommendations would indefinitely delay implementation of the May 1954 decision in Virginia and that it sought to encourage defiance beneath a façade of pretended conformity to the law. Its defenders argued that it was the most pragmatic approach for the South to take.

The Virginia brief was a mixture of evidence and fear that foreshadowed many of the techniques the South would use to resist the implementation of the school segregation decision in the years that followed. Its sharp contrast with the brief presented by the NAACP clearly illustrates the conflicting assumptions and legal strategies the two adversaries brought to the confrontation over school segregation. Each presented the Supreme Court with a historically reinforced, constitutionally valid, practical rationale for accepting its own particular definition of the problem before it, as well as the means to resolve it.

Moreover, the middle ground between the NAACP and the southern states occupied by the Kansas, Delaware, and District of Columbia briefs was a plausible position. As events were to prove, however, the real strength of the middle position came from beyond the briefs of the parties to the suit. The decision of the Eisenhower administration to support a gradual approach to school desegregation added immense prestige to that position. The reasons why the administration adopted that stance are thus a worthy topic for our consideration.

Chapter 7

Eisenhower's Moderate Approach to Implementation

As in other times of crisis, Americans looked to the president for leadership at the time of the school segregation decision. It was apparent to many that the reaction of the immensely popular, highly respected Dwight D. Eisenhower could be of crucial importance in influencing the reactions of Americans to the opinion. An examination of the Eisenhower administration's reaction to the May 1954 decision and the initial phase of the debate over its implementation suggests that the president continued to rely on the same moderate approach he had developed in the year and a half prior to the decision.

Political Implications

Eisenhower administration leaders certainly realized that the school decision was full of implications for the future of the GOP. Journalists, political commentators, and politicians carried on an extensive discussion of these implications for some weeks after the decision. Most agreed that it weakened the chances for Republican efforts to further dent the traditional Democratic domination of the South. A number predicted that the four southern Republican congressmen elected in 1952 and those Democrats who had supported Eisenhower's candidacy were in big political trouble.

Many southerners, according to these observers, held the Eisenhower administration directly responsible for the Supreme Court's ruling against segregation. They based this charge on two assumptions. Southerners blamed the president for naming the liberal Earl Warren as chief justice of the Supreme Court and because Attorney General Herbert Brownell had intervened on behalf of the federal government in support of the antisegregation forces in the school cases.[1]

Columnist Gould Lincoln, writing in the *Washington Star,* explained the basis of Eisenhower's appeal in the South prior to the school decision:

> Gen. Eisenhower carried four states of the Democratic "solid South. . . ." He ran strongly in other Southern States. His strength in the South was due to two things: He was regarded as a national hero rather than a Republican, and he gained from the Southern hatred of former President Truman, much of which was inherited by Adlai Stevenson. . . . Mr. Stevenson accepted the Truman civil rights program. The comment today among Southern Democrats was that Eisenhower would never carry a Southern State again.[2]

If the journalists were correct, the identification of the president with the school decision implied disaster for Republicanism in the South. Their comments suggest that a great deal of the president's support was rooted in the assumption of many southerners that he would leave racial matters to the states. A later Republican administration sensing the potency of this feeling would use it as the basis of a "southern strategy" to build its power in the South.

The pessimistic picture drawn by the political pundits was reinforced by the letters the administration received from federal officials in the South. Typical of these was the 5 October

1954 letter from Hardy A. Sullivan, director of the Tampa, Florida, office of the Federal Housing Administration, to Presidential Press Secretary James C. Hagerty. Emphasizing the changed attitude of southerners toward the president, he stated:

> I had lunch today at Valencia restaurant, near here, and heard three businessmen talking. . . . They looked at the enclosed headlines [regarding disorders over integration in D.C. schools] and said "I am dam [*sic*] glad it is now happening in Washington where *he* can see it," another man "I voted for him as he said he would leave it up to the states or give us real states rights," the other man "I wont [*sic*] make that mistake again." There was much more conversation all along the same veing [*sic*] and anti-integration.[3]

Such pessimistic judgments as these raised a question: Could the administration do anything to escape the blame that southerners heaped upon it for the school decision?

Sullivan did suggest an approach to implementation which he felt would offset the alienation he had observed:

> Jim—The Texas attorney general came forth with the suggestion that the States be allowed to gradually integrate the races in the schools as they would determine themselves. I believe Florida endorsed practically the same plan. It might be wise to adopt such a plan. . . . This would re-assure on states rights yet not attempt to revoke the supreme court decision. . . . This would put the onus on the respective governors of the states where it belongs. . . . The issue is hot right now and something should be done promptly or the whole thing will backfire.[4]

The message coming from federal officials in the South contained one main theme: Go slow on implementation.

There was, of course, another aspect of the political impact of the school decision. Many of the same commentators who predicted that the decision would lead to disaster in the South felt that it would be partially offset by Republican gains among normally black voters in the urban areas of the North who would credit the administration for the Court's opinion. Most agreed, however, that the possibility that such feelings would break the loyalty of northern blacks to the liberal wing of the Democratic party, which also supported the school decision, was by no means as certain as the loss of Republican and conservative Democratic support in the South.[5]

Thus, the Eisenhower administration was certainly aware that the school segregation decision could have far-reaching effects on American politics. Unfortunately, that knowledge did not solve the political dilemma the decision caused for the GOP. Whatever position the administration took could conceivably endanger the hopes it cherished to improve its standing with an important segment of American voters. Would a conciliatory mood placate the alarmed white South? Would it destroy Republican hopes to gain black votes through its previous impressive accomplishments in the area of civil rights? Worst of all, no one could predict the consequences for either major party of a knock-down drag-out fight on the question in national politics. The lack of certainty about these and similar questions encouraged President Eisenhower to adopt a cautious stance on the implementation of the school decision.

The Art of Caution

Probably Dwight D. Eisenhower's most controversial position in the realm of civil rights, certainly the one that earned him the most criticism, was his refusal to publicly voice his approval of the 1954 decision in the school segregation cases while he was in office. He later explained the reasons for this stance in his memoirs:

> After the Supreme Court's 1954 ruling, I refused to say whether I either approved or disapproved of it. The Court's

judgment was law, I said, and I would abide by it. This determination was one of principle. I believed that if I should express, publicly, either approval or disapproval of a Supreme Court decision in one case, I would be obliged to do so in many, if not all, cases. Inevitably I would eventually be drawn into a public statement of disagreement with some decision, creating a suspicion that my vigor of enforcement would, in such cases, be in doubt.[6]

Despite his rationale, which he stated repeatedly from 1954 to 1960, the exponents of school integration charged him with vacillation, arguing that he owed the nation a more positive stand in view of the critical nature of the segregation issue. Many charged that his neutral position encouraged intransigence and defiance on the part of segregationists. Such complaints fell on deaf ears, however, because the president and his most influential advisors were convinced that such a personal stance would further inflame an extremely emotional situation. His position was one of the major arguments used by a whole series of critics who charged him with a general lack of leadership. It ranks as one of the chief examples why such diverse critics as Emmet John Hughes, Earl Warren, Richard Kluger, and Paul L. Murphy have referred to the president's refusal to make adequate use of the power and prestige he possessed.[7]

One strong influence lurking behind Eisenhower's public position (and perhaps controlling it) in the spring of 1954 was his fear, later to be vindicated in Virginia, that the southern states would close down their public school systems rather than integrate them. Indications of the importance of this fear appear in the notes summarizing the president's 18 May 1954 pre–press conference briefing. As Presidential Press Secretary Hagerty noted in his diary:

The president is considerably concerned, as are all of us, on the effect of the ruling. There is a strong possibility that some of the southern states will take steps to virtually cancel out their public education system and through legislative devices within their states place most of their schools on a "private" school basis, giving state aid to such "private" institutions. The president expressed the fear that such a plan if it were followed through would not only handicap Negro children but would work to the detriment of the so-called "poor whites" in the South.[8]

Such concerns, when coupled with the president's beliefs, explain the moderation and caution with which he approached the school desegregation issue.

The president's moderation was also very much in evidence in his public comments about the desegregation issue in the period between the first *Brown* decision and the implementation decision which followed it a year later. In his 19 May 1954 press conference, the president was asked by a southern reporter if he had any advice for the South as to how it should react to the decision. He replied:

Not in the slightest. I thought that Governor Byrnes made a very fine statement when he said let us be calm, and let us be reasonable, and let us look this thing in the face.

The Supreme Court has spoken, and I am sworn to uphold the Constitutional process in this country. And I am trying—I will obey it.[9]

The president carefully avoided any references to the fear he had expressed privately the previous day.

When asked whether the decision would put those southerners who had supported the Eisenhower ticket in 1952 on the spot and whether it would alienate his southern supporters, the president drew a sharp distinction between the Court's decision and the administration's responsibility for it.

The Supreme Court, as I understand it, is not under any administration. . . . That is all I will say. I have stood, so far as I know, for honest, decent government since I was first mentioned as a political figure. I am still standing for it. And they will have to make their own decision as to whether they decide that I have got any sense, or haven't.[10]

The president, utterly consistent with his personal beliefs, attempted to stake out an independent position on the desegregation question despite the brief his attorney general had presented to the Supreme Court supporting desegregation. Such a position was in line with his beliefs about the importance of separation of powers in the federal government, his already cited reservations about the wisdom of administration involvement in the case, and his perception of the political situation.

Not surprisingly, then, in his 16 June 1954 press conference the president publicly stated his skepticism about the chances of overcoming segregation solely by legal action. In reference to a question about whether he intended to take action to try and get bills banning segregation in interstate travel out of committee in the House, he responded that he believed in "progress accomplished through the intelligence of people, and through the cooperation of people, more than law, when we can get it that way."[11] That belief explains much about the president's approach to the desegregation question, particularly his reluctance to take executive action and to recommend legislation dealing with the issue.

The extension of his moderate approach was also evident in the message he sent to the Forty-fifth Annual Meeting of the NAACP on 29 June 1954. Citing the school segregation decision as a "milestone of social advance," he praised the mature response of Americans to it and argued that the times required the continued demonstration of that maturity. The president defined what he meant by that maturity:

> We must have patience without compromise of principle. We must have understanding without disregard for differences of opinion which actually exist. We must have continued social progress, calmly but persistently made. . . .[12]

The president obviously saw an important role for himself as a calming influence, as a mediator between the major protagonists on the segregation issue. His words failed to inhibit the

NAACP's continuing efforts for rapid desegregation.

Another aspect of Eisenhower's attempt to avoid controversy on the desegregation question appeared in his treatment of the members of the black press. As Presidential Press Secretary Hagerty noted in his diary, Eisenhower mentioned that because he did not want to be charged with ignoring the black press he was going out of his way to recognize Ethel Payne, a black reporter for *Defender Publications,* despite his belief that many of her questions were foolish.[13] The president stated the basis of his action:

> You know, Jim, I suppose nobody knows how they feel or how many pressures or insults they have to take. I guess the only way you can realize exactly how they feel is to have a black skin for several weeks. I'm going to continue to give them a break at the press conferences despite the questions they ask.[14]

While Eisenhower might have been gulity of condescension here, he must also be credited with compassion and empathy.

There was an important reason why the president was critical of the questions asked by black reporters. He found them annoying because he felt they pushed him into an advocacy or activist position on the desegregation question. During the president's press conference on 7 July, Payne asked whether his administration was supporting a bill to bar segregation in interstate travel in light of his Justice Department's position that there was a legal basis for such a law and because his Bureau of the Budget approved of it. The president's retort was sharp:

> I don't know by what right you say that you have to have Administration support. The Administration is trying to do what it thinks to be—believes decent and just in this country, and it is not in the effort to support any particular or special group of any kind. These opinions were sent down. These beliefs are held as part of Administration belief, because we think this is just and right, and that is the answer.[15]

The distinction he drew between doing something because it was right and doing the same thing for the purpose of advancing a certain group proved ultimately to be difficult to maintain in the highly charged atmosphere that surrounded the school segregation cases.

The president's attitude toward implementation of the desegregation decision was greatly influenced by his continued faith in the efficacy of always taking a moderate approach to tough problems. Writing to his old personal friend Swede Hazlett on 23 October 1954, he stated:

> The segregation issue will, I think, become acute or tend to die out according to the character of the procedure orders that the Court will probably issue this winter. My own guess is this—they will be very moderate and secure a maximum of initiative to local courts.[16]

The Hazlett letter indicates that the president in late 1954 had much confidence in the moderating potential of a Court decree which allowed a gradual process of desegregation. He was the prisoner of his own philosophy on the point. Reason, he soon learned, could not overcome emotion on the segregation issue.

Further evidence of the polarizing effect of the school decision came to the administration in the deluge of letters the president received from ordinary citizens discussing the issue. It is this author's personal estimate, after examining the massive collection of that correspondence in the Dwight D. Eisenhower Presidential Library that the overwhelming number of the letters the president received (80 percent) were from southern and border states, and nearly all of them condemned the decision and the Supreme Court. The correspondence represented a vast geographical and occupational cross-section of southern whites. The range of criticism in the letters included: scholarly constitutional dispositions on states' rights, arguments based on the *Plessy* doctrine, openly racist arguments emphasizing the inferiority of blacks, and charges that the decision was part of a Communist plot designed to destroy America by race mixing.[17] The predominant mood of the letters was fear.

Many held the president personally responsible for the decision and accused him of betraying them. Still others expressed confidence that Eisenhower would use his power to check the Supreme Court. The letters presented a striking exhibition of the intensity of southern feelings on the Court's action. The manner in which the administration responded to the correspondence suggests that it was an influential factor in pushing the president toward a cautious stance on the integration question.

After considerable experimentation and discussion, Maxwell M. Rabb, President Eisenhower's secretary of the cabinet and his chief advisor on civil rights affairs, decided that a rather generalized, nonoffensive answer by one of the lesser-known men on the White House staff would be the best means of responding to the opponents of the Court decision. As Rabb emphasized in a memorandum to J. William Barba, assistant to the special counsel to the president, concerning the proper way to answer prosegregation letters: "Ordinarily I find letters of this type that I think either you or Mr. Shanley should acknowledge. My name attached to this kind of response in behalf of the president would be like a red flag."[18]

Consequently, the administration developed a rather generalized response as typified by the following example:

> The president has asked me to acknowledge your letter of recent date in which you bring to his attention your views relative to the school segregation case. He has asked me to thank you for writing to him at such length and to tell you that he will bear in mind your comments.[19]

Nothing in its wording revealed the administration's attitude toward the decision.

The administration's response to the minority of Americans, nearly all from outside the South, who wrote supporting the school segregation decision contrasted sharply with that sent to its critics. A typical example was the 20 July 1954 letter from Maxwell M. Rabb to the Reverend L. K. Jackson of the St. Paul Baptist Church in Gary, Indiana, which stated in part:

> The president wants you to know that he is deeply grateful to you for your kind comments about his part in urging an end to second-class citizenship. It is the expressed objective of the president that a "cardinal ideal of this heritage we cherish is the equality of rights of citizens of every race and color and creed." You may be assured that we will strive to realize this objective.[20]

The contrast between the two types of letters symbolizes the dilemma the administration found itself in after the May 1954 decision. The Supreme Court had unintentionally placed the administration on the spot.

What about the impact of the outpouring of correspondence on the president? Eisenhower's actions from May 1954 to May 1955 suggest that he became convinced during that time that the school decision had created a politically explosive crisis, one which sharply divided Americans. He was fully aware that the heart of the crisis lay in the unique racial attitudes of white southerners. The increasing caution of his public statements on the segregation issue suggest that he hoped a moderate position on the part of his administration would lessen that polarization. For whatever reasons, the president moved to create a distinctly cautious position for himself on the desegregation question which contrasted sharply with his previous one. That he was aware of the political implications of the situation confronting him is certain. That his actions were governed by them is not.

The Administration's Brief

A hint of the position the administration would take in its brief on implementation of the 1954 decision appeared in the telegram President Eisenhower sent to Walter White on 29 June 1954 on the occasion of the NAACP's Forty-fifth Annual Meeting.[21] After greeting the delegates, the president assessed the significance of the school segregation decision:

> We have passed in the year 1954, a milestone of social advance in the United States. The social and political maturity of our people evidenced by the reception given the recent Supreme Court decision is of great significance to our nation and to the cause of freedom in the world.[22]

In a reference that suggested his own preference for restraint in the application of the school decision, the president continued:

> The times call for continuing demonstration of that maturity. We must have patience without compromise of principle. We must have understanding without disregard for differences of opinion which actually exist. We must have continued social progress, calmly but persistently made, so that we may prove without doubt to all the world that our nation and our people are truly dedicated to liberty and justice for all.[23]

The president's call for "patience without compromise of principle" suggests that he supported a cautious, gradual approach to implementation, one that would give the South time to adjust. Such an approach reflected the president's faith that reason and good will could resolve the crisis created in the South. His message gave the NAACP a clear indication that the government's brief on implementation would not support immediate integration.

On 23 November 1954, the day before the administration filed its brief, President Eisenhower revealed his thoughts on implementation at a press conference. In response to a question by Harry C. Dent of the *Columbia* (South Carolina) *State and Record* about his personal views, the president stated:

I am sure America wants to obey the Constitution, but there is a very great practical problem involved, and there are certainly deep-seated emotions. Now what I understand the Supreme Court has, and has undertaken, as its task, is to write its orders of procedure in such fashion as to take into consideration these great emotional strains and the practical problems, and try to devise a way where under some form of decentralized process we can bring this about. And I don't believe they intend to be arbitrary. At least this is my understanding.[24]

Eisenhower's remarks proved to be a fitting preface to the "gradualist" implementation brief the government filed the following day.

The president's position as reflected in the government's brief was disappointing to those Americans who hoped for rapid, massive desegregation supported by the federal judiciary and the executive branch. A number of individuals and groups accused Eisenhower of attempting to pressure the Court by commenting on the pending decision on implementation. One such example of this criticism appeared in a 25 November 1954 telegram from the officers of the all-black Louisiana Education Association, which charged:

An A.P. story of November 23, with comments accredited to you, which if true, indicate an encroachment by the executive upon the area of government reserved to the judiciary, seriously undermine that basic decision of May 17th.

It is not only precedent shattering for a President to comment upon a case pending in the Supreme Court, but in this instance these remarks are being construed as jeopardizing the rights of millions of people, injuring our prestige abroad and weakening our morale at home. For whatever reason the alleged statement was made these remarks are further being construed as pressure by the executive upon the judiciary.

We are deeply grieved by the alleged remarks and we join in heartfelt sympathy with those great Americans who moved ahead toward implementing the Supreme Court decision of last May 17th. . . . Please Mr. President clarify your position on de-segregation.[25]

The advocates of rapid desegregation regarded the president's remarks and the government's brief as dangerous rationales for delay that would be fully exploited by segregationists. There is no doubt that this feeling worked to create antagonism between the NAACP and the administration. The episode clearly illustrates the difficulties the president experienced when he tried to develop a position on an issue that was surrounded by conflicting moral principles and political necessities.

Attorney General Brownell filed the government's brief on implementation on 24 November 1954. The argument it presented was completely consistent with the moderate position the president had developed since the May 1954 decision. Beginning with the assumption that the Supreme Court had "full power to direct such relief as will be most effective and just," the government called for a prompt and feasible program to end segregated schools.[26]

Emphasizing that the "public interest required an intelligent, orderly and effective solution of the problems" that would be encountered by those complying with the segregation decision, the government reminded the Court that these problems would probably vary from area to area.[27] Consequently, the government recommended that the U.S. Supreme Court serve as the general supervisor of the desegregation process, and that it remand the cases to the federal district courts with directions to implement "as the particular circumstances permit."[28] The local school authorities were to formulate and execute desegregation programs under the supervision of the district courts which served the affected districts.[29] The gradual approach of the Eisenhower administration to the implementation question was in perfect character.

The administration's semiofficial newspaper, the *New York Herald Tribune,* painted an enthusiastic picture of what it regarded as the major advantages of the government's implementation plan in a 26 November 1954 editorial:

> The virtue of this plan is that it fits many local conditions. It offers understanding and good will; it leaves enforcement to the people themselves but insists that there must be enforcement. The objective is to get compliance from the ground up. . . . It is a practical application of common sense which allows each community to develop an acceptable solution.[30]

The administration hoped to bridge the gap between judicial principle and social reality in the South by the application of a mixture of local control and gradualism. On the surface, it appeared to be the most pragmatic approach. The crucial question yet to be faced was whether such an approach would be exploited as a sign of weakness by the more extreme opponents of desegregation. Much would depend on who controlled the process of desegregation at the local level. The Eisenhower administration's position was, of course, premised on the assumption that those who would shape the desegregation plans would do so in good faith. As events were to prove, that assumption was to be seriously challenged.

Summation

The predominant mood of the country during the year between the May 1954 segregation decision and the May 1955 implementation decision was one of apprehension. There were definite signs that the school segregation decision contained the potential for a struggle of major proportions. The conflicting stands on implementation taken by the NAACP, the government, and the southern states provided ample grounds for such a conclusion. President Eisenhower's attempt to stay aloof from the desegregation controversy and the exploitation of the issue by southern politicians added their own unique dimensions to the potential for conflict. The implementation decision of May 1955 brought all of these factors into interaction with each other. The time for waiting was over.

Chapter 8

The President Encounters Stiffening Resistance

The stiffening resistance to school desegregation which developed during the two years after the Supreme Court's May 1955 implementation decision severely tested the president's policy of moderation. Eisenhower's comments in that period indicate that, although the administration maintained its calm, noncoercive stance, he experienced growing disillusionment with the wisdom of the decision and the whole process of court-directed desegregation. Though ultimately the force of events in the 1955–1957 period led the president to exercise his executive powers with vigor in the Little Rock crisis, he undertook that action with a spirit of reluctance and the growing conviction that the more gradualistic approach he had long advocated was preferable to the one he felt was forced upon him by the Supreme Court.

Moderation in the Face of Defiance

One of the president's first public comments on the stiffening resistance to court-ordered integration occurred in his 8 February 1956 press conference. Alice Dunnigan of the Associated Negro Press asked whether the recent outbreak of violence during the attempted integration of the University of Alabama violated federal law and whether he planned to recommend that the Justice Department investigate the situation.[1] The president responded that the Justice Department was already looking into it without him ordering it because there were questions of federal law involved. He then publicly reiterated his view of the Court's implementation decision:

> But you must remember, the Supreme Court decision turned this whole process of integration back to the District Courts, and the District Courts were specifically instructed to handle it under the conditions that apply locally as far as they can.[2]

Integration, he insisted, was a judicial responsibility. Turning to the Alabama situation, he asserted:

> And while there has been an outbreak that all of us deplore when there is a defiance of the law, still the Chancellor and the Trustees, the local authorities, the student body, and all the rest of them, have not yet had an opportunity, I should think, to settle this thing as it ought to be settled. And I would certainly hope that we could avoid any interference with anybody else as long as that State, from its Governor on down, will do its best to straighten it out.[3]

The president was determined to avoid remarks that would further inflame the situation. Such a position was, of course, consistent with his desire to avoid confrontation and give the forces of moderation and conciliation time to operate.[4] Whether it was the wisest or most easily understood approach in the face of increasing violence and defiance of court-ordered integration is another matter.

The president received some support quite quickly for his position on the Alabama situation from some who were close to the scene and most opposed to integration. On 11 February 1956, Claude O. Vardaman, chairman of that state's Republican executive committee, wrote to the president commending him for the position he had taken regarding the events at the University of Alabama. Vardaman informed the president:

> Your expression that the Governor and the people of Alabama were obligated to keep law and order was well received by everyone, including the Governor himself. Everyone now realizes it is a bad situation and most people are exceedingly sorry it happened. Judge Hobart Grooms, (whom I recommended and you appointed) has postponed further hearings until February 29th, which will provide a "cooling off" period, which should be very helpful.[5]

The president's approach proved ineffective in the face of the growing spirit of defiance in the South. The black student, twenty-six-year-old Autherine Lucy, whose original admission by court order had precipitated the violence at Alabama, was ordered readmitted by a federal judge on 1 March 1956. She was subsequently expelled for allegedly making false charges against the university on 5 March 1956. When she again sought judicial relief, the federal district court refused to intervene on the grounds that she had not proven that the University of Alabama had expelled her arbitrarily because of her race.[6] The Eisenhower administration remained aloof, and many of those strongly opposed to integration became convinced that the federal government would not intervene in the South.

The president continued to maintain his position in the light of state-announced intentions of outright defiance of the Supreme Court's implementation decision. During the 29 February 1956 press conference, William V. Shannon of the *New York Post* noted that four southern states had passed interposition resolutions saying that the Court's desegregation decisions had no effect in their states. He asked the president what he thought about the concept of interposition and about the responsibility of the federal government for enforcement of desegregation decisions. Eisenhower answered that Shannon had raised the question of states' rights versus federal power and, more specifically, whether the Supreme Court was the last word in interpreting the Constitution. Carefully avoiding any statement of opinion about the constitutionality of interposition, he then asserted:

> Now, this is what I say: There are adequate legal means of determining all of these factors. The Supreme Court has issued its own operational directives and delegated power to the District Courts.
>
> I expect that we are going to make progress, and the Supreme Court itself said it does not expect revolutionary action suddenly executed.
>
> We will make progress, and I am not going to attempt to tell them how it is going to be done.[7]

Thus, the president again made it clear that he regarded the implementation question as one for the federal district courts and that he preferred a hands-off attitude.

Another powerful rationale for moderation came in the twenty-four page briefing that FBI Director J. Edgar Hoover presented to Eisenhower and his cabinet on 9 March 1956.[8] In it, Hoover emphasized the explosive nature of the situation created by the tactics of the NAACP and the White Citizens Councils. Hoover emphasized that there was a long historical background to the integration conflict, listed the reasons why white southerners opposed integration, summarized the crusade for integration, listed its proponents, and emphasized that the Communist party was attempting to infiltrate the civil rights movement and use it to foment social unrest. In summation, Hoover concluded: "Calm, judicious judgment, public education and real understanding are needed to avert explosive incidents. The area of danger lies in friction between extremists on both sides ready with violence."[9]

The conclusion of the FBI director's report seemed to epitomize the president's own views. Moreover, Hoover's emphasis on Communist involvement added a national security aspect to the situation which also inflated Eisenhower's already well-developed sense of caution. He became even more convinced that he should maintain a position between the extremes, one that would avoid creating the type of confrontation that, Hoover had warned, the Communists could turn to their advantage.

Evidence of the significant impact of Hoover's position on the president appeared in the 9 March 1956 cabinet meeting. Attorney General Brownell, in fulfillment of the president's remarks in his recent State of the Union Message, presented a draft statement which embraced the administration's civil rights recommendations to Congress. Brownell proposed a bipartisan commission, greater legal protections for the right to vote, strengthening of civil rights statutes to protect privileges and immunities of citizens, and a new assistant attorney general in charge of civil rights affairs in the Department of Justice.[10]

After the meeting, Maxwell Rabb, the secretary of the cabinet, sent Brownell a memorandum summarizing the president's reactions to the proposals. Rabb reminded Brownell that the president's remarks were not verbatim but drawn from notes and memories of several of those present. At the conclusion of his memorandum, he remarked: "You will also recall the Cabinet's feeling that the conclusions advanced by Director Hoover are good starting points for any statements on this subject."[11] There was no question about the administration's adherence to the Hoover approach.

The president's remarks left no doubt that he was favorably impressed by Brownell's proposals; and, typically, that he was also concerned that they be implemented with moderation. Regarding the increasing opposition to the Court's implementation decision, he reiterated his support of the federal courts' power to interpret the Constitution, but emphasized that the courts should do the enforcing. In granting his approval to the four-point program he restated his faith that the people would listen to those calling for calm and serenity and urged Brownell to include a statement with his proposals calling for that approach. He dismissed a cabinet member's charge that the proposals were too rapid a move toward desegregation with the response that they seemed more like "amelioration." He expressed confidence that Brownell's calls for greater protection of voting rights and the broadening of the federal civil rights laws were mild and that they would pour oil on the troubled waters.[12]

Eisenhower concluded his remarks by asserting that Brownell should present his proposal with a statement that many Americans understandably were separated by deep emotions on the subject. In explaining this point, he reportedly stated:

> One of the prime reasons for this is that, after all, another system was upheld by the Supreme Court for 60 years. These people in the South were not breaking the law for the 60 years, but, ever since the "separate but equal decision," they have been *obeying* the Constitution of the United States.[13]

The president's response to Brownell's proposals reveals much about his own ideas on the proper approach to the desegregation process. At its heart lay an insistence on gradual progress by the South and an understanding by all Americans of the immensity of the problem. These beliefs dominated his attitude toward school desegregation throughout his two presidential terms. Eisenhower was both a believer in and a practitioner of moderation.

There is no better evidence of the president's consistent adherence to this approach than his behavior during the early months of 1956. In March of that year, one hundred southern congressmen signed the so-called Southern Manifesto in which they pledged themselves to overturn the Supreme Court's decisions on segregation.[14] When questioned at his 14 March 1956 press conference about that action, the president made it clear that he was unwilling to provoke a confrontation on the issue. He emphasized that the signers of the manifesto promised to use every legal means and that no responsible person had talked about nullification. If they had, he continued, "there would be a place where we get to a very bad spot for the simple reason I am sworn to defend and uphold the Constitution of the United States and, of course, I can never abandon or refuse to carry out my own duty."[15]

The president softened the apparent firmness of his previous remarks by pointing out that the Supreme Court had acknowledged the emotions surrounding the segregation issue by holding that progress had to be gradual. He reminded his audience that there had been progress, that a quarter of a million black children were already in integrated schools in the border and southern states, and that the Texas Supreme Court had held that anything in the Texas Constitution or laws were void if they were in defiance of the United States Constitution. Such examples, he insisted, were proof that "there are people who are ready to approach this thing with the moderation, but with the determination to make progress that the Supreme Court asked for."[16] The president condemned those on both sides who took an extreme position, refused to predict the length of time that integration would take, and stated that it was his intention to achieve progress without coercion. He closed with his oft-repeated assertion that the American people could resolve the problem with patience and understanding.[17]

Eisenhower and Billy Graham

Significant insight into both the input that reinforced the president's approach to the segregation question and the way he attempted to apply it in early 1956 appears in his correspondence with the evangelist Billy Graham. The president and Graham discussed the segregation question in a 20 March 1956 meeting at the White House. There, Graham expressed his conviction that the Court's desegregation decisions had set back the cause of integration, which he was certain would come eventually. He admitted that the political and moral values were plain for all to see but that the social aspects were difficult because of the South's tradition of race relations— now compounded with fear and resentment. Graham promised the president that he was going to advise moderation and that he would try to get southern ministers to advocate that position.[18] Eisenhower had discovered an influential partner in moderation, one whom he felt he could work with effectively.

The president followed up his meeting with Graham with a letter on 22 March listing a number of specific proposals that he felt ministers could use to bring about a moderate solution to the desegregation crisis. After stating his belief that it was important to have steady progress toward integration even though complete success was years away, he described the conciliatory role he hoped ministers would play:

> Ministers know that peacemakers are blessed. They should also know that the most effective peacemaker is one who prevents a quarrel from developing, not the one who has to pick up the pieces remaining after an unfortunate fight. . . . All of us realize, I think, that success through conciliation will be more lasting and stronger than could be obtained through force and conflict.[19]

Eisenhower then listed a number of specific points for Graham's consideration. He suggested that efforts be made to elect a few qualified blacks to school boards, city and county commissions, and to admit university graduate students on the basis of merit rather than race. In deference to the Montgomery, Alabama, bus boycott then in progress, he urged the development of a flexible plan for filling up public conveyances with blacks who were standing while seats were held for whites.[20] The president expressed his hope that such actions might prove to have very practical results when he stated: "Thus these things would be called to the attention of federal judges, who themselves would be inclined to operate moderately and with complete regard to the sensibilities of the population."[21] The president was convinced that the federal judges enforcing the desegregation process could be led to practice moderation as long as there was *some* progress.

On 27 March 1956, Graham responded to the president with some advice of his own when he urged the president to stay out of racial matters until after the election even if his advisors felt that he could capitalize on the race issue in the North.[22] The evangelist based his warning on his conviction that any involvement would undermine the confidence of white and black leaders in the administration and work to the advantage of his political opponents. The president responded that it was a pity that the question was dragged into partisan politics and assured Graham that he would "always as a matter of conviction and as a champion of real, as opposed to spurious, progress remain a moderate in this regard."[23] Then, somewhat resignedly, he concluded: "There are foolish extremists on both sides of the question who will never be won over to a sensible course of action. But we have these with respect to every question. . . ."[24]

Eisenhower must have been pleased about the initial results of Graham's efforts on behalf of moderation. On 4 June 1956, Graham reported to the president that he had gone to work quickly among the denominational leaders in the South, had several private meetings with political as well as religious leaders, and that he had presented them with a sensible program for bettering race relations. He then stated:

> I believe the Lord is helping us, and if the Supreme Court will go slowly and the extremists on both sides will quiet down, we can have a peaceful social readjustment over the next ten-year period. I am more hopeful now than when I talked with you in March.[25]

Graham reiterated his earlier warning that Eisenhower should remain aloof from the racial issue until after the election. Here, despite some concern because the evangelist had shown his 22 March letter to others, was the kind of personality and approach which appealed strongly to the president. The calm, gradual movement toward integration which both preferred was one in which the process of change was directed by moderates.

Eisenhower and Judicial Activism

Graham's warnings about political involvement and his own cautious approach to controversial issues help to explain the president's increasingly critical attitude toward the Supreme Court's judicial activism, for which the late Chief Justice Earl Warren sharply criticized him.[26] Writing in retirement, Warren charged that when southern resistance stiffened,

> this was aggravated by the fact that no word of support for the decision emanated from the White House. The most that came from high officials in the administration was to the effect that they could not be blamed for anything done to enforce desegregation in education because it was the Supreme Court, not the administration, that determined desegregation to be the law, and the Executive Branch of the government is required to enforce the law as interpreted by the Supreme Court.[27]

The effect, according to the president's critics, was to weaken the authority behind the Court's decisions and thus strengthen those determined to defy them.

Such a result was diametrically opposed to the president's intentions. His increasing wariness about the Court grew out of his perception that its activism created serious problems for those like himself who practiced moderation on the race issue, problems that had immediate political ramifications as the 1956 reelection campaign approached. It explains much of the president's initial enthusiasm for the bipartisan commission that lay at the heart of his administration's proposed civil rights legislation in the spring of 1956.[28] The president hoped that such a commission would act as a buffer to keep the race issue out of partisan politics as well as develop viable means to lessen the chances of confrontation on the integration issue. Thus while the president was aware that it was unintentional, he was convinced that the Court had contributed to the confrontation psychology which permeated racial issues.

His concern, lest the issue become embroiled in political partisanship, was evident in his 21 March diary entry. There he expressed concern because of the increasing frequency which southerners referred to the desegregation decision as a Republican one. He noted that the appointment of Earl Warren as chief justice did not affect the outcome of the decision one bit.[29] While such a remark reflects naiveté about the crucial role Warren played in marshaling unanimous decisions in the 1954 and 1955 cases, it does, nevertheless, underscore how much the president feared the partisan use of that issue in the South.

The difficulty of separating the reasons behind the president's fears into narrow partisan and more altruistic motives is obvious; therefore, the human tendency to confuse what is in the self-interest with the national interest cannot be overlooked. Yet, Eisenhower's cautious nature and his genuine commitment to moderation must also be considered.[30] Part of the reason that the president's growing lack of enthusiasm for Supreme Court activism did not become apparent sooner can be attributed to the fact that his public stance on the desegregation issue remained unchanged. That is, he continued to emphasize in his press conferences the moderate aspects of the decision, the fact that the case had been remanded to the federal district courts, which would oversee local remedies that were tolerant of different situations. For example, at his 8 August 1956 press conference, when quizzed about whether or not his administration had any plans to enforce the "all deliberate speed" decision against the recalcitrant states, the president replied that the process was in the hands of the district court judges. He emphasized again that the Supreme Court had insisted that local conditions be taken into consideration. He reminded his audience that segregated schools had been legal from 1896 to 1954 under the "separate but equal" decision and then said:

> Now, as I have always believed, we have got to make certain reforms by education. No matter how much law we have, we have to—we have a job in education, in getting people to understand what are the issues here involved. I think that is the reason for the Supreme Court's reluctance just to issue an order for compliance, but instead gave this, created this term of "deliberate speed", and put the jurisdiction before the District Courts.[31]

The president completely avoided the issue of executive responsibility by asserting: "Now, I think that these district courts will have to take some cognizance, if there is no action taken at all in their areas."[32]

What the president said in private, however, was far different. On 14 August 1956, the president told his private secretary, Ann Whitman, that he felt that the trouble brought about by the Supreme Court's school decisions was the most important domestic problem facing the government. When she asked what alternative course the Court could have taken, he replied that it could have demanded that segregation be eliminated first from graduate school, later in colleges, and later still in high schools as a means of overcoming the emotional and intellectual attitudes that had developed over generations.[33]

The intensity of the president's feelings about the school decisions was illustrated in his telephone conversations with members of the Justice Department during the shaping of the

Republican civil rights platform plank at the 1956 National Convention in San Francisco. On 18 August 1956, the president telephoned William Rogers, deputy attorney general, stating the version of the platform plank that he preferred. As his secretary noted, it was apparently milder than the previous draft, for the president said to Rogers, "What are you going to do, get an injunction against the governor of Georgia, for instance?"[34] The president made it clear that he abhorred the thought of provoking a confrontation on the desegregation issue in spite of a state's defiance.

On the following day, the president became even more upset about the part of the plank dealing with his administration's attitudes toward the *Brown* decisions. In a telephone call to the attorney general in San Francisco, Eisenhower informed him that

> his quarrel was with efforts to insert the words "The Eisenhower Administration . . . and the Republican Party" have supported the Supreme Court in the desegregation business. He wanted the words "Eisenhower Administration" deleted. He reminded the Attorney General that the Attorney General was, in his brief before Supreme Court, appearing as a lawyer, not as a member of the Eisenhower Administration. President said he had always denied that the Administration took a stand on the matter. He said it had never come before Cabinet, for instance (and could the Attorney General imagine what a storm Mrs. Hobby would raise, had it?). The Attorney General agreed that was true. The President asked him to talk to Bush and Dirksen and if they did not come around, he would refuse to "go to San Francisco."[35]

Then in what was one of the most revealing statements the president ever made on the decisions, he informed the attorney general "that in this business he was between the compulsion of duty on one side, and his firm conviction, on the other, that because of the Supreme Court's rulling, [sic] the whole issue had been set back badly."[36] By August 1956, the president had become convinced that the Court's decisions on school segregation had created a dangerous situation.

The president's testiness about the platform plank on civil rights carried over into his press conferences. When asked at his 31 August 1956 press conference whether or not he was satisfied with the Republican civil rights plank, he snapped:

> I am not going again into the full discussion of what I believe about this subject. I think that no plank could satisfy everybody exactly. It couldn't possibly be done.
>
> Here is a problem that as I have said a thousand times is charged with emotionalism, where everybody has got to work hard with all of the strength he has, and I think that the more that work is done privately and behind the scenes rather than charging up on the platform and hammering desks, the better and more effective it will be.[37]

The president left no doubt as to the approach he preferred.

Events, however, seemed to leave little time for conciliation. When mob violence broke out in Clinton, Tennessee, and Mansfield, Texas, as school officials tried to carry out court-ordered school integration in the fall of 1956, the president, true to his approach, urged a change in spirit so that "extremists on both sides" would not dominate the situation. He criticized both the practitioners of violence and those who wanted the problem solved immediately. In so doing, he incurred the wrath of the NAACP's leadership.[38]

In a strongly worded letter, NAACP Chief Counsel Thurgood Marshall reminded the chief executive that citizens "continue to look to our president for forthright leadership in enforcement of the Constitution and laws of the United States as interpreted by the United States Supreme Court," and "an unequivocal stand against mob action wherever it occurs and regardless of who are the participants."[39] Marshall cited the president's recent remarks about the Clinton and Mansfield incidents, charging that they gave support to many in this country who have sought to confuse the issue by trying to divide responsibility for such situations between lawless mobs and other Americans who seek only their lawful rights in a lawful manner, often after unbelievably long periods of waiting.[40]

Marshall reminded the president that the real issue in the confrontations was not one of black citizens versus white citizens; rather,

it is a question of unlawful violent opposition against the orders of duly constituted federal courts. These are the only "two [sides]" involved. Surely, you do not mean to equate lawless mobs with federal courts as "extremists." Certainly the dozen Negro children involved in each instance trying to get an adequate education in a lawful manner could not be classified as "extremists."[41]

Marshall's letter underscores the type of attack to which the president's position left him open. It also foreshadowed one of the principal criticisms of his handling of the desegregation question—that he equivocated in a time of grave moral crisis.

Despite Marshall's impressive argument, the president continued to maintain his position. Resisting pressures for more vigorous action, he ordered the attorney general to ask that the Tennessee and Texas case records be sent to the Justice Department for study in the event that the district courts involved held some in contempt of its orders so evidence could be prepared if necessary.[42] The president's limited action made it clear that he had no taste for a confrontation on the integration issue and that his administration's response to such situations would be minimal. His earlier fear that court-ordered integration would ultimately cause a confrontation seemed to dominate his reaction at this time.

Occasionally, in the period of rising tensions, Eisenhower found evidence that supported the workability of his approach. On 11 September 1956, E. Frederic Morrow, a black economist and special projects advisor to the president, sent a memorandum to Press Secretary James Hagerty informing him that the public schools in Louisville were integrated the previous day without incident. The fact that Louisville was a border state city with a strong southern tradition seemed particularly encouraging. Morrow concluded his memorandum by noting: "It illustrates one of the president's wise observations made in a letter to me in June, 1954, that: 'Progress does not necessarily demand noisy conflict.' "[43] The president was so pleased with the Louisville experience that he remarked to an aide that the superintendent of schools there should be asked how his community was prepared and that those ideas should be used in other parts of the country.[44]

When the desegregation issue was raised in the 1956 presidential campaign, the president avoided extensive discussion of it. On 5 October 1956, for example, he was asked to comment on the charge of his Democratic opponent Adlai Stevenson that the Republicans were trying to take credit for the civil rights progress that the Democrats achieved. Eisenhower stated that during his first term there had been vigorous efforts to assure equal opportunity to people in areas where federal authority clearly extended. As examples, he cited the desegregation of the armed forces, government contracts, the District of Columbia, and the schools on army posts.[45] He carefully avoided any discussion of his administration's connection with the implementation of the segregation decision. He was still troubled with doubts about both the wisdom and the scope of the Supreme Court's activism in matters of state policy.

The Supreme Court's mid-November decision upholding desegregation of intrastate buses added to the president's fear that too much judicial activism would lead to further confrontations.[46] In reference to the decision that dealt with a

Montgomery, Alabama private bus company operating on a public franchise, the president asserted in his pre–press conference briefing that on issues such as this he was much more of a "states righter" than the Supreme Court. He was also frightened that such decisions would create troubles leading to setbacks for black civil rights.[47] Turning to the school question, his personal secretary noted:

> He referred to the schools—said how could the Federal Government enforce a ruling applying to schools supported by state funds. Said could have a general strike in the South. Feels that even the so-called great liberals are going to have to take a second look at the whole thing. He may say that the Supreme Court does not refer its decisions to him for approval or study. Governor of Mississippi said that they were going to ignore the ruling. President said that eventually a district court is going to cite someone for contempt, and then we are going to be up against it.[48]

The president's remarks illustrate how his philosophy of limited federal powers reinforced his fear that too much use of court-ordered desegregation would lead to an inevitable confrontation, one he felt the federal government might be unable to cope with given the widespread nature of resistance to integration. Therefore, his desire to maintain a sense of distance between the decisions of the Court and the actions of his administration became increasingly important to him during the growing crisis. Caught between his sworn duty to uphold the Constitution as interpreted by the courts and his own preference for a more gradual, moderate approach, the president continued to agonize and exercise restraint. However, by late 1956, time was running out. The growing pessimism and concern reflected in his remarks during that period suggest that he was becoming increasingly aware of the narrowing range of his options and resentful toward the institution whose actions, he felt, had created this situation.

The President Holds to His Course

Nothing in his own thinking at that time revealed an acceptance of the idea that strong action on his part would improve the situation. He was too tied to his approach and to his limited conception of the uses of presidential power to make the leap his contemporary and subsequent critics condemned him for not taking. While the question of whether a confrontation on the desegregation issue would still have occurred if he had acted more decisively is a debatable one, the president's fear of it was very real and in some ways the most controlling factor in his approach to the desegregation issue. It explains much about his hesitation to commit the executive branch in favor of integration.

The president's reaction to the March 1957 incident involving the remarks presidential advisor Bernard Shanley made to a New Jersey audience also underscores the nature of the president's attitude toward the desegregation decisions. The controversy grew out of Shanley's chance remark, in the midst of a speech praising the administration's record on desegregation, that some of the immediate results of the Court decisions had caused some problems.[49] When taken out of context, it appeared that one of the president's leading advisors had by extension expressed the administration's disapproval of the decisions. Eisenhower, after examining Shanley's statement, commented privately that his advisor was right but that he should not have made the remark. Moreover, in the event that he would be questioned on the remark at his upcoming press conference, he would refer reporters with questions about it to Shanley. He added the additional comment that he was not quarreling with the Supreme Court.[50] His reaction to the Shanley affair illustrates the gap between his feeling about the Court's desegregation decisions and his public position on the matter.

As southern resistance continued to manifest itself in various ways during the spring and summer of 1957, the president continued to adhere to his quiet, noncoercive course. On 6 May 1957, moderate Governor LeRoy Collins of Florida sent a letter to Eisenhower along with his state legislature's resolution and nullification of the Supreme Court's desegregation decisions. After assuring the president that the resolution had no force and effect in law and that it was not subject to his approval, Collins asserted: "I have nevertheless made it clear that I opposed this action to the extent that the same defies the authority of the United States Supreme Court."[51] Though his legal advisors actively researched the issue of nullification and concluded that such resolutions had no legal standing, the president made no public response to the matter and merely conveyed his thanks through a letter from Sherman Adams to the Florida governor for the position he took on the matter.[52] No statement from the White House supporting the Supreme Court and denying the doctrine of nullification was forthcoming in this instance or when other southern state legislatures followed suit.

The president's penchant for executive neutrality was reinforced by his advisors on racial affairs. On 3 July 1957, Maxwell Rabb wrote Press Secretary Hagerty that it was possible that the president would have to field a question about NAACP President Roy Wilkins' recent statement calling on Eisenhower to aid in protecting the NAACP from the "enemies of freedom" who were seeking to destroy it. Wilkins' references were to the increase in coercion against black citizens in the South and, more specifically, to the increasing legal restrictions placed on the organization's activities by southern state legislatures and state courts. Rabb advised:

The answer should be that while the president is sympathetic with any efforts for human justice, he cannot take sides with private organizations. The Court is the appropriate forum to determine matters of this kind where a private organization is concerned.[53]

Such advice reinforced the president's determination to avoid direct involvement and indirectly contributed to the charge that the president was insensitive to the moral issues in the controversy. The president's 19 November 1958 suggestion to cabinet members that federal judges and not NAACP lawyers fight school integration cases presents subsequent additional evidence of his feeling that the presence of the NAACP contributed to the emotions surrounding the desegregation issue.[54]

Yet another aspect of the president's approach to the desegregation cases is apparent in his writings. The perspective he felt he had gained on racial matters during his long periods of residence in the South should not be overlooked. That experience caused the president in the summer of 1957 to listen with tolerance and a great degree of patience when Senator Richard Russell of Georgia discussed with a great deal of emotion the reasons for his opposition to the administration's proposed civil rights bill.[55] So likewise it explains why on 23 July 1957 in reference to South Carolina Governor James Byrnes' request that the president show confidence in the people of the South to resolve their own racial problems, Eisenhower wrote:

> I am compelled to wonder why you have to express such a thought as nothing more than a hope. Many of my dearest friends are in that region, I spent a not inconsiderable part of my life in the South or in border states, and, moreover, this question of assuring the civil rights of all citizens does *not* apply exclusively to the southern areas.[56]

The president's southern experience left him convinced of the massiveness of the problems created in the South by the desegregation issue. It made him a believer in the wisdom of patience.

Perhaps the most comprehensive written exposition of the president's attitude during the desegregation crisis appeared in his 21 July 1957 letter to his old friend Swede Hazlett.[57] The chief executive opened his letter by restating his conviction that the Supreme Court's 1954 decision had a more disturbing effect on the domestic scene than any other recent event. He emphasized that it had greatly increased the responsibilities of the federal government in the area of protecting the constitutional rights of each citizen. He left no doubt that the decision had greatly added to the burdens of his office.

Eisenhower then explained that his own approach to the problem had been governed by several "obvious truths" and proceeded to list four of the most important ones:

(a). Laws are rarely effective unless they represent the will of the majority. In our prohibition experiment, we even saw local opinion openly and successfully defy Federal authority even though national public opinion then seemed to support the whole theory of prohibition.

(b). When emotions are deeply stirred, logic and reason must operate gradually and with consideration for human feelings or we will have a resultant disaster rather than human advancement.

(c). School segregation itself was, according to the Supreme Court decision of 1896, completely Constitutional until the reversal of that decision was accomplished in 1954. . . .

(d). After three score years of living under these patterns, it was impossible to expect complete and instant reversal of conduct by mere decision of the Supreme Court. The Court itself recognized this and provided a plan for the desegregation of schools which it believed to be moderate but effective.[58]

Though many might question the validity of his assumptions or their wisdom, the available evidence indicates that they were controlling determinants of his behavior.

Emphasizing that the court's plan must be binding on all Americans if our form of government was to survive, Eisenhower summarized the proposed civil rights bill his administration had submitted for congressional consideration.[59] His plan, he said, "was conceived in the thought that only moderation in legal compulsions, accompanied by a stepped-up program of education" could bring about peaceful integration.[60] He conceded that "some of the language used in the attempt to translate my basic purposes into legislative provisions has probably been too broad" and that this had made it subject to varying interpretations which he felt confident that Congress could correct.[61]

The president made it clear that, despite his concern for the Supreme Court's activism and his personal preference for a more gradual approach to the problem, there was one premise which he would uphold:

> There must be respect for the Constitution—which means the Supreme Court's interpretation of the Constitution—or we shall have chaos. We cannot possibly imagine a successful form of government in which every individual citizen would have the right to interpret the Constitution according to his own convictions, beliefs and prejudices. Chaos would develop. This I believe with all my heart—and shall always act accordingly.[62]

The last three and a half years of his presidency would sorely test Eisenhower's devotion to that principle.

Chapter 9

Little Rock: The President's Perspective

Dwight D. Eisenhower had little time to contemplate the emasculated version of the civil rights bill which passed Congress in August 1957. Less than one month later, his administration was embroiled in the Little Rock school crisis. Some see a direct link between the administration's efforts on behalf of the 1957 Civil Rights Act and that confrontation. Emmet John Hughes and others have charged that the president's weak efforts on behalf of that bill made possible the crippling jury trial amendment in contempt cases dealing with defiance of court-ordered desegregation. That behavior, they charged, encouraged the opponents of school desegregation by adding to the existing impression that he was not fully supportive of the courts.[1]

The question of his responsibility aside, the events surrounding the court-ordered attempt to desegregate Little Rock Central High School in the fall of 1957 brought the president face to face with what he had long feared: outright defiance of a federal court order by a state official.[2] The inflammatory actions and words of Arkansas Governor Orval E. Faubus finally put the president in a position where he had no choice

143

but to act. Eisenhower, despite his repeated pleas for moderation in the school desegregation question, had also stated publicly and privately on a number of occasions in the wake of the Court's 1955 implementation decision that he would honor his oath to defend the Constitution and that he considered the Supreme Court's interpretation of it as binding.[3] Couched as these statements were among pleas for moderation and a general policy of low-key Justice Department involvement only when a court requested it to help deal with defiance of its desegregation orders, it is easy to see why the president's statements were easily overlooked.[4]

Both the president's statements and actions during the crisis and his subsequent comments in his memoirs and an oral history interview indicate that he intervened at Little Rock because of Governor Faubus' defiance of federal court orders and not because of any enthusiasm for school integration.[5] The president's decision to send federal troops to preserve peace in Little Rock was undoubtedly one of the most difficult decisions of his presidency.[6]

What follows is an in-context examination of Eisenhower's words and deeds during the first three months of that crisis. It is a study of how the president was forced by events beyond his control to exercise his presidential powers in a way that he abhorred because of his determination to uphold his oath of office. It is not a story of the surrender of his moderation but rather its frustration. His experiences at Little Rock did not jar his conviction that the slower, low-key approach to school desegregation, which he preferred, was the better way. Moreover, the Little Rock experience did not markedly alter his preference for the cautious, limited application of federal power as his administration considered an expansion of civil rights legislation in the 1957–1960 period.

The Early Phase

The origins of the Little Rock crisis can be traced to a U.S. district court's acceptance of a desegregation plan submitted by that city's board of education in May 1955. That plan pledged the integration of the Little Rock Public Schools by 1963.[7] When the board's plan was challenged by the Arkansas NAACP on the grounds that it took too long to accomplish its purpose, the court held that it was in good faith and, as a result of three separate court orders, the board announced that it would initiate the plan by permitting black students to attend the previously all-white Central High School in the fall 1957 term. The integration plan sharply divided the community.[8] At the opening of that school term, Governor Faubus, on the premise that it was necessary to avoid violence, used the Arkansas National Guard to prevent blacks from entering Central High School. Faubus thus received nationwide publicity (notoriety?) for his vociferous denunciation and defiance of the federal court's integration orders. His behavior greatly inflamed the situation in Little Rock. Faubus' actions set the scene for the direct confrontation of state and federal authority that the president had long feared would be the result of court-directed desegregation.

Eisenhower's involvement in the Little Rock crisis was unenthusiastic from the very beginning. On 3 September 1957, immediately after Faubus had used the National Guard to block integration, the president reviewed the situation with his staff and made it clear that he had no desire to get the administration involved in the controversy. He expressed doubt that the Justice Department had a right to intervene and stated that in the end the administration was up against the same thing, "these people who believe you are going to reform the human heart by law."[9] Despite this attitude, the president soon found himself deeply involved in the situation.

Faced with a blatant defiance of his order, Federal Judge Ronald N. Davies requested that the Justice Department begin collecting facts regarding those persons, including the governor, who were interfering with or failing to comply with the district court's integration order. At this point, Faubus telegraphed the president on 4 September requesting his assurance, understanding, and cooperation with the actions he had taken to delay integration. In his 5 September response, the president informed Faubus that he would honor his oath to support and defend the Constitution by all the legal means at his command. The president also strongly denounced Faubus' assertions that federal authorities were considering taking him into custody and that his telephone had been tapped. The president closed his telegram by informing Faubus that the Justice Department was investigating the question of interference with the district court's orders and that he expected the governor, other state officials, and the National Guard to cooperate with the court.[10] On 9 September, the attorney general informed the president that the Justice Department was in the process of fulfilling the request of the district court.

It is apparent that at this point moderate attempts were being made to defuse the crisis and that the president was initially confident of their success. The agent of moderation in this case was Arkansas Democratic Congressman Brooks Hays, who informed the president through Presidential Assistant Sherman Adams that Faubus was anxious to find a way out of the impasse he had gotten himself into and that he would like to have a meeting with the president.[11] Unfortunately, as both Hays and the president were to soon discover, Faubus used both of them for his own purposes.

The president received conflicting advice from his own advisors about the wisdom of such a meeting. Adams informed Eisenhower that he had discussed the idea with Attorney General Brownell, who was opposed to such a meeting. Brownell was certain that Faubus had "soiled" himself badly and should be left to suffer for it. Adams, on the other hand, accepted Hays' appealing argument that Faubus realized that he had made a mistake and was looking for a way out of the situation.[12]

Attorney General Brownell had insisted that the district

court orders were the law and that Faubus should be forced to comply with them. Eisenhower, however, rejected that argument because it failed to take into consideration the situation in the South. He further informed Adams that

> he believed the Justice Department itself must make very clear that it is appearing in court only as a friend of the court to make sure that the National Guard is not being used to prevent carrying out of court orders. By no means does the Federal government want to interfere with governor's responsibilities.[13]

Eisenhower agreed that he would talk with the Arkansas governor at his request. Adams further reinforced the president's decision when he informed him that Faubus was not essentially a segregationist, that his son attended an integrated college, but that the governor believed that integration should begin in the first grade and proceed on a grade a year basis.[14]

The president's choice of options regarding his approach to Little Rock is revealing. It is apparent that he was hopeful that a meeting with Faubus might head off an ugly confrontation of state and local power. The picture Adams presented of Faubus' motives made such an approach irresistible. The president's remarks also underscore his reluctance to promote federal interference in areas which he felt were under state responsibility.

Eisenhower then telephoned Brownell and informed him that he had talked to Adams and listed four points that he wanted to make clear about his approach to the Little Rock crisis. He told Brownell that it was important that the federal government avoid implying that it was seeking to interfere with a state's responsibility for preservation of law and order. He further stated that he also wanted to avoid the appearance of questioning the governor's right to call out the National Guard. He informed Brownell of his decision to meet with Faubus, provided that the Arkansas governor express his willingness to comply with the orders of the federal court. Finally, the chief executive noted the American public's misconception that he could go in and automatically tell a mob to disperse and integrate the high school.[15]

Still openly skeptical about the value of a meeting with Faubus, Brownell reminded the president that Brooks Hays' intervention with Faubus was the fifth attempt—that Senator John McClellen, Winthrop Rockefeller, Harry Ashmore, the editor of the Little Rock *Arkansas Gazette,* and ex-Governor James McCann had all concluded that it was hopeless. The president countered with the argument that maybe the time was now ripe when it might not have been previously and insisted that he would go ahead with a meeting if Faubus assured him in a telegram asking him for an appointment that he would be "guided by federal court orders."[16] On 11 September, the president announced the receipt of such a telegram from Faubus and that he had invited the Arkansas governor to meet with him at the vacation White House at the Newport, Rhode Island, Naval Air Station on the forthcoming weekend.[17]

The Meeting

Faubus and Eisenhower met on 14 September at the president's tiny office in his vacation quarters. After a twenty-minute private conversation there, they adjourned to a larger office where they were joined by Adams, Hays, and Brownell.[18] The president's version of his visit with Faubus suggests that his initial reaction was one of hope that the crisis could be resolved by compromise.

Eisenhower recalled in his dictated notes that Faubus "protested again and again he was a law abiding citizen . . . and that everybody recognizes that the Federal law is supreme to State law."[19] The president reported that he discussed the Little Rock situation with a firm but conciliatory approach, one which gave the Arkansas governor a way out and permitted him to save face.

I suggested to him that he go home and not necessarily withdraw his National Guard troops, but just change their orders to say that having been assured that there was no attempt to do anything except to obey the Courts and that the Federal government was not trying to do anything that had not been already agreed to by the School Board and directed by the Courts; that he should tell the Guard to continue to preserve order but to allow the Negro children to attend Central High School.[20]

Continuing, the president held out the following incentive to Faubus: "I urged him to take this action promptly whereupon the Justice Department would go to the Court and ask that the Governor not be brought into Court."[21] Such an action would be in Faubus' interest, the president told him.

I did not believe it was beneficial to anybody to have a trial of strength between the President and a Governor because in any area where the Federal government had assumed jurisdiction and this was upheld by the Supreme Court, there could be only one outcome—that is, the State would lose, and I did not want to see any Governor humiliated.[22]

The president thus combined firmness with moderation in an attempt to depolarize the Little Rock crisis.

And what of Faubus' response? Eisenhower was convinced that the governor had promised that he would change his position.

He seemed to be very appreciative of this attitude and I got definitely the understanding that he was going back to Arkansas to act within a matter of hours to revoke his orders to the Guard to prevent re-entry of the Negro children into the school.[23]

Eisenhower noted that Faubus reiterated his intentions to change the guard's orders when Adams, Hays, and Brownell joined them.

The separate public communiqués which Eisenhower and Faubus issued both referred to the "constructive discussions" the two men had held. But as Emmet John Hughes has pointed out, the two could not agree on a joint statement. Consequently, the two statements led to differing interpretations of what the leaders had agreed on at the conference.[24] Eisenhower's statement praised Faubus for his promise to respect the orders of the federal district court and his assertion that it was his responsibility to preserve law and order in Arkansas. The president concluded by expressing confidence that Faubus would use his office to insure progress in the elimination of segregation as ordered by the court.[25] Faubus' statement admitted that the 1954 decision outlawing segregation in the schools was the law of the land and that it had to be obeyed, promised to support the people of Little Rock in their obedience to federal court orders, and emphasized that the federal government did not have any thought of challenging his responsibility as governor to protect the people of Arkansas from violence. He closed with a plea that the complexities of integration be patiently understood by the federal government.[26] At no point in his statement did Faubus refer to his promise to change the orders of the National Guard.

Despite the president's conviction that Faubus had promised that he would change the troops' orders, there was little optimism on his staff about the outcome of the meeting at Newport. Ann Whitman wrote in her diary on 14 September, the day of the Faubus meeting:

> I got the impression that the meeting had not gone as well as had been hoped, that the Federal government would have to be as tough as possible in the situation. I gather, too, that Governor Faubus has seized this opportunity and stirred the whole thing up for his own political advantage, a feeling that is, I believe, borne out by the FBI report. If that report becomes public in the hearing, the consensus is that it will backfire badly for Governor Faubus.
>
> There was certainly a great frenzy around here. The test comes tomorrow morning when we will know whether Governor Faubus will, or will not, withdraw the troops.[27]

The administration's fears were confirmed when Faubus upon his return to Little Rock continued to do nothing about changing the National Guard's orders. The president's attempt at compromise had failed.

The Confrontation

Word that Faubus was not going to amend his orders reached the White House on 19 September. Informants reported that Faubus was not going to obey the federal court's order to appear and that he intended to engage in some publicity-gaining legal maneuvers.[28] Though the president was so angered by Faubus' duplicity that he initially decided to make a statement at that time, he was talked out of it by Sherman Adams and Herbert Brownell, who counseled him to remain silent for the time being. In the event the press raised questions about Faubus' actions, these advisors had determined that Press Secretary James Hagerty would say that the president was disappointed because voluntary means to resolve the crisis had not been found and the court proceedings would go forward.

At the same time, it became apparent that Faubus' behavior was pushing the administration toward a crucial decision. For as presidential aide General Andrew Goodpaster mentioned in his memorandum to Hagerty, Adams and Brownell had decided that:

> At the time the Court issues a directive to admit the children forthwith, and Governor Faubus refuses to comply, then an obligation falls upon the Federal government to require Faubus to do so by whatever means may be necessary. At this time the President should speak to the country.[29]

The administration was beginning, however unenthusiastically, to toughen its position.

Faubus proceeded to play his role to the hilt. On 20 September, a hearing was held in the federal district court in Little Rock in which Faubus had been ordered to appear and show cause why he should not be enjoined from using the National Guard for preventing the integration of Central High School. Faubus did not appear personally but instead sent lawyers who read a statement questioning the federal court's authority and emphasized that the governor's absence did not mean that he would refuse to comply with the court's orders.[30] Upon completion of this statement, Faubus' lawyers departed and District Judge Ronald N. Davies promptly enjoined the Arkansas governor and the National Guard from interfering with the progress of court-ordered integration at Central High School. That evening, Faubus withdrew the National Guard from the high school leaving the police in control.

While the events of 20 September were taking place in Judge Davies' courtroom in Little Rock, the president received a telephone call from Brownell, who informed him of Faubus' failure to appear in court, and that the FBI was talking to the Little Rock chief of police about deputizing citizens. Brownell also told the president that assuming Judge Davies issued the injunction against Faubus, the governor would have two courses of action open to him: one would be to withdraw the National Guard (which he did that same evening) and the other would be to simply defy the court order. Brownell emphasized that whatever option Faubus followed, it would require important decisions on the president's part. The attorney general informed Eisenhower that Secretary of the Army Wilbur Brucker was coming over to discuss the use of the army with the attorney general in the event it became necessary.[31]

The president agonized. He told the attorney general he was loath to use troops because he felt the resistance to school integration might spread and that violence would occur. He was convinced that he had the authority to call out the troops, although he insisted he could not use them to preserve law and order, but to see that the black children were protected. Then, showing his bitterness at what he regarded as Faubus' duplicity, he expressed hope that someone would tell Hays just how low Faubus had fallen in Eisenhower's estimation since the governor had broken his promise.[32]

Reflecting his long-standing fear that a confrontation over integration might lead to the closing of the public schools, Eisenhower asked Brownell whether Faubus had the legal authority to close the schools if an attempt was made to force entry of the black children. Brownell responded that he would check into the matter. Eisenhower then reiterated his concern lest Faubus in Arkansas and leaders in other parts of the South seek to abolish the public schools.[33] The president's abhorrence of confrontation in the Little Rock crisis was a manifestation of his long-held fear that the federal government might be helpless in the face of extensive use of that tactic throughout the South, and that the precedent set for defiance of constitutional authority would have devastating results.

A glimmer of hope that the crisis might be resolved without federal executive action appeared on the evening of 20 September when, as previously stated, the unpredictable Faubus ordered the National Guard withdrawn from Central High School. The president's public statement on the following day reflected his relief that a direct confrontation of state and federal authority had been averted. He still hoped that moderation might triumph in the Little Rock situation. He expressed confidence that the citizens of Little Rock would oppose violent action by extremists and called for their sympathetic understanding of the ordeal that the nine black children who had been prevented from entering the school had experienced.[34]

Unfortunately, the president's hopes for moderation and progress were not shared by all of the citizens of Little Rock. On 23 September, enraged by Faubus' inflammatory remarks, their hostility to integration, and the churning tides of rumor, a screaming mob of several thousand whites gathered at Central High School to protest the admission of the black students. That same day, upon receipt of information that local law enforcement agencies were having problems controlling the mob around the school, Eisenhower issued a Proclamation of Obstruction of Justice, ordering all persons attempting to interfere with the federal court's integration order to cease and desist.[35] Attached to the proclamation were excerpts from Chapter 15, Title 10, Sections 332–34 of the United States Code which empowered the president to make his proclamation. All three of these sections justified the president's use of either state militia or federal troops to end unlawful obstructions of justice. Eisenhower was thus forced to the threshold of decision.

The events of the following day would prove crucial. At 8:35 A.M. the president, who was still at the vacation White House in Newport, telephoned Brownell informing him that he was working on a statement regarding the actions of the mob at Little Rock but that it would not be issued unless or until something happened.[36] Always the moderate, the president noted that he had softened up the draft statement sent by his staff in Washington by striking out the phrase "the law had been defied" and substituting one stating that his sympathy was with the people of Little Rock.

The attorney general, after agreeing with the president that it would look better if the chief executive went about his normal routine, mentioned that General Maxwell Taylor was anxious to use the National Guard rather than resorting to regular army troops. Eisenhower agreed but felt that the Little Rock units should not be used because it might be a "case of brother against brother." Brownell said that it would take six to nine hours to call them up, but both men felt that at that point it would not matter.[37]

Later that morning, the White House received Mayor Woodrow Wilson Mann's telegram (sent at 9:06 A.M., CST) urging that the president call out federal troops to preserve order in Little Rock. Mann minced no words in describing the reasons for his request:

The mob is much larger in numbers at 8 A.M. than at any time yesterday. People are converging on the scene from all directions. Mob is armed and engaging in fisticuffs and other acts of violence. Situation is out of control and police cannot disperse the mob.[38]

There would be no more waiting on the president's part.

At eight minutes past noon (EDT), spurred on by Mayor Mann's request, the president told his staff that he would sign the order for federal troops to restore peace in Little Rock.[39] The rapidity with which the president shifted from his initial decision of a few hours earlier to rely on Arkansas National Guard units is indicative of the impact of the mayor's request. The same could be said of the reversal of his earlier decision to remain at Newport in order to give the impression of preserving his original routine.

The swiftness of his change of mind is clearly portrayed in a letter to his old friend General Alfred M. Gruenther, written just prior to his reception of Mayor Mann's telegram.[40] In that letter, the president rejected Gruenther's suggestion that he could more effectively deal with the Little Rock crisis from Washington. Eisenhower argued that the office was wherever the president happened to be and that if he ran back to Washington in the midst of every crisis, it "would be a confession that a change of scenery is truly a 'vacation' for the President and is not merely a change of his working locale. This is untrue."[41] The second reason, he informed Gruenther, was that he did not want to "exaggerate the significance of the admittedly serious situation in Arkansas."[42] As he put it:

I do not want to give a picture of a Cabinet in constant session, of fretting and worrying about the actions of a misguided governor who, in my opinion, has been motivated entirely by what he believes to be political advantage in a particular locality.[43]

Despite his letter to Gruenther, the president did fly to Washington on the evening of the twenty-fourth and read his statement on Little Rock from the White House. Ann Whitman explained that his change of mind had two causes: the technical problem of setting up the necessary communications from Providence and because some of his staff advised him that his speech would be more effective if he made it from the White House.[44] Logistics, politics, and the seriousness of the Little Rock situation combined to bring the president back to Washington.

The president's letter to Gruenther also presented a valuable insight into the state of his thinking at the peak of that crisis. Most striking was his statement that:

> The Federal government has ample resources with which to cope with this kind of thing. The great need is to act calmly, deliberately, and giving every offender opportunity to cease his defiance of Federal law and to peaceably obey the proper orders of the Federal court. In this way the actions of the Executive in enforcing the law—even if it becomes necessary to employ considerable force—are understood by all, and the individuals who have offended are not falsely transformed into martyrs.[45]

As late as the same morning of the twenty-fourth, then, Eisenhower was confident that his moderation could be successfully combined with firmness and practicality. However, the raging mob that encircled Little Rock Central High School on that morning destroyed the chances for calm deliberation. Moreover, the emotions and the political opportunism generated by the president's decision to resort to federal troops added yet another dimension of tension to the situation.

Executive Order No. 10730, which the president signed on 24 September 1957, simply asserted that the willful obstruction of the court's order was continuing and directed the secretary of defense to nationalize all Arkansas National Guard units for duty and to make such use of the regular armed forces of the United States as was necessary.[46] It was justified with the same references cited in the presidential proclamation of the previous day. Later that same day the battle-hardened veterans of Korea in the 101st Airborne Division were flown to Arkansas and deployed around the high school. The president then confronted the task of explaining his role in the events at Little Rock to a nation already deeply divided on the segregation issue.

The president delivered the statement he had worked on for two days over a nationwide radio and television hookup at 9:00 P.M., EDT on the twenty-fourth. He began his remarks by expressing sadness about the events that had occurred at Little Rock and by reiterating the firmness of his intention to see that the federal court's orders there were carried out. He summarized the causes of his decision to intervene—placing the blame squarely on demagogic extremists—and emphasized that as president he was duty bound to uphold the federal court.[47]

Next he turned to a more precise explanation of the reasons for the use of federal troops. Eisenhower cited the Supreme Court's desegregation decrees, emphasizing that his personal feelings had no bearing on the matter of their enforcement. He pointed out that several communities in the South had instituted plans for gradual integration and, in so doing, had demonstrated to the world that we were a nation of laws. The chief executive explained that he had been forced to take presidential action at Little Rock because the acceptance of the primacy of law had broken down there.[48]

Eisenhower traced the sequence of events beginning in May 1957 which had led to his intervention. Carefully avoiding any specific reference to Faubus, he placed the blame for the crisis on those "certain misguided persons, many of them imported into Little Rock by agitators, [who] have insisted upon defying the law and have sought to bring it into disrepute . . ." thus frustrating the court's orders.[49] Such a situation, he emphasized, would lead to anarchy if allowed to continue.

In an attempt to head off those who would seek to exploit the federal intervention for demagogic purposes, he stated that federal troops were not being used to "relieve" local and state authorities of their primary responsibility to preserve law and order or to run the schools. Instead, he reiterated that the troops were there to prevent interference with the orders of the court. As he put it:

> The proper use of the powers of the Executive Branch to enforce the orders of a Federal Court is limited to extraordinary and compelling circumstances. Manifestly, such an extreme situation has been created in Little Rock.[50]

In a gesture of conciliation toward the South, the president stated that the overwhelming majority of Americans in all sections of the country were law-abiding and that they deplored extremists' calls to violence. He admitted the school integration decision affected the South more seriously than the other sections, but that he had observed firsthand that the "overwhelming majority of the people in the South—including those of Arkansas and of Little Rock—are of good will, united in their efforts to preserve and respect the law even when they disagree with it."[51]

Neither did the president ignore the international implications of Little Rock. He remarked with sadness that the events there had done a tremendous disservice to the people of Arkansas in the eyes of the nation, and the nation in the eyes of the world. He noted that our Communist enemies were "gloating over this incident and using it everywhere to misrepresent our whole nation."[52] In this case, the cold war provided him with an excuse to insist on better behavior. Eisenhower concluded by calling on the citizens of Arkansas "to assist in bringing to an immediate end all interference with the law and its processes."[53]

While the president's statement was certainly a clear explanation of his reasons for using federal troops, it did little to resolve the impasse in Little Rock and in some ways perhaps contributed to its prolongation. As his personal secretary noted, White House mail on reactions to Eisenhower's use of troops at Little Rock ran about even, with a sharp division on the basis of geographic location.[54]

Defense and Withdrawal

Consequently, the administration found itself involved in a double-barreled effort as a result of its intervention. On the one hand, it was forced to defend its actions from a variety of critics who, mostly for political reasons, sought to obliterate the distinction the president made between using troops to uphold the orders of a federal court rather than to force integration. On the other hand, the administration sought means to restore calm so that the president could remove the federal troops quickly. Both these efforts were greatly complicated by Governor Faubus' attempts to capitalize on the presence of the troops to whip up support for his efforts to win another term as governor. What better way to accomplish this than by charging the administration with carrying out military occupation to force integration.[55] In this situation, the administration's efforts were sometimes so intertwined and concurrent that they can be best understood by viewing them in chronological order.

The pattern of emotional segregationist charges followed by patient administration response was established early in the crisis. On 26 September, one day after the 101st Airborne Division had secured the entry of the nine black students to Central High School, the president received a telegram from Senator Richard Russell of Georgia. In it, he vigorously protested the "highhanded and illegal methods being employed by the Armed Forces of the United States under your command who are carrying out your orders to mix the races in the public schools of Little Rock, Arkansas."[56] Charging that the troops, according to newpaper reports, were using Hitler-like storm trooper tactics on American citizens, Russell proceeded to list a series of beatings, bayonet-point crowd control, illegal jailings, and other denials of constitutional rights which he insisted the troops had inflicted on the innocent citizens of Little Rock.[57] Expectedly, Russell's telegram also included a wide-ranging attack on the Supreme Court whose illegal decisions, he insisted, had precipitated the defiance of the federal court orders.

The president's 28 September telegram to Russell left no doubt as to where he placed the blame for his use of troops. Admitting that he was greatly saddened because the obligations of his office forced him to call out the federal troops, the president proceeded to state his case bluntly:

> My conviction is that had the police powers of the state of Arkansas been utilized not to frustrate the orders of the court but to support them, the ensuing violence and open disrespect for the law and the federal judiciary would never have occurred. The Arkansas National Guard could have handled the situation with ease had it been instructed to do so. As a matter of fact, had the integration of Central High School been permitted to take place without the intervention of the National Guard, there is little doubt that the process would have gone along quite as smoothly and quietly as it has in other Arkansas communities. When a state, by seeking to frustrate the orders of a federal court, encourages mobs of extremists to flout the orders of a federal court, and when a state refuses to utilize its police powers to protect against mobs persons who are peaceably exercising their right under the Constitution as defined in such court order, the oath of office of the President required that he take action to give that protection. Failure to act in such a case would be tantamount to acquiescence in anarchy and the dissolution of the Union.[58]

Though he stopped short of naming Orval Faubus, the thrust of his remarks was unmistakable. He subsequently indicated that he was certain that the Arkansas governor not only precipitated the crisis, but was also responsible for its continuation.

The president also completely rejected Russell's charge that the troops had acted like storm troopers because: "In one case military power was used to further the ambitions and institutions of free government."[59] He closed his telegram by assuring Russell that his allegations of wrongdoing on the part of individual soldiers at Little Rock would be investigated by the secretary of the army and passed on to the senator.[60]

Subsequent investigation proved that Russell's charges were groundless—that the troops had acted with a great deal of restraint in the face of repeated provocations. Secretary of the Army Brucker's letter rebutted Russell's allegations point by point and concluded that there were no instances of unjustified use of force by the federal troops against the citizens of Little Rock.[61]

And so began a war of words over the president's actions. Many of the administration's opponents were either incapable or unwilling to accept the premise which it presented for intervention there.

By coincidence, the events at Little Rock climaxed during the time the Southern Governors Conference was meeting. After the president sent troops, members of the conference requested that he meet with a committee of five governors regarding the crisis. That committee originally consisted of Frank G. Clement of Tennessee, LeRoy Collins of Florida, Luther Hodges of North Carolina, Theodore McKeldin of Maryland, and Marvin Griffin of Georgia, the last an ardent advocate of segregation. Griffin subsequently refused to attend the meeting with the president, charging that the president broadened the scope of the meeting to include the entire integration question instead of confining it to the Little Rock situation.[62]

The president met the four remaining southern governors at the White House on 1 October 1957. At that meeting, according to the official press release,

> the Governors informed the President that the Governor of Arkansas had authorized them to state that he is prepared to assume full responsibility for maintaining law and order in Little Rock and, in connection therewith, will not obstruct the orders of the Federal Courts.[63]

Though the news from the governors was encouraging, the president had been the victim of Faubus' unkept promises before. Consequently, he informed Faubus and the press that

> upon a declaration on the part of the Governor of Arkansas that he will not obstruct the orders of the Federal Courts and will in connection therewith maintain law and order in Little Rock, the President will direct the Secretary of Defense to return the command of the Arkansas National Guard to the Governor. Thereupon, as soon as practicable, all Federal troops will be withdrawn.[64]

This time, the president was determined that there would be no room for misunderstanding of his or Faubus' words. Nevertheless, the southern governors left the conference full of hope that there might be a speedy removal of federal troops and a rapid end to the confrontation. But the Arkansas governor, playing to a full grandstand on an issue which he was confident would reassure his reelection, chose to perpetuate confrontation between the federal troops and his government.

Faubus' public statement interpreting his supposed agreement with the president was far different from that which he asked the southern governors to convey to the president. He stated that if the national guardsmen were returned to his control he would not use them to prevent the black children from going to school and that there would be no obstruction of court orders "by me," meaning that he would not actively prevent others from obstructing. Certainly the most discouraging part of his statement to the president must have been the governor's promise to act "as he had done in the past."[65] Faubus' interpretation of the proposed agreement was so different that the four southern governors who had tendered it to the president accused Faubus of changing the meaning of his statement after Eisenhower had accepted it.

Faubus' actions left the president in the position of either having to surrender to the governor's definition of the agreement or to leave the federal troops at Little Rock and the Arkansas National Guard under federal control. On the evening of 1 October, the president issued a public statement announcing that since Faubus' statement "does not constitute in my opinion the assurance that he intends to use his full powers as Governor to prevent the obstruction of the orders of the United States District Court," the president had no recourse but to maintain federal presence in Little Rock.[66] The president concluded by thanking the four southern governors for their efforts at mediation and expressed hope that they would continue to create the conditions necessary to withdraw the troops.

As a further means of justifying its actions in Little Rock, the administration on 3 October released a summary of the legal principles that had guided the president in the Little Rock crisis. The four principles were:

1. The Executive Branch of the Federal Government does not participate in the formulation of plans effecting desegregation. . . .
2. The period of time within which any such plan should be put into effect likewise must be proposed by the local authorities and approved by the Courts. . . .
3. A final order of a Federal Court giving effect to a desegregation public school plan must be obeyed by State authorities and all citizens as the law of the land. . . .

4. Powers of a State Governor may not be used to defeat a valid order of a Federal Court. . . .[67]

The document made it clear that the administration's decision to intervene in Little Rock was based on the premise that it had no other choice short of the sacrifice of constitutional government and that its only involvement in the integration process occurred when courts requested its assistance to see that their orders were carried out.

The voluminous correspondence which the administration carried on with the critics of its actions at Little Rock adhered strictly to the four principles cited in its 3 October position paper. Letters sent over the signature of the president, Sherman Adams, and all other members of the administration emphasized that while there was room for disagreement about the wisdom of the Court's desegregation decisions, there was no question about the president's duty to see that district court orders were upheld.[68] The administration adhered strictly to the position that it had been confronted with a grave constitutional challenge.

Administration Attempts to Extricate Itself

Insights about the president's own state of mind regarding Little Rock can be gleaned from the notes his secretary took during his 3 October 1957 pre-press conference briefing.[69] The president first noted that his public position would be that the Governors' Committee was still working and that, while he was not confident, he was hopeful that something satisfactory could be worked out. He said that he would also mention that the troops were there to see that the court's orders were being carried out and that they would be withdrawn only on assurance that they were not needed and after a period of calm in which civilian authorities prove they can maintain peace. He emphasized that he would reiterate his belief that respect for court decisions must be maintained.[70]

So much for his public position. Then he expressed his own thoughts on the situation. He made it clear that he was much more pessimistic about the crisis than he could publicly admit. He was more doubtful than ever about the wisdom of court-directed desegregation, and it is clear that his skepticism received strong reinforcement from Sherman Adams. As Ann Whitman noted:

> The President said there was a grave situation raised by Governor Adams as to the right of the Supreme Court to go ahead after they find a thing unconstitutional—to work out plans and lay down schemes for implementing plans. Gets into area of individual liberties and states' rights. President said we might have ground torn out from under us by an amendment to the constitution or "some law."[71]

Eisenhower was clearly worried about the vulnerable position that he felt court-ordered integration had created for his administration.

Turning to the question of how he intended to deal with the crisis, the president stressed that his main effort would be directed toward playing down the situation in Little Rock by being as quiet as possible about it. He noted that the other southern governors did not agree with the school decisions either but that they were trying in good faith to do something to make it a livable situation. Faubus, he was convinced, was deliberately trying to keep the crisis going with the goal of stirring up so much trouble in the South that it would be beyond the ability of federal troops to control the situation.[72] The president thus hoped to use the same strategy of silence against Faubus that he had used against Senator Joseph McCarthy previously. Unfortunately, the emotions and the opposition here were far different than in the McCarthy controversy.

Despite the president's strategy, the Little Rock crisis refused to go away. On the contrary, it ended up absorbing much of the administration's attention and energy for almost two years after Eisenhower intervened with federal troops. Much energy was dissipated in responding to Faubus' continued exploitation of the situation. On 1 October 1957, for example, the governor charged that federal troops had invaded the privacy of the girls' dressing room at Central High School. The White House denied the charges.[73] During his 9 October pre–press conference briefing, the president and his aides discussed ways to handle any reporters' questions that might arise about it. Eisenhower thought that it might provide a good opportunity to praise the discipline of the troops. In the event of a possible question about whether there would have been trouble in Little Rock if Faubus had not called out the guard, the president said he would respond that it was difficult to answer a hypothetical question but that he might mention that integration had proceeded in other places in Arkansas without incident.

Despite its tough public stance against Faubus, there was never any desire on the part of the administration for a prolongation of the federal troop presence in Little Rock. The president and key members of his administration began seeking ways to achieve rapid withdrawal of federal troops almost immediately after their arrival. A 15 October memorandum summarizing a conference between the president, Attorney General Brownell, Assistant Attorney General William Rogers, Secretary of the Army Wilber Brucker, and generals Maxwell Taylor, Wilton Persons, and Andrew Goodpaster reflected unanimity on the wisdom of getting the federal troop contingent reduced in size and out as quickly as possible.[74]

On 16 October, Maxwell Rabb sent a memorandum to Sherman Adams noting that several cabinet members had requested that their meetings include a review of the situation in Little Rock. In rationalizing the need for the cabinet-level discussions, Rabb said:

> There is no doubt that this question is one of the most significant to come before the Executive since the turn of the

century. Its judicial, legislative, political, domestic and international ramifications are everywhere. What we have done
already and, more important, what we will do from now on,
will affect the entire Administration's program, its Federal–
State relations and its dealings with the reconvening Congress. It probably cannot be ignored in the State of the
Union Message.[75]

Preoccupation with this crisis was widespread in the administration.

One of the many problems confronting the administration
as it tried to extricate itself from the Little Rock dilemma was
its inability to attract substantial support for its position
among moderate southern leaders. On 19 October, the president discussed that problem in a telephone call with HEW
Secretary Oveta Culp Hobby, a Texan. In that conversation,
the president mentioned that only Ralph McGill, the outspoken
editor of the *Atlanta Constitution,* had openly supported the
administration's actions. When Hobby suggested bringing
southern leaders up to Washington for a conference, the president replied that none of them were in a position to take a
forthright stand.[76] With the collapse of the earlier Governors'
Committee attempt, the administration could neither claim
any southern support for its actions nor utilize it as a possible
vehicle for mediation of the crisis. The intense emotional
reaction the confrontation had stirred in the South hastened
the administration's desire to end the Little Rock incubus as
soon as possible.

The president's advisors also wrestled with the problem
with less-than-successful results. A 19 October transcript of
a telephone call from Sherman Adams to Assistant Attorney
General William Rogers presents a view of the options considered and the narrow range of the choices the administration
possessed. When Adams, calling on behalf of the president,
asked Rogers for his suggestions, he responded that the one
thing to do would be to reduce troop strength gradually.

Adams then mentioned that Press Secretary Hagerty had suggested wiring Faubus asking him if he was ready to grant the rights of the black children. Both Adams and Rogers agreed that such a move would be a mistake. Adams told Rogers that he had two suggestions: first, that the administration call in the Civil Rights Commission and negotiate with local authorities concerning their readiness to take on responsibility for assuring that black children could go to Central High School; or second, that the administration itself could negotiate in that manner.[77]

Despite Faubus' refusal to budge, the administration did move methodically to reduce its military presence at Little Rock. The president listed the major steps in that process in his memoirs.

> On October 14 I approved Secretary Brucker's order to withdraw half the Army troops and to defederalize four-fifths of the National Guardsmen. On October 23, Negro students left Central High for the first time without a military escort.[78]

Still working to milk as much advantage as possible from the situation, Faubus on 25 October telegraphed Eisenhower and Secretary of the Army Brucker condemning the use of the guardsmen at Central High School as "a violation of their rights," and demanding the release of the eighteen hundred who had been retained on federalized status.[79] It was important to his purposes that federal involvement be pictured as an arbitrary occupation.

The resignation the previous week of Attorney General Brownell, who had long expressed a desire to return to private law practice, gave Faubus the occasion to express his hope that the attitude of the Justice Department would shift "from political motivation to one of impartial enforcement."[80] As Herbert Parmet has noted in a recent work, the reaction to Brownell's resignation in the South indicates that he was regarded as the major villain in the Little Rock affair.[81] Such an approach made it easier to sidestep the problem of explaining Eisenhower's role. Brownell's ringing defense of the administration's actions in an Official Opinion issued in November 1957 was a persuasive rebuttal of such charges, but it had little effect on those who, like Faubus, chose to portray him as the director of forced integration by an army of occupation.

Painfully aware of Faubus' intentions, the president continued to move toward disengagement. However, as he admitted in his 30 October pre-press conference briefing, his efforts were still partially stalemated. One reason for this was that attempts to further reduce its military forces had been stymied because of the refusal of the Little Rock police and mayor to take responsibility for maintaining law and order in the city.[82] That condition, fortunately, proved to be a temporary one.

Subsequent administration attempts to renew its moderate approach to the integration question appeared in the 20 November announcement that the Justice Department had decided not to prosecute agitators or troublemakers at Central High as long as no further trouble occurred.[83] The Justice Department's action was accompanied by continued reduction of the federal government military presence. Eisenhower later wrote:

> By November 15 the National Guard took over the control of the school area. By November 27 the last of the 101st Airborne Division left Little Rock. . . . On May 8, 1958, I announced that when school ended, the Guard would leave.[84]

Such actions on the part of the administration should not be construed as signifying the end of the struggle surrounding the desegregation of Central High School.

However, it is not the purpose of this study to present a comprehensive history of the two years of judicial and political attack and counterattack that occurred before Little Rock Central High was finally reopened on an integrated basis without incident in the fall of 1959. The means to examine that story are readily available through a variety of works.[85] The emphasis here, rather, has been on a characterization of the thinking and reactions of Dwight D. Eisenhower and key members of his administration in the initial, critical phases of that crisis.

Critical Perspectives

The president's reaction to the Little Rock crisis has provoked a variety of assessments. One of the sharpest criticisms came from Virgil T. Blossom, a moderate superintendent of the Little Rock Public Schools at the time of the crisis. Writing in 1959 from the perspective of one who not only experienced the crisis but was also a victim of the subsequent segregationist-inspired purge of the school administration, he argues that Little Rock caught the Eisenhower administration unprepared. He insists that it should have taken strong civil actions against Faubus for defying the court and, further, that its decision to intervene militarily came too late. This, in turn, helped provoke the tragic reaction and bitterness which made it easy for the moderates to be pushed aside by the segregationists. In summation, Blossom charged that the administration waited too long to respond and when it did it was with the wrong means, making a difficult situation impossible.[86]

Blossom's arguments have proven to be telling ones. They have been restated by numerous academic and political critics since 1959.[87] The overwhelming bulk of this criticism of Eisenhower's actions dealt with the problems created by the effects of his reactions to Little Rock. Very little of it has been directed at an understanding of the causes of his behavior.

It is apparent from the president's remarks during the confrontation and the actions that he did finally take that his skepticism about the viability of court-ordered desegregation and his preference for a moderate approach explain much about his behavior. The president was fearful lest the federal courts precipitate a crisis in the South which would lead to a tragic confrontation of state and federal power on such a broad scale that the administration could not cope with it. It is also important to note that the president was the victim of conflicting advice from his staff and that he was strongly attracted to Sherman Adams' arguments that he could arrive at an accommodation with Faubus.

Undoubtedly, Eisenhower regarded the Little Rock confrontation as primarily a constitutional crisis in which he faced the unpleasant task of fulfilling his oath of office to uphold the Constitution (i.e., a government of laws) against those who sought to defy it. The enormity of that duty, his awareness of how deeply the South felt about the race issue, and the hope that he and many others held initially—that Faubus was negotiating in good faith—explains his slowness to act. Ultimately, he did act but on a battleground which he feared with weapons which, though certainly constitutional, he abhorred because they pitted American against American and seemed to perpetuate an already dangerous crisis.

Eisenhower's response to Little Rock can be judged from several perspectives. Regardless of which approach is chosen, it seems clear that the president's actions were consistent extensions of his style of leadership and his previous experience in the segregation controversy. Whether or not those previous experiences blinded the president to some realities or caused him to place too much faith in his low-key approach to racial problems is another matter. One thing is certain. The mixture of moderation and firmness which marked his behavior during the Little Rock confrontation symbolized the tension between the approach he preferred and the one created by his duty to uphold the Constitution.

There is no question as to the sincerity of his remarks to his good friend Ogden R. Reid on 28 September 1957: "As I am sure you realize, the Little Rock situation has been troublesome beyond imagination. Thank you for your approval of the decision that I was duty-bound to make."[88]

Chapter 10

The Closing Years: 1958-1960

The confrontation at Little Rock proved to be a bitter experience for Dwight D. Eisenhower. It did not, however, destroy his faith in the efficacy of a gradual, low-key approach to the desegregation question. If anything, it reinforced it. The president's public and private words and deeds during the last three years of his presidency, as this chapter illustrates, substantiate this point. Even his decision to introduce the additional civil rights legislation as suggested by his advisors during that period did not represent a surrender of his moderation. The aspects of the proposals relevant to the school desegregation issue were aimed at easing the tensions surrounding it. Moreover, his willingness to push hard for protection of voting rights while offering only lukewarm support for the measures aimed at facilitating school desegregation in the face of determined congressional opposition stands as proof of his continuing doubts about the wisdom of relying too heavily on desegregation by judicial or legislative fiat.

Late 1957–1958

The president reiterated his preference for a gradual, long-range approach to desegregation in a number of personal letters, some written during the height of the Little Rock confrontation. Writing on 21 October 1957 to retired Major General I. T. Wyche, Eisenhower stated:

> I share your concern over the antagonisms created by racial problems. It is the kind of thing that seems to preclude any easy and quick answer. For example, were there a Constitutional Amendment affecting the matter, it would certainly eliminate arguments as to what is the true meaning of the Constitution. But, assuming that such action would tend to uphold the 1954 decision of the Supreme Court, we would be little further along in the elimination of the emotions and arguments that have developed around the problem itself.
>
> So far as I am concerned, I am still clear in my mind that, regardless of all corrections attempted by legal means of whatever character, we still have a great task of education and conciliation.[1]

The president continued to receive reinforcement for his cautious approach from those members of his own staff charged with civil rights matters. On 12 November 1957, Maxwell Rabb sent a memorandum to Sherman Adams detailing a number of points for the president's consideration about the makeup and funding of the Civil Rights Commission created by the 1957 Civil Rights Act.[2]

Among the seven substantive and procedural aspects discussed in the memorandum, three stand out. First, the report advised the president to avoid permitting the relationship between the White House and the commission from becoming too closely knit for fear of creating adverse criticism in Congress and the press. Second, it expressed the hope that the commission could assist the government in overcoming the "profound" public ignorance about what the Justice Department can and cannot do in civil rights cases. Third, it recommended that the commission investigate highly explosive situations such as the Montgomery, Alabama, bus boycott and the Autherine Lucy affair, with the hope that such early analysis could prevent the outbreak of violence.[3]

Eisenhower's civil rights advisors thus perceived of the bipartisan Civil Rights Commission as something of a buffer which would absorb much of the shock, controversy, and criticism the administration faced in the civil rights realm. There is evidence that the White House "separatist" position proved disappointing to key members of the Civil Rights Commission such as John Hannah and Gordon Tiffany. This was certainly true in late 1958 when the White House balked at coordinating policy statements of the administration and the commission.[4] Administration advisors reasoned that such coordination was impossible on two grounds: first, the commission was a bipartisan one with independent status; and second, because it would be practically impossible to coordinate statements with all of the offices of the executive branch. The administration's perception of its relations with the Civil Rights Commission was based on its desire to separate itself from embroilment in the desegregation issue. This guaranteed that the commission initially got precious little in the way of direct guidance in its activities and functions from the very administration which had urged its creation.

Critical insights regarding the president's attitude toward desegregation emerged from his 23 June 1958 meeting with Martin Luther King, Jr., A. Philip Randolph, Roy Wilkins, and Lester Granger. That meeting was held at the request of the black leaders who hoped they could persuade Eisenhower to take a more sympathetic public position in the struggle for desegregation. The meeting came one month after Clarence Mitchell, an associate of Wilkins, had issued an extremely critical statement on the president's attitude toward the black struggle for civil rights.[5]

Randolph opened the meeting by commending the president's efforts to improve the political and economic status of blacks and praising him for his courage. Randolph read a list of nine recommendations which the leaders hoped to see the administration put into effect.[6] Each of the respective leaders spoke in detail about some of the recommendations.

King spoke in support of the first three recommendations,

which he regarded as crucial to the mobilization of the spirit needed to fight segregation. These recommendations included a call for a presidential announcement in support of the desegregation decision, a White House conference to be used as a forum for the expression of good will between blacks and whites, and dissemination of progress reports toward integration by government as the basis of education in the desegregation process. At the end of his presentation, Rocco C. Siciliano noted, King said:

> He agrees that morals cannot be legislated (only education and religion can do this, he said) and that internal attitudes are hard to change, but that action is possible to attempt to control the external effects of such attitudes.[7]

King's statement reveals a sharp contrast between his and Eisenhower's approach to the desegregation issue. While both shared the same premise, the civil rights leader insisted that the difficulty in the heart and mind should not become an excuse for inaction. The president regarded such actions, and particularly the direct confrontation techniques King advocated and practiced, as counterproductive because of the antagonisms they developed.

Roy Wilkins also spoke. He praised the president's orders relating to desegregation of the armed forces and urged that the administration work to get the deleted sections of the 1957 Civil Rights Act enacted into law.[8] The major proposal that he cited was that which would have granted the attorney general increased statutory weapons to use against those who defied federal court orders. Wilkins also encouraged the president to increase his efforts on behalf of securing the right to vote for blacks in the South as the basis of peaceful change and adjustment in that section. Wilkins' recommendations must have surprised and delighted Eisenhower because they were things he had long advocated. Much to the relief of many, Wilkins did not choose to restate his recent criticism of the president either in the meeting or in the press conference which followed.

Ironically, the most discouraging statement came from the most moderate of the leaders. Lester Granger emphasized that in his long lifetime of involvement with civil rights activities, he had never seen a time when the bitterness of blacks showed "more signs of congealing" then at present.[9] Granger asserted that this frustration developed because many blacks had been led to believe that there was hope and progress, yet it had suddenly at present appeared to stop. He discussed some of the confusion created in the public mind by well-meaning whites who misstated or misunderstood the significance of black involvement in the desegregation process.

William Rogers, who had recently replaced Herbert Brownell as attorney general, commented that he felt that bitterness was growing among American blacks because of the frustration caused by occasional temporary setbacks in the midst of true progress. He explained that the bitterness was not evident before because most blacks had not really seen any reasons to be hopeful.[10] Rogers told the black leaders that the Justice Department was defending the law by aggressive court action whenever and wherever it felt there were sufficient legal grounds to be successful but that it was unwise for the cause of civil rights to institute actions in each individual complaint situation. Rogers also reminded Wilkins that he had demonstrated willingness to abandon the criminal penalties portions of the administration's civil rights bill during the debate which had occurred prior to its passage.[11]

Then it was Eisenhower's turn to speak. He was obviously hurt and upset by the remarks about black bitterness. As Siciliano further noted in his memorandum:

> He was extremely dismayed to hear that after 5½ years of effort and action in this field these gentlemen were saying that bitterness on the part of the Negro people was at its

height. He wondered if further constructive action in this field would not only result in more bitterness.[12]

Granger assured the president that the bitterness the leaders had mentioned was not directed at him or his administration, but rather toward the localities where progress had been made initially and then halted.[13]

Siciliano further noted in his memorandum that:

> The President spoke forceably [sic] about the need for diligent and careful perusal by the Federal Government of any actions in this field. . . . He said he did not propose to comment—and knew they did not expect him to—on the recommendations which he had before him, but said that he would obviously be glad to consider them. He then said that there might be at first blush some value in convoking a White House conference, but added that he was doubtful if it would be productive of anything.[14]

Randolph interrupted at that point and argued that the president's participation might "give it a high moral tone, to which the President replied there was only so much any President could do in opening such a meeting."[15]

Attorney General Rogers proceeded to summarize the administration's position for the black leaders. He expressed his personal skepticism about the value of a White House conference on desegregation, arguing that it would "only serve as a sounding board for the reaffirmation of previously announced positions."[16] He assured the leaders that the administration would take aggressive action in all areas under federal authority. Eisenhower expressed his agreement with Rogers' remarks and stressed his own belief in the particular importance of voting rights.[17]

It was apparent that Eisenhower saw the possible effects of more direct presidential action on behalf of desegregation in far different terms than did the four black leaders. He interpreted the bitterness of blacks as proof that too much agitation and confrontation on civil rights was harmful while they viewed it as reflecting the lack of enough progress toward desegregation. The leaders also had far more confidence than the president in his ability to effectively exert moral leadership in the desegregation crisis. He was convinced that such overt behavior on his part would increase the tensions already present because of judicial activism. The suggestions of the black leaders, with the exception of their strong pleas for expanded protection of voting rights, ran counter to his hopes for less direct administration involvement in the desegregation question. The chasm between him and the black leaders, despite the polite tone of their subsequent joint statement and the latter's press conference regarding the meeting, was a vast one. It was the product of totally different approaches and perspectives on the desegregation question.[18]

Further evidence of the president's unwillingness to adopt a tough stance against the opponents of desegregation appeared in his remarks during his 8 August 1958, pre–press conference briefing. His comments on the attempt of the Virginia legislature to evade desegregation by closing its public schools and creating a system of private segregated ones reveal his continued sympathy for white southerners caught in the throes of the crisis. The president announced that he got very annoyed at the refusal of the North to see how deeply the people of the South feel about the integration issue.[19]

Discussion then shifted to New York Democratic Congressman James Roosevelt's recent letter to the president asking if the administration had made preparations in the event that clashes over desegregation occurred when the 1958 school year opened. Eisenhower commented that it was not his responsibility to keep order everywhere, but only to see that the orders of the federal judges were carried out.[20] Such comments indicate the president's attitude toward the school desegregation issue was the same as it was prior to Little Rock.

Evidence that he still held hopes for a peaceful solution to the school desegregation problem appeared in his 3 October 1958 letter to Ralph McGill, who had suggested that the closing of the schools might eventually help the cause of desegregation. Eisenhower's comments are particularly significant because they came after Virginia had shut down its public schools. In commenting on McGill's point, he told the editor:

> It is quite possible that your statement that the schools must be closed for a period before there is hope of acceptance of the decision is a correct one. I tend to believe that the students themselves will eventually resolve the issue, merely by their desire to have the educational processes resumed, despite the objections they may have to the conditions under which it may proceed. Incidentally, it is curious how the extra-curricular activities of school life—the football team, the band, etc.—seem to become more important levers in urging the reopening of the schools than does educational opportunity. The children will likely be helpful in bringing pressure upon parents, school boards, and local authorities, for the reopening of the schools.[21]

His faith in common sense and good will seemed undiminished.

When questioned about Virginia's defiance in his 21 January 1959 press conference, the president took a somewhat equivocal position. He said that HEW was authorized by law to provide desegregated education on the military bases but that the proper means to educate the fifty-five hundred government and military dependents who had attended the now-closed public schools were "not so clear."[22] He further noted that the federal government provided huge grants to the public schools, including those in Norfolk, Virginia, which were "impacted" because of large numbers of children of federal civilian and military employees. However, when a reporter asked him whether he was considering requesting Congress to stop aid to schools if they did not desegregate, he sharply denied the charge.[23]

Another reporter raised the question about the president's reaction to recent statements by the governor of Virginia calling on the citizens of his state to increase their defiance to the Court's decisions. Eisenhower responded that he did not know what the governor meant, because the Virginia school closing policy which gave aid to some districts and not others had been declared unconstitutional by their own state supreme court and by subsequent federal courts. The real issue, Eisenhower emphasized, was whether a U.S. citizen inside or outside of government should be "ready to obey the laws of his state and of his nation."[24] The president maintained his position that when court orders were defied in desegregation cases the major point was not a question of integration but obedience to the law. However, missing from his remarks was any firm promise to see that the laws would be enforced like those he had made prior to Little Rock. He was convinced that confrontation would resolve nothing; therefore, he was determined to allow the tactic of avoidance and delay to operate in the Virginia situation. His stance was essentially a verbal position, unreinforced by any positive action on the part of his administration.

The post-Little Rock era also saw the president, with the same rationale as previously, refusing to express public approval or disapproval of the desegregation decisions, even though he had many opportunities to do so. One such occasion occurred on 13 June 1959 in a meeting with Charles B. Shuman, president of the American Farm Bureau, regarding that organization's legislative program. During the meeting, Shuman gave the chief executive a pamphlet entitled "The Supreme Court of the United States" in which the Farm Bureau head had criticized him for acquiescing in a number of the Court's controversial decisions. The president's response left no doubt about his continued devotion to the principle that the Court's interpretation had to be respected.

After assuring Shuman that he did not quarrel with a number of Shuman's conclusions or his right to assert them, the president took up the charge of presidential acquiescence.

> The oath of the President is to support and defend the Constitution of the United States—not to interpret it. I am afraid we would have chaos if each started giving his own interpretation to the words of the Constitution.
>
> In any event, I have one simple question. Do you have anything to suggest that a President should do, if he should personally disagree with a decision? I remind you that if ever he made such disagreement public, then he would always be under the suspicion that in such cases he would probably not be interested in enforcing the law faithfully. . . .[25]

Though the frustrating disputes over the civil rights bill, federal aid to education, and the Little Rock crisis were all in a sense the products of the judicial activism which he feared, the president's faith in the correctness of his noncommittal position on Supreme Court decisions remained unshaken.

Toward the Civil Rights Act of 1960

The confrontation at Little Rock left the president a sadder but wiser man in at least one way. Though he never lost his preference for a gradual, low-key approach to desegregation based on education and conciliation, he did accept the need for strengthened federal civil rights legislation to deal with those who fomented violence or defiance of court-ordered desegregation. The development of such proposed legislation was consistent with his determination to see that the courts' interpretation of constitutional rights was upheld. The hesitation and sporadic nature of his efforts reflected Eisenhower's unenthusiastic acceptance of the need to make the best of the situation created by judicially directed desegregation.

The issue of school desegregation had been present as something more than the ghost at the banquet in the year-and-a-half struggle which had culminated in the Civil Rights Act of 1957, though it certainly took a back seat in the president's eyes to his major objective of increased protection of voting rights. The result of a bipartisan compromise, the final version of the 1957 act had created a Civil Rights Commission with limited investigatory and reporting powers and increased protection for voting rights. The act's effectiveness against the foes of school integration was severely inhibited when a coalition of liberals and southerners sought to overwhelm administration opposition and added a jury trial requirement to the section of the bill aimed at those charged with contempt of court.[26]

The subsequent efforts which culminated in the Civil Rights Act of 1960 reflected continuing administration attempts to obtain greater protection for voting rights, and more effective legislation against those who advocated and practiced defiance to obstruct school desegregation. On 19 November 1958, the president in a meeting with the attorney general, secretary of labor, secretary of HEW, and several members of his own staff discussed his civil rights policies and stated his desire to go forward with both administrative and legislative action.[27] In his typically cautious manner, the president expressed his hope that some means could be found for federal judges to fight out segregation cases rather than leaving them to NAACP lawyers who he felt would inflame them. Evidence that key administration members preferred a toughened legislative approach was soon forthcoming. On 28 January 1959, Eisenhower received an eight-point memorandum outlining a proposed civil rights program from the attorney general and the secretaries of labor, defense, and HEW. In addition to voting rights proposals, it contained several features aimed at strengthening the federal government's position against the opponents of school desegregation.[28]

The Justice Department's suggestions included, in addition to its call for a two-year renewal of the Civil Rights Commission, the adoption of specific criminal penalties against those who interfered with desegregation. It sought up to $10,000 in fines and ten years' imprisonment or both for those traveling in interstate and foreign commerce to avoid state and local criminal prosecution for use of explosives and firearms on buildings used for religious or educational purposes. Another penalty of up to $10,000 in fines and two years in prison was proposed for those obstructing federal court orders relating to the administration of schools, admission of racial minorities to schools, or state and local plans for such admissions.[29] Still another Justice Department proposal aimed at permitting, with judicial approval, the federal government to file suits on behalf of persons denied equal protection of the laws in situations where an individual might be threatened with reprisal. The criminal penalties and the more protective attitude of the Justice Department contrast sharply with the administration's 1957 proposals for the use of civil contempt citations against the opponents of school desegregation.

Not all of the administration's proposals were coercive. HEW proposed the creation of grants to assist local districts in bearing the cost of shifting from dual to integrated school systems. They also sought authorization from the commissioner of education to provide, on request, information and technical assistance to those districts making the transition. These suggestions were accompanied by predictions that such actions would help increase incentives for compliance.[30]

HEW's second proposal authorized the commissioner of education to provide public education for children of military personnel, whether they resided on bases or not, if local authorities refused or were unable to do so. One of HEW's proposals did reflect a toughened position on desegregation. Its final proposal required that henceforth any public schools built in federally affected areas with federal funds would be open to all children or the involved districts would be forced to turn the buildings over to the commissioner of education.[31] The latter proposal indicated that some elements of the administration were willing to exert greater pressure for desegregation in the borderline area of federal-state relations which the president had initially felt was not within the realm of federal responsibility. Despite disclaimers about their coercive nature, the proposals submitted to the president were distinctly tougher than those brought forth earlier. Stiffening resistance had convinced many members of the administration to belatedly seek stronger legal weapons.

The proposed civil rights legislation was one of the major topics for discussion when the president met with his party's legislative leaders on 3 February 1959. A recently declassified confidential memorandum written by Presidential Assistant Lewis Arthur Minnich, Jr., aptly portrays the president's attitude and indicates that his administration's approach was conditioned by ever-present political demands.[32]

Attorney General Rogers opened the meeting by reviewing the federal role in Arkansas, its deliberate decision to maintain a hands-off position toward the Virginia situation while it continued to closely monitor events there, and the moderate nature of administration actions in the civil rights field. He then summarized the Justice Department's portion of the proposed civil rights legislation. In the course of this discussion, it became apparent that House Minority Leader Charles Halleck of Indiana was not convinced of the need for additional civil rights legislation. As Minnich noted: "Mr. Halleck questioned the need for further action in this field in view of the dissension created by new legislation and in view of the progress being made around the country in civil rights matters."[33] Despite vigorous defense of the proposals by Attorney General Rogers and Vice President Richard M. Nixon, Halleck continued his critique by raising a similar objection about HEW's legislative proposals.[34] Nixon responded that the HEW proposals were necessary to assuage a difficult situation.

When some of the senators and congressmen called attention to the adverse effects the civil rights proposals would have on Republican efforts to secure southern Democratic votes on budgetary issues, the president himself responded. According to Minnich, he

> stated his concern with this question but his belief that the Administration must advance some moderate and constructive proposal in view of the provisions of our Constitution, the Supreme Court decision, and the large number of citizens not enjoying their proper rights. The President did not wish to make any proposal that gave rise to arguments and dissension but he was convinced that these proposals were essentially moderate and something the Administration must do.[35]

This position was reinforced by Nixon, who emphasized that the administration's proposals were workable and that most Republicans preferred their own to some more radical Democratic ones or none at all.

After some further suggestions by Senator Leverett Saltonstall of Massachusetts about changing the HEW proposal to a general statement that it stands ready to help any state asking assistance, Minnich related:

> The President added a word on the need for money for schools on military bases, then stated something of a feeling that there was an element of expecting the worst and of acknowledging defeat in this provision. He felt the proposals generally could be regarded as spreading a little oil on troubled waters. He repeated his belief in the need for an Administration proposal.[36]

Despite skepticism and attempts on the part of the GOP legislative leadership to water down the administration's proposals, the message the president sent to Congress on 5 February 1959 included all of them save one.[37] The proposal to protect individuals from reprisals in civil rights cases was deleted because of strong objections among some Republican legislators who feared that such a provision might get the Justice Department involved in labor union disputes.[38]

The administration's supporters in Congress thus entered what proved to be another long and frustrating battle on behalf of its civil rights proposals. They later found that they would receive only lukewarm support from the president on those parts of the program not connected with voting rights. However, that fact was not apparent in the initial discussions which accompanied the administration's introduction of its program in 1959.

During the legislative leadership meeting of 17 February 1959, Senator Everett Dirksen of Illinois reported that the chances for approval would be much improved if it included the conciliation service idea suggested by Senate Democratic Majority Leader Lyndon Johnson. Regardless, Dirksen predicted the Senate would handle the proposals very quickly.[39] House Minority Leader Halleck commented on the absence of attacks by southerners and that he was very pleased with the proposals as they were finally submitted.[40] Eisenhower then concluded the discussion by emphasizing how the "very nature of these things required the moderate, constructive action as a matter of decency without regard to the pressure or absence of political benefit."[41]

The president's continued preference for a restrained approach to the civil liberties question was apparent in his attitude toward the role he envisioned for the Civil Rights Commission. It is obvious that though the administration initially refused to coordinate its civil rights policy statements with those of the commission, it did shift to a more cooperative attitude toward it. Minutes of a 27 February 1959 meeting reveal that the president and the attorney general reiterated their support for a renewal of the Civil Rights Commission and pledged the cooperation of the executive branch, including closer communication between it and the commission. Moreover, they concurred with its chairman, John Hannah, that in the event Congress created a civil rights conciliation service it should be operated by the Civil Rights Commission.[42]

The president's conservative heart was gladdened when Hannah emphasized that the solution to civil rights problems would occur only if people recognized the importance of developing local solutions to them. Minnich noted in his minutes:

> The President spoke with emphasis on the importance of feelings rather than laws in the solution of these problems. He hoped that the members of the Commission would keep on with their work despite their individual preferences for other activities.[43]

Whether the president was consciously trying to steer the commission members away from calls for more legislation is difficult to say. Nevertheless, his remarks do indicate that he maintained his preference for an approach to the desegregation question far different from one based on begrudging or forced conformity to court orders. It was his hope that the Civil Rights Commission could be an agent for depolarization.[44]

As his remarks to Congressman Halleck in the 11 August 1959 legislative leadership meeting indicated, the president was also concerned about his proposed civil rights legislation for another reason. When Halleck informed him that it was stalled in the House Rules Committee, Eisenhower warned him that if Congress failed to act, the administration would be subjected to immense pressure to give up its moderate program in favor of a more drastic approach.[45] The warning had little effect on Halleck or his congressional colleagues.

Though the administration did succeed in winning congressional renewal of the Civil Rights Commission, a staff memorandum dated 3 February 1960 noted that its other six proposals were still pending.[46] Four of those six dealt directly with school segregation. These included proposed legislation to make obstruction of court-ordered school desegregation a federal offense, additional investigative authority for the FBI in cases dealing with attempted destruction of schools or churches, financial and technical aid to state and local agencies to assist them in bringing about school desegregation, and the authorizing of the commissioner of education to provide on a temporary basis for education of children of armed forces members where state-administered public schools were closed to avoid desegregation. The other two involved extension of voting rights protection and creation of a government committee on contracts discrimination. How much support the administration could bring to bear on their behalf in Congress would prove to be critically important in 1960.

What of Eisenhower's own attitude regarding the pending proposals? The president gave some indication of where his priorities lay in a 24 January 1960 legislative leadership meeting when he reported his oft-stated warning about the dangers of too many laws on civil rights. Despite the fact that he had approved the submission of his administration proposals, he concluded the discussion on civil rights by expressing the conviction that if voting rights were protected, the administration's responsibility would be fulfilled.[47]

Another clear statement of his attitude appeared in his remarks during the 2 February 1960 legislative leadership meeting. In the midst of a long discussion about the ways to most effectively protect black voting rights, Eisenhower cited the difficulty of determining the political impact of civil rights matters. Citing the example of how little the Republicans' excellent civil rights record had helped them among blacks in metropolitan New York, the chief executive was, as he had always been, skeptical about the potential for political gain in the civil rights area.[48]

The president then asserted that his interest in civil rights legislation was based on two principles which, while not necessarily detached from politics, were certainly beyond the realm of narrow partisanship. First, according to the person who took notes at the meeting, he wanted to make sure that the "Administration was doing whatever might be necessary to carry out the Constitution, and secondly, to have a bill which, while moderate, would be regarded even by the extremists as a definite step forward."[49] The president informed his leadership that he would give full support to the proposal that federal referees be appointed in cases where the denial of voting rights existed. He was convinced that the critical right above all others was voting and that once it was achieved others would soon follow.

The extremists whom the president cited in this instance were those who were calling for more rapid, decisive action against the opponents of desegregation. The president's support for civil rights legislation was thus based on his genuine fear that there had to be some action by the moderates if they were to maintain control of the situation. It is also apparent from his remarks that he did not really place the high priority on the rest of his administration's civil rights proposals that he did on the protection of voting rights. This was exemplified by the willingness of the president and the attorney general to be flexible about the precise details of the antibombing proposal when questioned by Senator Dirksen in that same meeting.

Further evidence of this lower priority for the school desegregation aspects of the civil rights proposals appeared in the president's meeting with the Republican leadership during the time the battle for the civil rights bill raged in Congress. In the 8 March 1960 legislative leadership meeting, Senator Dirksen discussed the deadlock in the Senate over the administration's proposals to grant assistance to desegregating school districts and to create a statutory basis for a committee on contracts to enforce nondiscrimination in businesses doing work for the federal government. Senator Saltonstall informed the president that the language of the bill put the Congress on record as confirming a Supreme Court decision, and Ohio

Representative William M. McCulloch noted that the House committee had struck out that portion of the bill and that it would not be restored on the floor of the House.[50] Minnich recalled in his notes:

> The President made clear that his interest was in getting the essentials that he had originally recommended, and particularly the one big objective of protecting the sanctity of voting. The educational grants, he said, were something he had accepted but had not ever deemed essential.[51]

He then added that if parts of his program were knocked out, the administration should not have to bear the blame for it, but that it should be placed on his opponents in Congress where it belonged.

When the president was asked at his 18 March 1960 press conference whether or not he would attempt to have the Senate restore two key parts of his civil rights bill which the House had struck from it, he became evasive:

> Well, I shall continue to say that this bill was brought up, after all kinds of conferences I could get, as you know, I am trying to find a moderate, reasonable path that points to progress, and so I believe in this bill, and I'm going to ask for it.
>
> Now, of course, I want the best bill the Congress will give me in this very troublesome and sensitive area.[52]

Both Eisenhower's public and his private remarks reveal his lack of genuine commitment to those parts of the administration bill beyond the protection of voting rights.

The legislative proposals that became the Civil Rights Act of 1960 included all of the administration's original proposals except the federal grants to desegregating school districts and the committee on contracts.[53] Coming as it did in the wake of the disastrous 1958 midterm elections and the extended recession which marred his second term, some scholars have argued that the 1960 act was at least the partial product of the need of both parties to prove that they could provide decisive leadership in the midst of the expanding civil rights revolution as the presidential campaign of 1960 approached.[54] The president's own assessment also underscores the fact that the Civil Rights Act did not evolve in a political vacuum.

On 26 April, Eisenhower congratulated the Republican legislative leaders on their role in obtaining passage of the Civil Rights Act. He took an active part in the discussion of ways to make it clear to the people that the Republicans had played a primary role in the passage of the legislation. The minutes of the meeting noted that the president felt that "were it not for the political gain that was involved, he would have no concern as to whom got credit; the important thing was the actual accomplishment of the things that were needed."[55] The impossibility of separating legislation from its political consequences is clearly illustrated here.

Through it all, the president never lost his preference for a more gradual approach to the desegregation problem than the one which he felt the courts had thrust upon him. On 16 August 1960 in a legislative leadership meeting, he stated that he thought his administration had an excellent record on civil rights, in that he had made practical moves that were possible and desirable. Typically, he expressed skepticism about the viability of using the law to enforce desegregation. He commented that he had preached for years that progress would come from education and from the kinds of practical ideas he had endorsed. Then, with his eye on the upcoming presidential election, he agreed with those on his staff who said an election year is no time to try any "spectacular stuff" in the civil rights realm.[56] Dwight D. Eisenhower remained convinced that basic changes in race relations were dependent not on the compulsions of law, but rather on the creation of changes in the hearts and minds of people.

Such assumptions governed his behavior during the desegregation crisis which spanned his presidency. They contributed much to the frustration civil rights advocates experienced during that period. They also encouraged intransigence on the part of those who mistook them for weakness. Moreover, they made him singularly unenthusiastic about the position in which the desegregation decisions placed him from 1954 to 1960 and certainly slowed his movement toward decisive action in the face of defiance of federal court orders at Little Rock. In an important sense, Eisenhower completed his involvement with the school segregation question where he had started it—not really wishing to become involved in what he perceived to be a dangerous situation created by the excessive use of judicial power.

The interim period between the presidential election of 1960 and Eisenhower's departure from office saw no change in his attitudes or policies. One example will suffice. In that period there was a great deal of violence and open defiance surrounding the court-ordered desegregation of the New Orleans, Louisiana, public schools. On 30 November, New York Republican Senator Jacob K. Javits, the frustrated liberal advocate of more active Republican support of civil rights, telegraphed the president requesting a meeting and urging him to speak out as "the conscience of the country."[57] Javits urged the president to do this because he was convinced "that the New Orleans situation is a test for us all and offers an excellent occasion to most eloquently affirm this moral issue in a direct public way in order to invoke support for the forces of law."[58]

Javits' twin requests were not to be fulfilled. On 1 December, Eisenhower wrote to the New York senator, informing him that the meeting he had requested would be "inadvisable" at that time. With his characteristic caution reinforced by his awareness that the incoming Kennedy administration would soon have the responsibility for dealing with the desegregation issue, the president refused to issue a statement. As he explained:

> Obviously the timing and nature of statements and actions whether by myself or other Executive Branch officials in respect to this situation would be matters of great delicacy. I will not fail to keep your views in mind as the situation unfolds.[59]

The president's perspective on the potential impact of a statement was far different from that of Javits.

Thus, even at the end of his administration, after he was freed from any political impingements and campaign obligations, Eisenhower chose to remain aloof from what many Americans regarded as a critical moral crisis. He was convinced that the desegregation crisis would not be resolved by such means. It is also possible that his refusal to speak out on the New Orleans situation was because of his experiences at Little Rock. The closing days of his administration reiterated the triumph of caution in his approach to the school desegregation issue. In more ways than even the president realized, he left the presidency and the school desegregation crisis in much the same state that he had found them—the former, full of potential, and the latter, full of conflict.

Chapter 11

Mixing Oil and Water

There is no clearer illustration of the paralyzing effects of the school desegregation issue and the challenge it posed for presidential leadership than that which appeared when the Eisenhower administration and the Congress took up the issue of federal aid to public education. Nowhere did the Eisenhower administration labor harder with less satisfying results than in its efforts to keep the controversy which surrounded desegregation from jeopardizing what many regarded as the critical necessity for federal assistance to beleaguered school districts in many states. These districts had simply been unable to keep up with the demand for new classrooms caused by the rapid increase in school age population created by the post–World War II baby boom.[1]

The rapidity with which desegregation and federal aid became entangled in spite of the persistent efforts of the Eisenhower administration to keep them separate stands as powerful testimony to the explosiveness of the desegregation issue, the controversial nature of the federal aid proposals, and the catalytic effect which both had on the public mind and on congressional politics. The merger of the two issues presented incredibly complex problems for the advocates of school desegregation and federal aid and a whole new set of opportunities for those who sought to block their implementation or turn them to partisan advantage.

Neither the crisis in education nor the controversy over the use of federal aid to alleviate it had their origins in the years of the Eisenhower presidency. Both had already precipitated strong arguments in the Truman years. That administration's proposals had floundered on a combination of black-liberal demands for desegregation riders on congressional bills, white southern fears that federal aid would be used to bring school integration, and Catholic demands that federal aid also be extended to parochial schools. The questions raised had proven to be so politically divisive that the congressional leadership of the already sharply divided, contentious Democratic party carefully avoided taking a stand on the issue.[2]

The change of administrations following the Eisenhower landslide of 1952 did nothing to remove the controversy surrounding the federal aid to education issue. As even a cursory examination of the *New York Times Index* for the 1952–1960 period indicates, the potential for conflict between the diverse groups that had taken stands on the federal aid issue was enormous.[3] Obviously, the federal aid question created crosscurrents involving church-state relations, conservative-versus-liberal conceptions of the role of government, partisan political pressures, and the positions of vested social and economic interests. The groups lining up on one side or another of the issue included many of the major pressure groups in the country. Much of the rhetoric in the debate between the conflicting groups centered on the question of whether or not the proposed aid would lead to federal control of education. The emergence of the desegregation issue added another critical dimension to the already complex, explosive character of the federal aid question. As events soon proved, it was truly an issue that would challenge both the wisdom and depth of

President Eisenhower's commitment to a moderate approach to civil liberties, his belief in the limited scope of federal powers, and his abilities as a presidential leader.

Origins of the Eisenhower Approach

The Eisenhower administration's response to the repeated calls of the NEA, the AAUP, and other groups of like mind for increased federal assistance to public education was, like so many other aspects of its behavior, a moderate, even conservative one. President Eisenhower was, after all, a firm believer in state and local financial support and control of the public schools.[4] Many conservative Republicans and Democrats in and out of the Congress opposed federal aid on the grounds that it constituted a dangerous threat to states' rights and individual freedom. Eisenhower shared many of these fears. Consequently, when his administration, under the guidance of Commissioner of Education Samuel Brownell and others in the Department of Health, Education and Welfare, confronted the question of federal aid to education, they did so with the president's traditional beliefs, those of the conservative wing of his own party, and, not surprisingly, the sensitivity of race-conscious southerners in mind.

The administration's resultant proposed federal aid to education policy thus centered on attempts to identify the area of greatest need for public school districts, and from that decision determine what kind of help the federal government could provide without in any significant way threatening local control of the public schools. While the origins of its decision to assist classroom construction are clouded, internal administration memoranda indicate that during the first year of the Eisenhower administration both the Bureau of the Budget and the Office of Education were opposed to any federal subsidization of school construction or teachers' salaries because of the numerous serious financial and policy problems such aid might involve.[5] Commissioner of Education Brownell preferred, instead, that the administration sponsor a series of "grass roots" conferences in the states to study educational problems, including classroom construction, and then take those matters to a national White House Conference on Education which would formulate proposals from their recommendations.[6]

Consequently, with HEW Secretary Oveta Culp Hobby's concurrence, Commissioner Brownell's recommendation was passed on to the White House for inclusion in the forthcoming 1954 State of the Union Message. In late December 1953, however, Bryce N. Harlow of the president's staff called Nelson Rockefeller, an undersecretary at HEW, and stated

> that at a White House Conference it had been felt that the section on education was too weak and that Dr. Flemming had written a paragraph for inclusion in the message. Mr. Rockefeller pointed out that it went further in regard to Federal aid to education than the Secretary was ready to go at this time, but that if the White House wanted it included in the message, we would, of course, agree. Mr. Harlow had previously read the section to Dr. Brownell.[7]

Thus, the desire to strengthen the education section of the State of the Union Message became the basis of a major policy position.

The passage authored by ex-college-president Arthur Flemming, who was at the time director of the Office of Civil Defense Mobilization, against the wishes of the officials in charge of HEW and its Office of Education thus went into the January 1954 State of the Union Message and placed the Eisenhower administration on record in favor of federal assistance to states that were demonstrably unable to finance the scheduled construction costs. In a memorandum dated 8 January, Joseph N. Dodge, director of the Bureau of the Budget, noted: "The declaration in this year's State of the Union Message appears to be an extremely important policy decision and equivalent to a policy commitment."[8] And so it was, the

Eisenhower administration, with what appeared to be major reservations from many of its education experts, entered the thicket of controversy surrounding the federal aid issue.

The division in the administration and the president's strong reservations about any federal aid help to explain why it took the administration over a year after the president's January 1954 State of the Union Message to introduce a specific plan to Congress.[9] That delay was to ultimately prove to be of critical importance, for the Republicans lost control of Congress in the 1954 midterm elections. The administration's initial effort, which the president outlined in his 1 February 1955 letter to Congress, emphasized the size and immediacy of the problems created by the critical shortage of classrooms. Commenting later in his memoirs on his proposed solution to this problem, President Eisenhower stated:

> The main responsibility for education was still to rest with the states and localities within them. But federal assistance would be available, under the administration's plan, for any district showing a need. . . . I asked the Congress to authorize, over the next three years, the investment of more than a billion dollars in federal loans and grants, which would stimulate a total investment in that time of more than $7 billion in new school buildings. I opposed involving the federal government in the operation of the schools, such as in paying teachers' salaries.[10]

Despite the charges of its critics, including many professional educators, that it was an inadequate plan which, in effect, demanded a pauper's oath, the president's proposal was completely consistent with his own philosophy of limited federal involvement and a genuine desire on his part to leave control of education in the hands of state and local authorities.[11]

Impact of the Desegregation Issue

Any chance that the Eisenhower administration had to develop a program that would quickly alleviate the classroom shortage evaporated with the United States Supreme Court's May 1954 decision in the school segregation cases. That decision focused national attention on the controversial aspects of American education in a way that nothing else could. Those who desired the rapid destruction of segregated education and those who desired its preservation assessed all proposals for federal aid to education in terms of how they would affect their primary interests. It was in the emotionally charged atmosphere created by such reactions to the *Brown* decision that the Eisenhower administration was forced to develop and advocate its policies. Small wonder that it found its efforts embroiled in controversy and ultimately frustrated.

Evidence of increasing concern about the impact of the school segregation decision on the administration's federal aid to education proposals surfaced in Secretary Hobby's 14 October 1954 press conference. Reporter Sarah McClendon raised the issue when she asked a double-barreled question: "Mrs. Hobby, will there not be a need for legislation in education on school integration? Don't they have to have more legislation to implement that?"[12] Secretary Hobby responded by asserting that the administration at that point did not know, that it was already in the process of desegregating schools on federal establishments prior to the decision. Turning to the question of the specific means of implementing the May 1954 *Brown* decision, she stated:

> Now, when the Supreme Court formulates its specific decrees, then we will be in a better position to know exactly how it affects us. . . .
>
> And until the specific decrees of the Supreme Court come down, there is no—there would be no change here because there is no reason for [construction of schools in federally affected areas].[13]

Secretary Hobby here expressed what was to become a basic tenet of the administration's position prior to the Court's May 1955 implementation decision in the school segregation cases: although the federal government would continue its policy of desegregating facilities totally in the sphere of federal authority, there would be no change in current administration education policies in such areas as grants to federally "impacted" school districts or aid to segregated land grant colleges until the implementation decision was announced.

The administration had no intention of going out of its way to seek trouble. Its policy was one of temporizing and emphasizing the limited scope of federal authority in the realm of education. In this way it hoped to avoid becoming embroiled in the desegregation controversy as it developed its federal aid to education program. Unfortunately, its hopes that the two policies could be developed independently of each other soon came to naught.

Some three months after the administration's announcement of its "wait and see" policy on the desegregation issue, President Eisenhower, in a begrudging departure from his personal philosophic beliefs in the face of mounting national need, sent his 1 February 1955 letter to the Congress, unveiling his proposal for limited, selected federal aid to the states for classroom construction.[14] It became apparent almost immediately that the administration's attempts to avert the commingling of its federal aid to education policies and the segregation issue faced heavy odds. On 4 February 1955, Roy Wilkins wrote to Sherman Adams:

> The National Association for the Advancement of Colored People is keenly interested in putting safeguards in the proposed legislation on school construction which will make certain that Federal funds are nor [*sic*] appropriated to subsidize school systems in states which refuse to comply with the United States Supreme Court opinion holding racially segregated schools to be unconstitutional.[15]

The NAACP left no doubt that it and its growing constituency were unwilling to perceive the crisis in American education as something unrelated to their long, bitter struggle against segregated education. It was, as events were to prove, a short step from the Wilkins letter to the Powell Amendment.

Despite such reactions, the administration was determined to keep its school construction program and the segregation issue separated. As James Hagerty in his diary entry for 9 February 1955 noted:

> At the staff meeting we were particularly concerned about questions on the school construction program which would deal with segregation. It was agreed that the President, if asked, should say the present school construction program is one of an emergency nature, that the Supreme Court was presently discussing the implementation of its decision and the injection of segregation into the emergency construction program would do nothing except delay the building.[16]

The position articulated at the presidential staff meeting quickly became the official public position of the administration. While certainly logical and typically moderate in its tone, the administration's position was based on an overestimation of the willingness of the American people and their elected representatives to see the question of federal aid as something totally distinct from the desegregation question.

This was also illustrated by the persistent questions which reporters continued to raise in the administration's press conferences about the impact of desegregation on federal aid to education. While President Eisenhower, much to Hagerty's relief, did not have to field a question about the topic in his 9 February 1955 press conference, Secretary Hobby was not so fortunate the following day. When questioned about whether or not the federal government would have any control over states which would want to take advantage of the proposed school construction plans and build schools for whites only, she responded: "I would say that since the Supreme Court decision has been handed down, since its decrees implementing the decision have not been made, that we probably wouldn't."[17] While such a hands-off attitude was justified by administration spokespersons on the grounds that they did not desire to second-guess the Supreme Court, it failed to convince many that the administration's classroom construction proposal could be implemented without considering the impact of the pending school desegregation decision. In effect, the emotional impact of the desegregation issue was such that it undercut the administration's argument that the classroom shortage was so critical that it should be judged on its own merits.

The Zelenko Letter and Administration Strategy

Despite growing pressure from a number of sources including the NAACP, the administration stuck to its position. This was apparent in its handling of the Zelenko letter. On 30 March 1955, Congressman Herbert Zelenko, New York Democrat and a member of the House Education and Labor Committee, wrote a letter to President Eisenhower asking him to state his views regarding segregation in the schools, because questions had arisen about that point during committee testimony about the administration's classroom construction bill.[18] As Zelenko stated, he had decided to write the president after hearing Congressman Adam Clayton Powell, New York Democrat, urge that such a bill contain an antisegregation rider that would forbid any state supporting segregated schools from receiving federal funds under the program.[19]

It is difficult to determine whether Congressman Zelenko was seeking to politically embarrass the president, or perhaps to block federal aid proposals, or whether he was sincerely interested in seeking clarification of how the president's attitude on segregation would affect the administration of the proposed classroom construction program. It would seem that, regardless of his motives, Zelenko's request was a reasonable one in light of Powell's demand for an amendment that would most certainly lessen the chances of passing the federal aid to education bill and the confusion which surrounded the administration's noncommittal position regarding the way the funds would be allocated. Congress, whether the administration accepted the fact or not, had proven unable to keep the school construction and desegregation issues separated.

Congressman Zelenko's letter created both a crisis and an opportunity for the administration. On one hand, it sought to evoke a statement from the president in a context which again underscored the volatile, but perhaps inevitable commingling of the federal aid and desegregation issues, something the administration was trying to avoid. Any clear, highly publicized strong statement by the president for one side or the other of the desegregation matter would embroil him in controversy. On the other hand, the Zelenko letter did give the president an opportunity to clarify and restate his moderate position before a committee whose support was crucial to the passage of its proposed school construction bill. Small wonder that the administration weighed its answer very carefully.

Upon receipt of the Zelenko letter, Bryce N. Harlow, an administrative assistant to the president, requested assistance from HEW Secretary Hobby in framing an answer to it. At that time he stated: "You will note that I have simply acknowledged the letter. I doubt that the president should become personally involved in the matter. Possibly, also the White House should not be connected with the reply."[20] Harlow was obviously determined to keep the president from becoming personally embroiled in a controversy about segregation while action on the school construction bill was pending before the House Education and Labor Committee.

On 18 April, Roswell B. Perkins, acting HEW Secretary in Hobby's absence due to illness, sent a memorandum and the draft of a suggested reply to Congressman Zelenko. In the memorandum, Perkins recommended that Harlow rather than the president respond to Zelenko and presented Harlow with two suggested paragraphs which became the critical part of Harlow's response. The two were:

> The Supreme Court is presently considering the nature of the decrees it should issue to give practical effect to its decision of May 17, 1954, on the question of segregated schools. When these decrees have been issued, the general conditions under which Federal agencies must execute programs which are related to schools will have been determined.
>
> Because of these facts, it would be unfortunate if consideration of critically needed school legislation should be delayed.[21]

The letter, which was finally sent to Congressman Zelenko on 21 April 1955 under Harlow's signature with the concurrence of HEW Secretary Hobby and presidential staffers Sherman Adams, Wilton Persons, James Hagerty, Gerald Morgan, Jack Martin, and Maxwell Rabb, sought to leave the president on the middle ground where he could avoid committing himself.[22] It was a classic expression of the administration's moderation in the face of potential conflict.

Prior to his insertion of the previously cited paragraphs authored by Perkins, Harlow presented a clear statement of the principles that had guided President Eisenhower's approach to the desegregation question. It emphasized the president's determination to end racial segregation because wherever

> an undertaking involving the use of Federal funds is predominantly Federal in its application, there can no more be racial segregation in the application of those funds than there can be in the application of the tax laws which produce the government's revenue.[23]

Continuing, Harlow noted that "it is [Eisenhower's] view that when an undertaking is predominantly local in character, the Federal involvement should be restrained to avoid federalization of the activity concerned."[24] Education was obviously one such local activity. Harlow further pointed out that such principles had resulted in exceptional advances during the two years that Eisenhower had been president. On these grounds, the administration rested its case for the exercise of moderation and the separation of the school construction and desegregation issues. Congressman Zelenko, upon receipt of the Harlow letter, promptly placed it and his original letter in the official record of the committee's hearings. As their numerous subsequent letters to Eisenhower were to prove, many congressmen did not regard Harlow's response as either satisfactory or realistic because it left the president uncommitted and the two issues still inextricably conjoined.

HEW Secretary Hobby's characterization of the status of the administration's classroom construction proposal in the 22 April 1955 cabinet meeting provides an interesting view of the political strategy the administration had used in support of its school construction bill in both houses of Congress, some perspective as to how it regarded the bill's current status, and the conclusion it had reached about its prospects.[25]

The secretary began by acknowledging that the administration faced a severe challenge from the Democrats who sought to upstage the Republicans with a much more comprehensive plan for school construction. She pointed out that Democratic Senator Lester Hill of Alabama had held hearings in the Senate Education and Labor Committee on federal aid to education even prior to Eisenhower's 8 February message announcing the administration's plan. She further noted that Hill's drive for a school construction bill, "providing nothing but large-scale grants to the States," had been effectively slowed by moving Eisenhower's education message up one week.[26]

Continuing, she related how Hill's committee had not met to consider the school construction question since shortly after the administration had testified on 16 February on behalf of its bill because "the issue of segregation has stopped any school construction measure on the Senate side, at least temporarily."[27] Turning to the situation in the House, Hobby reported that hearings on the federal aid to education bill were currently in progress in the House Committee on Education and Labor but that its conservative chairman was dragging them out in order to avoid holding hearings on minimum wage legislation. As a result, Secretary Hobby predicted that no federal aid to education bill would come out of committee until June at the earliest.[28] She then summed up her comments with a discouraging prediction about the fate of the pending school construction bill.

> My guess is that the chances of any school construction measure being enacted this year are not greater than 50–50, in view of the segregation issue and other issues which may be thrown into the picture. If a bill should be enacted, it will probably be much changed from the Administration bill and will place emphasis on outright grants in larger amounts than the grants in . . . the Administration bill.[29]

The mixture of the volatile desegregation issue and political partisanship thus placed formidable obstacles in the path of the administration's school construction plan.

Continued Separation

The Supreme Court's May 1955 implementation decision calling for the desegregation of public school systems "with all deliberate speed" under the supervision of federal district courts did not alter the administration's determination to keep the issues of school construction and desegregation separated. Although the administration did drop its "wait and see" position, which it had articulated prior to the implementation decision, it continued to emphasize judicial rather than executive and legislative responsibility for the desegregation process and that the school construction question should be approached on its own merits because of its proven need. As before, those challenging the administration's position remained adamant.

Nowhere was this more apparent than in President Eisenhower's press conferences in the year following the implementation decision in the school desegregation cases. The tone and content of the president's responses to questions about school construction and segregation indicate that he was both frustrated and disgusted by the continuing attempts of many of his congressional opponents to merge the two issues in the face of his continued insistence that they be treated separately. The president's responses reveal much about the problems he encountered when he tried to put his moderate philosophy into practice.

One of the favorite techniques used by Congressman Adam Clayton Powell and other exponents of rapid desegregation was the attachment of antisegregation riders and amendments on important appropriations bills, such as those covering military reserve appropriations and, not surprisingly, the administration's federal aid bill. In his 8 June 1955 press conference, a reporter noted that the administration's school construction bill was bottled up in committee by a dispute over such an amendment and asked the president to give his opinion about the uses of such antisegregation amendments. The president's response was frank:

> My own feeling about legislation is a simple one. If you get an idea of real importance, a substantive subject, and you want to get it enacted into law, then I believe the Congress and I believe our people should have a right to decide upon that issue by itself, and not be clouding it with amendments that are extraneous.[30]

Though he denied he was referring to any specific bill, it was obvious that the president was angry at those, like Powell, who had resorted to such techniques against what he regarded as high priority items in his legislative program.

In his 7 July 1955 press conference, in response to a question by May Craig of the *Portland* (Maine) *Press-Herald* about whether he would "oppose and consider as extraneous" an antisegregation amendment to the administration's school construction bill, the president became more specific: "Well, I would think it was extraneous, yes, for the simple reason that we need the schools, and I think that the other ought to be handled on its own merits."[31] The president reiterated his belief that Congress should leave the desegregation process to the localities which were already under Supreme Court order to carry out this process under the direction of the district courts. As he put it: "Now, why do we go muddying the water?"[32] It is difficult, given what we know of his own philosophy, to be certain whether Eisenhower's remarks about the willingness of Americans to desegregate their schools voluntarily were based on trust or merely on hope. It must be kept in mind here that the president expressed his reservations about the ability of courts and laws to overcome the attitudes reinforcing segregation.

Eisenhower's most emphatic statement in favor of keeping desegregation and school construction separate came in his 25 January 1956 press conference in response to a question about an antisegregation amendment to the school construction bill.[33] After reiterating his determination to uphold the Constitution and the unanimous decision of the Supreme Court, the president explained his reasons for opposing such an amendment:

> The Supreme Court, in reaching its decision as to what the law was, provided and specifically provided there be a gradual implementation, and referred it back to the District Courts so that it should be gradual.
>
> But in the meantime the need of the American children for schools is right now—immediately—today.

So I think there should be nothing that is put on this thing that delays the construction of the bill. Now when you come down, though, to ask a man to vote against something that he believes to be in furtherance of the Constitutional provisions, then you have got a tough one.[34]

Though the president indicated his awareness of the tough choice that those favoring desegregation would have to make when desegregation riders are attached to bills, he made it clear that he felt it was still in the national interest to keep the school construction bill separate. While there may be reason to fault his perception of political reality here, there is no reason to question his sincerity.

Ten days prior to the 25 January press conference, the president had discussed the problems raised by antisegregation amendments with House Minority Leader Charles Halleck.[35] At that time Halleck had expressed concern that such an amendment would survive a committee vote on a school construction bill and that Republicans would then be confronted with the problem of having to vote for it on grounds of political expediency or to leave themselves open to the charge that they favored segregation. Eisenhower responded that his strong civil rights record had not gained the GOP any more votes in 1954 than it had in 1952 and that he was thus very skeptical of any statements about how Republican behavior would affect votes. Continuing, the president also expressed concern about how the nation would get its needed classrooms if a Powell Amendment were hung on the school bill and the Senate proceeded to filibuster it to death. Later in that same conversation he admitted that in view of the Supreme Court's segregation decision, a vote against the Powell Amendment would seem to be a vote against the Constitution.[36]

Despite the president's beliefs then and because of the potential political difficulties the Powell Amendment created for many Republican congressmen, the administration did not make an attempt to formally hold them to the president's position. A 24 January memorandum by Lewis Arthur Minnich of the president's staff noted that there would be no administration directed opposition to antisegregation amendments offered for the school construction bill for the time being and that further consideration of the question would be given when the exact nature of the education bill was known.[37] Such a position, at least temporarily, let many concerned Republican congressmen off the hook and seemed to be a prudent measure, given the administration's awareness that the school construction bill probably would not get out of the committee. Thus, although the president never altered his public stance on the issue, he did understand the difficult position in which the Powell Amendment placed the Republican members of Congress, a group already conscious of its minority position and ideological disparities.

One liability of maintaining a policy of moderation on the segregation question became powerfully clear with the release of the 7 August 1955 Gallup Poll which assessed Eisenhower's presidential leadership. Although he received generally high marks from those surveyed, one of the five areas in which he did draw significant criticism centered on the idea that the president's actions "encouraged segregation."[38] That particular result of the poll did not go unnoticed by the administration's civil rights experts.

The following day, Maxwell Rabb wrote a memorandum to Howard Pyle, the president's administrative assistant, in which he stated:

> You will note that one of the chief criticisms of the President's leadership was that he "encourages segregation." This is, of course, outrageous. We have an extraordinary record in this field. However, in my opinion, if such a feeling exists we are probably to blame. We have been more than tender in soft-pedalling our accomplishments.[39]

Continuing, Rabb pinpointed the effect of the president's stand on antisegregation amendments on public opinion.

> The only time that people are aware of an Administration stand on this issue is when the President discusses the amendments to the School and Reserve Bills (and the Negroes feel it is unfair that he scold them without also chastising the Southern attitude). . . .
>
> Perhaps it is time to give some serious thought to this whole problem.[40]

Rabb's suggestion did not go unheeded.

On 22 December 1955, Joseph H. Douglass, special representative of HEW Secretary Marion B. Folsom, presented a detailed memorandum to Rabb on ways to counteract the president's negative image on the desegregation question.[41] In his "Analysis of Problems and Suggested Proposals for Improving Relations with the Negro Group," Douglass pinpointed six major causes of the administration's failure to improve its standing among black Americans. Two of the flaws he pinpointed—the administration's nonaggressive approach and the absence of a clearly systematic plan on civil rights—seemed particularly germane to the president's position on school construction.[42] Douglass then went on to detail a suggested plan to counteract the administration's poor image, including the recommendation that both President Eisenhower and Vice President Nixon "take strong stands on the issues."[43] This proposal was, of course, never implemented for a number of reasons, not the least of which was that it violated the canon of moderation which the president hoped would prevail in the realm of race relations. Despite the administration's toughened stand against the opponents of school desegregation in subsequent years, it never shifted from its basic position that the classroom construction and school segregation issues be treated separately.

Chapter 12

The Administration Defends Its Position

On 28 November 1955, frustrated by the failure of the Eighty-fourth Congress to pass a federal aid to education bill, President Eisenhower convened the White House Conference on Education.[1] The four-day conference of two thousand educators and interested citizens was the culmination of a series of earlier meetings which had been held on the local, state, and regional levels to define the country's educational needs and the best ways to meet them. As President Eisenhower later related in his memoirs:

> At the end of the four-day series of meetings, the conference adopted a report calling for federal funds for public schools, opposing funds for nonpublic schools. . . . Using the findings of this conference, we hoped to get a sound school-construction bill through the Congress the following year.[2]

The administration was optimistic that such a strong recommendation for federal assistance would lend respectability to its classroom construction proposal and create pressure on Congress for its passage, even though its plan was far more modest than what many of the conference participants desired. The administration also hoped that the conference's

213

decision that questions about desegregation be left to local school districts would not go unnoticed by Congress.

Quite expectedly, when the president presented his revised program for federal aid to classroom construction in a special message to Congress in January 1956, he incorporated a number of the recommendations of the White House Conference.[3] While the administration's revised proposal was somewhat more broadened in scope (it included $1 billion in matching school construction funds for needy school districts over a five-year period and $750 million to purchase school construction bonds), it still adhered basically to the president's twin desires to channel federal aid to needy school districts and to minimize federal controls on education.[4] True to the president's fiscally conservative heart, the administration's plan also contrasted sharply with the far more expensive proposal sponsored by Democratic Representative Augustine Kelly of Pennsylvania containing an aid distribution formula based on the school-age population in each state. The president's message made no direct reference to the threat of Adam Clayton Powell and others to attach antisegregation riders to all proposed federal aid to education.

Members of the administration were heartened when the White House staff's survey of twenty major newspaper editors and two national columnists revealed that thirteen endorsed his proposals, five were friendly though they neither endorsed nor opposed the program, while only four were definitely unfavorable.[5] Several of the editors who favored the plan also expressed the hope, as did the editor of the *Chicago Sun-Times,* that "this well-thought-out Eisenhower plan will not be handicapped by attempts to relate it to efforts to end segregation in public schools."[6] Hopes ran high among members of the administration and this group of editors that the president's decision to broaden his plan for classroom construction would make it palatable enough to many hesitant congressmen to offset the threats of an antisegregation rider. It was crucial that the two issues not be tied together. Unfortunately, this was not to be.

Emotion and political partisanship often conspire in American politics to create an atmosphere that is hostile to moderation, the trait most central to Eisenhower's attitude toward racial issues. By 1956, the president was confronted with two groups that, on the desegregation question, were unalterably opposed to each other, as well as a third group that opposed federal aid to education for a variety of philosophic and economic reasons. Each group had a substantial power base in Congress and used the legislative process to support its position. Just as the advocates of desegregation started to attach their riders to every bill in sight so the segregationists used their control of committee chairpersons, the congressional seniority system, the threat of filibuster, and presented manifestos vowing the legislative overthrow of the school segregation decisions. The third group had little difficulty achieving its goals by encouraging the stalemate created by the desegregation struggle. The administration's attempt to steer its classroom construction bill through such stormy legislative waters thus faced odds too great to overcome.

As Eisenhower noted bitterly in his memoirs, proposals for federal aid for classroom construction, which he felt were greatly improved because they incorporated proposals of the White House Conference on Education, were defeated in both 1956 and 1957 when they were brought to the floor of the House with the Powell Amendment attached.[7] That amendment, authored by Congressman Adam Clayton Powell, simply forbade the federal government to give money to any state which operated segregated schools in defiance of the school segregation decisions.

The six-year struggle of the administration to secure a school construction bill without the Powell Amendment is significant, even though it ended in defeat. It provides additional evidence of the inability of the Eisenhower administration to control the effects of the segregation issue with its policy of moderation. Though it is a story of frustration, disappointment, and, in some cases, indecision and unrealistic political judgments, it is worth telling for those interested in an accurate history of the nature of Eisenhower's presidential leadership and the way policies were formulated in his administration.

Congressional Appeals to the President

On 10 February 1956, eight Democratic members of the House who favored the school construction bill wrote to President Eisenhower expressing their concern that the classroom construction proposal might fail "because of the proposed inclusion of an anti-segregation amendment."[8] Noting critically that Republican Minority Leader Joseph W. Martin of Massachusetts had announced his support for such an amendment, the representatives expressed their opinion that "such an amendment would win enough votes in an unrecorded teller vote in the Committee of the Whole so as to insure its inclusion in the bill as presented to the House for a final vote."[9] The result, they warned, was that the bill would "either be defeated in the House, or filibustered to death in the Senate— by a combination of foes of integrated schools and of Federal aid for school construction."[10] Such a result, the congressmen argued, would be tragic to those like themselves who believed in both federal aid for school construction and the desegregation decision of the Supreme Court.

According to the congressmen, what was missing was some assurance that federal funds would not be used to assist those school systems which practiced open defiance of the Supreme Court's implementation decree.[11] Turning to the cause of this lack of assurance, the congressmen cited two basic points: first, the administration's statements that enforcing compliance with the Court's decree is not the responsibility of the executive; and second, the existence of the *Massachusetts* v. *Mel-*

lon case precedent, denying a taxpayer standing to enjoin the federal executive from using funds in an unconstitutional manner, had created fear that funds would be allocated to defiant school systems.[12] The congressmen insisted that the threat of open defiance was very real and that it "must not be fed and encouraged by allocating to its support Federal funds."[13]

The solution to the dilemma thus created by the antisegregation amendment was, according to the eight representatives, in the hands of the president. As they said:

> The vexing moral and political problem posed by the antisegregation amendment can be solved quite simply by your declaring publicly that you will not allocate funds to any school system which you find is not in "good faith" compliance with the minimum requirements of the Court's decree to "make a prompt and reasonable start" toward integration; and that where any doubt exists . . . you will direct the Attorney General to submit the matter for a declaratory judgment or some similar procedure by the appropriate Federal Court.[14]

The congressmen emphasized, in deference to Eisenhower's limited conception of executive powers, that they were not asking him to assume a judicial function, but "simply the executive function of insuring that Federal funds are not spent to further an unconstitutional purpose."[15]

They insisted that the results of such an action on the part of President Eisenhower would be the removal of the necessity for the antisegregation amendment. They reasoned that Congressman Powell had indicated that he would not offer his antisegregation amendment if the president would make such a statement.[16] A further result, they argued, would be to make the school construction bill acceptable to a number of congressmen who could not accept it with an antisegregation amendment for political reasons. The result would be that "this number may well be just sufficient to make possible passage of the school aid bill in both House and Senate."[17]

The congressmen concluded their letter by stating that the presidential declaration which they suggested would clarify the administration's position on school construction, thus giving federal aid proposals an even chance for passage. They insisted that "without such a declaration, it will surely fail."[18] They left no doubt that they felt the responsibility for the failure or success of the school construction bill was up to the president. Would he bring his moral and political prestige to bear to end the legislative deadlock on that bill? Would he change from a policy of restraint to one of active support of the desegregation edict?

The pleas of the Democratic representatives fell on deaf ears. On 13 February 1956, Bryce N. Harlow forwarded the letter from the eight congressmen to J. Lee Rankin, assistant attorney general in the Office of Legal Counsel, asking for his recommendations regarding an appropriate reply on behalf of the president.[19] Rankin's reply reiterated the president's insistence that school construction and discrimination were two distinct issues, that the president was opposed to anything that would delay the enactment of the school construction bill, and that he was dedicated to the Court decision, which had decreed gradual implementation of school desegregation under the supervision of the federal courts.[20]

Harlow's response to the congressmen on 1 March 1956 touched lightly on one of Rankin's points, extensively expanded another, and added still a third point which Rankin had totally ignored.[21] The bulk of Harlow's cold, totally formal letter summarized the Supreme Court's implementation decision in the *Brown* case. He then made it very clear that the administration had a hands-off policy toward the implementation of the school desegregation decision. As he put it:

> It is thus apparent that under the Supreme Court decision, the Federal judiciary, not the executive branch of the Federal Government, is to determine how compliance with the Supreme Court mandate is to be brought about and what con-

stitutes compliance in good faith. The course of action you request the President to take would be, therefore, inconsistent both in act and in spirit with the decision of the Supreme Court.[22]

The administration's refusal to become involved in the controversy over the implementation of the desegregation decrees by "hiding behind the skirts" of the judicial decision reflected a continuation of its policy of keeping President Eisenhower out of potentially divisive situations while it sought gradual, moderate, voluntary solutions to controversial issues. It was a constitutionally justifiable one, much in keeping with the moderate tone and nature of the Court's implementation decree which in turn reflected the administration's brief on the question. That position, though, ignored the fact that the school construction and desegregation issues had become hopelessly entangled and that resistance to implementation had proven more formidable than many had anticipated.

The eight congressmen had made a strong argument in their first letter that a promise to see that public funds were not expended for unconstitutional purposes might be enough to separate the two issues at least enough to assure passage of the classroom construction bill. Such a position was also constitutionally viable, given an activist conception of executive powers. Ironically, the Harlow letter reveals that the administration's perception of the scope of executive leadership was very restricted, while the representatives' letter proves that theirs was more expansive.

Harlow closed by expressing appreciation that the representatives shared Eisenhower's desire that a school construction bill be passed without delay. He reminded them that it was still the president's view that

> many of the problems of the type to which you refer could be eased through the establishment of the bipartisan civil rights commission he recommended last January to the Congress. He is hopeful that you and your colleagues can find

your way clear to help advance this legislation in this session.[23]

Harlow's plug for the administration's proposed bipartisan civil rights commission was indicative of its desire to keep the desegregation issue out of partisan politics or, as some critics said, to minimize its involvement with it. The limited scope of executive power expressed in the Harlow letter had doubly adverse effects. It was interpreted by the segregationists as a sign of fear on the part of the administration. On the other hand, it represented an abdication of responsibility to those like the eight Democrats who had urged the president to speak out.

Not surprisingly, the eight Democrats found Harlow's response to their plea for presidential support highly unsatisfactory. So much so, as a matter of fact, that on 6 March 1956 they sent a second letter to the president.[24] Addressing themselves directly to Eisenhower, they brushed aside Harlow's letter as an inadequate explanation of the president's position. They rejected the argument that a presidential statement on the issues would be inconsistent with the Supreme Court's decision that the federal judiciary direct the desegregation process. They insisted that such a response missed the point of their request:

> We recognize and applaud the moderate and gradual approach of the Supreme Court's decision. . . . The only assurance we seek, Mr. President, is that you will take the necessary steps to make possible judicial consideration, in order to determine whether the Supreme Court's mandate is in a specific case being met.[25]

In this manner, they hoped to keep the president from hiding behind the Court decision.

The congressmen added a further compelling argument: since the desegregation question was "the most vital domestic issue of our time, the responsibility to speak out is yours alone."[26] Reminding Eisenhower that he had spoken out on the issue in the past as in his 19 March 1953 press conference when he had condemned segregated schools on military posts and the use of federal funds to support segregated facilities, the congressmen pleaded:

> If you still feel that no American can "legally, logically or morally" justify discrimination in the expenditure of Federal school aid funds, we hope that you will not let silence imply your agreement with the statement of Mr. Harlow.[27]

Such a reiteration, they were convinced, might be enough to head off the antisegregation rider which would destroy the school construction bill.

Hopeful that their strongly worded letter would offset the corps of advisors around the president who, like Harlow, had counseled silence on the desegregation question, the representatives urged the president to make a public answer to the following specific question:

> If the pending school construction legislation (which contains no specific anti-segregation amendment) is enacted, and if a state whose governor and legislature have publicly proclaimed their defiance of the Supreme Court decision and their intention never "to make a prompt and reasonable start toward integration" requests funds to build further segregated schools and thus perpetuate segregation, would you direct that Federal school construction funds be paid over to that state, or would you (as we urge) reserve such payments in order to permit a ruling by the appropriate Federal District Court, in a declaratory action brought by the Federal Government or in an action brought by the state to determine whether it was in compliance with the Supreme Court's decree and hence eligible for funds?[28]

The representatives closed their second letter by reminding the president that his answer would be of vital importance in determining the fate of the school construction bill.

This second attempt to get the president to speak out proved no more successful than the first. It did, however, succeed in attracting an answer from another member of the president's staff. On 8 March 1956, Bryce Harlow forwarded the congressmen's second letter to Gerald D. Morgan, special counsel to the president, with a memorandum that stated: "General Persons and I think this letter needs a reply over your signature—that obviously I cannot again reply in view of the nature of this rebuttal. WBP is leery of referring this to Justice."[29] The last sentence of the note suggests that there was disagreement between the members of the president's staff and some members of the Justice Department about whether or not the president should maintain his position of noninvolvement with the Court's implementation decision. Such an assumption is not unreasonable, given the disagreement and lack of communication between the presidential and Justice Department staffs over the scope of executive responsibility and enforcement powers of what became the Civil Rights Act of 1957.

The letter Morgan wrote on 15 March 1956 merely reiterated the main point of Harlow's first letter: the administration's position remained unchanged.[30] It refused to accept the premise that it had a supportive role to play in the implementation of the *Brown* decision. Morgan concluded his letter by emphasizing that the president felt that judicial implementation of desegregation and the construction of urgently needed schools could go on at the same time. Moreover, he stated: "[Eisenhower] will not assume that it is essential, in order that progress may be made in the former, to reserve or withhold funds necessary to progress in the latter."[31] The president's assumption proved to be wrong. His continued refusal to assure the Congress that he would withhold federal school construction funds from defiant states—as the eight Democrats had urged him to do—contributed to the attachment of the Powell Amendment to the school construction bill, thus assuring its defeat in the 1956 and 1957 congressional sessions.

On 6 March 1956, Attorney General Brownell sent a message to the president advising him about the position he should take if questioned about the Powell Amendment in his forthcoming press conference. In it, Brownell urged the president to reiterate his stand that the Powell Amendment was a separate proposal which should not be allowed to delay a school construction bill, and noted that this position was supported by educational leaders and leading newspaper editors.[32] In his 14 March 1956 press conference, Eisenhower turned aside the question about the Powell Amendment by saying that he never made any declaration on any law in advance of when it was delivered to him.[33] Similarly, one week later, in his 21 March press conference, when asked if he had any ideas about a positive approach that would get the stalled school construction bill off dead center, he asserted that he had expressed himself several times previously on the matter and that he had nothing more to say about it.[34]

Despite its wishes to the contrary, the administration's desire to keep the president as aloof as possible from the politically explosive desegregation issue worked to frustrate its hopes for a school construction bill by denying it the means to develop a flexible approach consistent with the political realities which governed the Congress at the time. Eisenhower's insistence in both volumes of his memoirs that the blame for the defeat of the school construction legislation rested more with the Democratic majority overlooks the fact that his stance encouraged the disastrous attachments of antisegregation amendments to school construction bills in the Eighty-fourth and Eighty-fifth Congresses.[35] His refusal to speak out on the desegregation issue undoubtedly deprived the moderates in both parties of a rallying point from which they might have carried the day, particularly in light of Powell's repeated promise that he would not introduce his amendment if the president pledged to withhold federal aid from defiant school districts.

Causes of the Administration's Position

An understanding of the reasons for the frustration of its attempts to secure a classroom construction bill requires careful investigation of the forces shaping the Eisenhower administration's behavior. For example, what caused the administration to insist up to early 1959 that all questions of compliance with the school desegregation implementation decision be left to the courts? Why did it develop such a limited perception of its responsibilities in the face of mounting political pressure that it do otherwise?

One significant reinforcement of its cautious attitude came from educators whose institutions would be greatly affected by the administration's desegregation and federal aid policies. Some of that input was at a very high level. On 2 March 1956, the president's brother Milton, who was then president of Pennsylvania State University, forwarded a copy of a memorandum to Sherman Adams. This memorandum was written by Russell I. Thackrey, president of the Association of Land-Grant Colleges. Originally intended for Commissioner of Education Samuel Brownell, it dealt with the question of whether or not the president should consider withholding federal funds by administrative action from land-grant colleges in segregated states.[36] Thackrey stressed the difficult situation an action on behalf of the president would create for the administrators and trustees who found themselves caught between conflicting federal and state laws.

> They recognize the supremacy of Federal law, and the ultimate necessity and desirability of complying with it. But in cases in which effective public opinion is predominantly and emotionally ranged on one side, it is a necessity that they be able clearly to show that there was no legal alternative to compliance. The courts are accepted as the final determinants of law.[37]

Thus, Thackrey argued that matters of compliance should be left up to the courts and that the administration should emphasize that that would continue to be its policy.

Any announcement of administrative action to force desegregation, Thackrey insisted, would be taken as proof that

> the Executive Branch is to move generally into the field of withholding all funds which flow through it to the States ... through administrative decision on compliance or noncompliance, rather than through the processes of court action. . . . In short, I think that at the minimum, *every relationship of any department or agency of the Federal Government with public educational institutions at any level will be affected by administrative action in this case.*[38]

Here, then, was a compelling practical reason for administration noninvolvement: there would be danger of further inflaming an already serious situation.

Such thinking, of course, strengthened the hand of those among Eisenhower's advisors who felt that the compliance question should be left to the courts. This, coupled with the president's well-known personal abhorrence of federal interference in state and local matters, created a powerful rationale against the president taking a strong stand on the withholding of federal funds.

There was also another important reason which helps explain why mounting congressional pressure for presidential leadership on the school desegregation question had little effect on the administration. By late March 1956, a number of the president's advisors were convinced that the Democrats were trying to exploit his moderate stand for partisan gain. In a memorandum to Bryce Harlow dated 27 March 1956, Maxwell Rabb attached an excerpt from the 26 March *Congressional Record* as evidence that the Democrats "are on the way to making capital of the civil rights issue."[39] Rabb's references were to the charges of Congressman John Dingell,

Michigan Democrat, that the president had shirked his duty as chief executive and failed to give his support and leadership to those striving for racial equality.[40] Dingell, it should be noted, had written the president on 27 January, 8 February, and 8 March 1956 urging the president to throw his support behind the Powell Amendment and publicly pledge that he would withhold federal funds to states announcing their defiance of the Court's desegregation decisions.[41]

The administration's response, as in its letters to the eight Democratic representatives cited previously, adhered to its familiar line that the courts were capable of implementing their decisions gradually and that the school construction bill should be passed quickly because of urgent need.[42]

Dingell, finding this argument unacceptable, used it as an excuse to openly chide Eisenhower for his lack of leadership on the issue of civil rights enforcement. Those Democrats who were supporting civil rights legislation were, as Dingell readily acknowledged in his first letter, seeking bipartisan support to avoid letting the Powell Amendment become the basis of a split in the Democratic party. Many, like Dingell, were no doubt sincere in their desire to gain school construction legislation which would be applied on a desegregated basis. They were fully aware that the opponents of federal aid could hide behind the Powell Amendment, whereas they would have had much greater difficulty masking their opposition in light of a statement from the president which would cause the amendment's removal.[43]

Faced with this charge and the highly publicized attempt, led by Representative James Roosevelt, New York Democrat, of a bipartisan group of congressmen to obtain the discharge of an omnibus civil rights bill sponsored by Emanuel Celler, New York Democrat, from the House Rules Committee, Maxwell Rabb suggested measures which the administration could take to counter what he regarded as opportunism. He suggested three major steps:

1. We should have the Republicans who are especially concerned with the civil rights issue advised to keep hands-off these maneuvers which are obviously intended to help the Democrats.
2. Our GOP friends should be prepared to answer the kind of statement that people like Dingell are making. . . . All we need to do is have someone rise and point out that the President's quiet approach in the field of civil rights has been extraordinarily effective in the District of Columbia, our Armed Forces, the federal establishment, etc. and that his work has served as a model in today's atmosphere of tension and bitterness.
3. I think that the Republicans in the House feel neglected on this. Possibly I could take them in hand—perhaps with a group here for breakfast.[44]

The administration's attempts to assuage Republican congressmen proved ineffective because the Powell Amendment tied the school construction and desegregation issues firmly together in the House. Moreover, 1956 was a presidential election year, a time when it is more difficult than usual to keep issues beyond the reach of partisan maneuvering. Yet, it seems apparent that Eisenhower's position virtually guaranteed the defeat of the school construction bill. The charge of partisanship against the Democratic efforts was undoubtedly valid, but there is also no doubt that it served as a convenient rationale to justify the administration's already well-formulated position.

Similarly, the efforts to keep the two issues separated also caused the administration to take a negative position toward proposals which sought to use federal aid to education as a means of facilitating desegregation by paying for the costs of the transition. Such an approach had been suggested prior to the first *Brown* decision by the head of the Federal Civil Defense Administration, Val Peterson, who had been a school administrator prior to his service as governor of Nebraska.[45] His proposal, however, had never gained support among the other members of the president's staff because of their fears that it would commingle the construction and desegregation issues.

Peterson was not the only person who saw federal aid as a means of easing the desegregation process. Democratic Representative Stewart Udall of Arizona introduced a bill (H.R. 6803) on 14 June 1955 providing federal aid to all districts carrying out, or announcing their intention to carry out, school integration.[46] The Udall plan proved even more challenging because the day after he introduced his bill he wrote directly to the president seeking his approval and support. Noting that Eisenhower had recently expressed concern lest the segregation issue delay congressional action on other important legislation, Udall stated:

> I believe that the approach which I have suggested might well operate to prevent such delay, for it would stimulate cooperation in the Congress by uniting those who are now in disagreement. It would produce national unity in place of division. . . .[47]

Here, the administration faced a challenge to its separatist policies because of the potential appeal of the Udall plan to many moderates who were seeking ways to depolarize the desegregation crisis.

A few days later Harlow wrote Udall informing him that his bill would receive earnest consideration.[48] Harlow's letter was the last thing which Udall heard from the administration about his proposal. The promised evaluation of the plan finally appeared in a 27 March 1956 letter to Chairman Graham A. Barden, North Carolina Democrat and a member of the House Education and Labor Committee, in response to his 10 October 1955 request for an assessment of it.[49]

In that letter, Harold C. Hunt, acting HEW secretary, reiterated his department's sympathy with the objective of facilitating adjustment necessitated by the Court's desegregation decisions but stated that he had grave reservations about the practical wisdom of the approach proposed in the Udall bill.

> We seriously question whether it is possible to distinguish, in such manner as is necessary for determinations of the amounts to be paid under the bill, between that portion of the cost for a needed school building which is occasioned by a program for racial desegregation and the portion due to other causes, such as population growth, obsolescence, etc.[50]

In its place, Hunt urged consideration of a substitute proposal:

> We believe that Federal assistance in the provision of school buildings, where and as needed for whatever reason, would be more effectively afforded by a general school construction bill along the lines of S. 2905, which would provide for larger amounts of Federal funds proportionately for these States with low per capita income and a high proportion of school-age children to the total population. Such a bill would be of major assistance in aiding public school construction in those States where the problems of school desegregation will be the most difficult.[51]

Hunt's combination of practical objections and incidental effects enabled him to reject the Udall approach, to hint that the federal money might be used to ease desegregation, and, at the same time, to preserve the administration's noncoercive separatist stance.

On 30 April 1956, HEW Secretary Marion Folsom restated the administration's unyielding position on the school construction issue in a speech before the Detroit Economic Club. Folsom was blunt:

> But another issue—unrelated to the merits of the school construction proposal itself—has become an obstacle to progress of the school bill in Congress. This is the issue of racial integration in public schools.
>
> The commingling of these two issues profits neither

school construction nor integration. They are separate issues and they should not be confused. The problems of integration can best be solved under the procedures and the spirit set forth in the Supreme Court's opinions. The proposal to help wipe out the classroom shortage can best be solved on its own merits.[52]

The two paragraphs had been cleared by presidential staffers Morgan and Harlow, and they represent part of the administration's attempt to "get the message out." Despite such efforts to sway influential private citizens, Congress remained unconvinced.

The problem of building support for the administration's position had not been ignored. As early as May 1956, Eisenhower's advisors came close to sending the Democratic House leadership a formal letter urging them to work to keep the school construction and desegregation issues separated. That idea had its inception in HEW. On 6 May 1956, Secretary Folsom sent a memorandum to Presidential Assistant Sherman Adams along with two copies of a draft of a letter which he proposed to send to House Speaker Sam Rayburn.[53] In the memorandum, Folsom mentioned that he had briefly conversed with Jack Martin and Bryce Harlow and that he hoped he could bring up the subject at a forthcoming legislative leadership meeting. By 11 May, Folsom had submitted what by then was a third draft of his proposed letter.[54] Careful examination of the three drafts reveals that, though they went through a process of abbreviation and refinement, their essential points were the same as the HEW secretary's remarks to the Detroit Economic Club; though they were more mildly stated and with the nature of the appeal for congressional action being considerably toned down by the time the third draft was completed.

On Sunday, 20 May, Presidential Assistant Harlow completed yet another attempt at editing what by that time had become the Folsom letter and press statement.[55] Harlow's revision struck out references to the "voice of extremism" and those who would spread race hatred among the American people. It was at that point that Harlow, whose advice was highly valued by the president, asserted: "It strikes me that, as edited, this could be used as a press statement—but I still doubt the advisability of its being sent as a letter to the Republican and Democratic leadership."[56] Harlow's remark underscores the serious disagreement in the administration about the values to be gained from letters to the Democratic House leadership, whose continued cooperation was essential for the passage of other high-priority administration bills that were less divisive than the school construction and desegregation issues. As usual, the president's own advisors came down on the side of caution.

The result of the Folsom effort was a draft statement prepared for President Eisenhower to read at his 6 June 1956 press conference. In it, the president reiterated his "deep conviction of the need for legislation to provide Federal assistance for construction of public schools."[57] His statement emphasized that the need was real, that the basic responsibility for such construction ordinarily rested with the states, but that they were presently unable to keep up with the demand created by the most rapid and sustained enrollment increase in our history. He then restated the kind of proposal he desired:

> Federal assistance for classroom construction should be provided promptly. Federal assistance should be designed to encourage even greater State and local effort, should be distributed where needs are greatest, and should avoid any vestige of Federal control of education.[58]

The president thus recapped both the motives and the approach which he felt would best benefit American public education. Both reflected his grudging acceptance of the necessity of federal aid.

Turning to the integration question, the president asserted that congressional action had been delayed because

> of a proposed amendment which would deny Federal funds for school construction under certain conditions relating to racial integration in public schools. I have been advised that if this amendment is adopted, school construction legislation most probably will be defeated in this session of Congress.[59]

Emphasizing that such an amendment would benefit neither those who need the schools nor the integration process, the president urged the Congress to treat integration and school construction as separate issues, leaving the matter of integration to solutions "under the letter and spirit of the Supreme Court's decisions."[60] The message concluded with a reminder: "Schools are needed now. The education of children is at stake—children of all races."[61]

That position unfortunately failed to take into account the political realities at work in Congress, including the impact of the Powell Amendment on the school construction bills. Congressmen opposing that antisegregation rider joined other opponents of the Democratic plan and defeated the Kelly bill by a 224 to 194 count. The administration's refusal to modify its position in the face of certain defeat suggests that it was either deeply devoted to the president's policy of moderation and his conservative approach to school construction, or totally unrealistic about the divisive impact school desegregation had on Congress, or extremely cautious about getting involved in the controversy for political reasons. Regardless of the motives, the impact of that approach on the Congress was highly limited and even negative.

The president made little mention of the federal aid and integration questions in his 1956 reelection campaign. When the issue was raised, his position insulated him from controversy. On 2 October 1956, L. E. McConnell, a Wichita Falls, Texas, oilman, wrote the White House asking whether "Federal Aid for education which Pres. Eisenhower mentioned in the Lexington Ky. speech was only to be issued to schools that accepted negroes as students?[62] McConnell's letter was routed from Maxwell Rabb to Lewis Arthur Minnich, assistant staff secretary and campaign advisor, for comment because a presidential speech and policy were involved.

Minnich responded: "I don't think the question has been answered in the campaign. Is it advisable to recall one of the Press Conference remarks about the need for schools (in answer to questions about the Powell Amendment)?"[63] Rabb answered that question affirmatively.

The political value of the president's position on the school construction-desegregation issues vis-à-vis the administration's attempt to avoid antagonizing potential supporters—in this case white southerners—was apparent in the letter Rabb wrote to McConnell. In it, Rabb stated:

> We have checked the President's speeches and statements on this subject and, thus far, there has been no discussion of the issue which you raise. You will recall that during the past year this question was raised in connection with an amendment to the bill offered in Congress for aid to school construction; at that time, the President stated that he believed that the most important matter was to get the aid to the school systems and he opposed the amendment which would have denied aid to schools which were not integrated.[64]

Rabb's response made no mention of the president's insistence that desegregation matters be left to the courts, which by 1956 were embroiled in controversies with southern segregationists. McConnell was left with the impression that the president opposed desegregation enforcement.

Ironically, what in the context of congressional politics seemed to be an unyielding, inflexible position came off in electoral politics as a sensible occupation of moderate, even conservative ground. Viewed solely from a public political viewpoint, the administration's position was a marvelously practical one for an election year. Any attempt of the Democrats to exploit the school construction and desegregation issues would have had highly divisive, perhaps even disastrous, results on that party's unity.

During the 10 May 1957 cabinet meeting, HEW Secretary Folsom outlined the background and the current status of attempts to get a classroom construction bill through Congress.[65] His summation provides an interesting view of the administration's perception of its efforts and its explanation of the causes of its lack of success.

In tracing the background of the administration's efforts, Folsom emphasized that its 1956 proposal had been defeated because of the Powell Amendment, adding that the administration had gotten no help from the congressional leadership either.[66] Turning to his present proposal, he reported that the current bill recently voted out of committee was closer to the administration's original bill than that of the Democratic alternatives, and that the Republicans on the House Education and Labor Committee had done a fine job. Though the bill differed in the amount it would spend and its allocation formula, the president's principles, such as a time limit, aid restricted to the needy, and the encouragement of local and state efforts, were preserved.[67] He concluded that the bill was as good as the administration could get and that it should give its full support while emphasizing that it would still like a formula more favorable to needy states.[68] Folsom then summarized and rebutted the arguments presented against the bill, noting that polls indicated that the American people favored federal aid to classroom building by a four to one margin and concluded that: "If leaders get back of it, have good chance to defeat Powell amendment & pass bill."[69]

The reason for Secretary Folsom's optimism in light of the administration's continued unwillingness to move away from the rigid distinction between the classroom construction and school segregation issues is difficult to fathom. True, the president's smashing reelection triumph in 1956 had proven how highly he was esteemed by the American people, but it had not broken the Democratic control of Congress, nor convinced many recalcitrant southerners to accept the process of court-ordered desegregation which he was obliged to enforce.

The politically divisive and explosive issues which swirled around the Powell Amendment showed signs of becoming even more complex. A president's electoral mandate, as Franklin D. Roosevelt had learned in 1936, seldom guarantees him dominance of the legislative process. Both the opponents and supporters of segregation took advantage of the vacuum created by the president's stance to buttress their positions. This unwillingness of the administration to accept the idea that the desegregation crisis affected the classroom construction issue again contributed to the defeat of that bill with the Powell Amendment attached, on 25 July 1957 when 97 Democrats and 111 Republicans voted for the bill while 126 Democrats and 77 Republicans voted "no."[70]

The effect of the president's stance in Congress was the same as no leadership at all. That, when combined with indecision and parliamentary maneuvering on both sides, assured the defeat of the bill.

Chapter 13

Principles and Continued Deadlock

Ironically, the deadlock over federal aid to education was only broken during the Eisenhower years by the impact of international rather than domestic events, and these occurred in such a spectacular manner as to completely alter the nature of the federal aid issue for a brief period of time. The success of the Soviet Union's rocket technology, reflected in its successful launching of Sputnik I on 4 October 1957, injected an increasing sense of immediacy by tying the rationalization of cold-war defense needs to the federal aid to education issue.[1] Pressure for action was so great that the Joint House-Senate Conference Committee was able to delete the anti-segregation amendment which had been attached to the bill.[2] The resulting National Defense Education Act of 1958 was signed into law by President Eisenhower on 2 September.[3] The legislation provided federal government loans for college students planning teaching careers and large amounts of money for the development of enrichment programs in science, math, and modern foreign languages, as well as graduate fellowships for potential college teachers.

Though successful in allaying public fears that the Congress and the president were doing nothing in the face of a growing Soviet threat to American national security, the legislation failed to even address the basic impasse which the desegregation issue had created for the administration's classroom construction proposals.

In early 1959, the administration, in the face of bitter and often violent opposition to court-ordered attempts to implement school desegregation plans and signs of increasing black activism, adopted a more openly supportive position on school integration. An important feature of this program was its proposal to provide federal financial assistance to help school districts bear the cost of desegregation, something which the administration had previously rejected as impractical when suggested by a member of its own staff and by Congressman Stewart Udall.[4]

A Surplus of Opponents

The shift in policy did not come easily. It was opposed by some important members of the administration. On 28 January 1959, Maurice Stans, director of the Bureau of the Budget, sent a memorandum to General Wilton B. Persons, presidential assistant, dealing with the school proposal portions of the civil rights legislation that the administration had recently drafted. In referring to the section dealing with the education of children of military personnel in areas where the public schools had been closed and with the question of federal aid to help pay the costs of desegregation, Stans was blunt: "We doubt that the proposals are either necessary or desirable but in view of their political overtones, we will not oppose their submission to the Congress."[5]

With reference to the proposed desegregation aid, he asserted:

No information has been presented which would indicate that transitional costs of desegregation have impeded or prevented school districts from complying with court decisions. Hence, there is no indication that such grants would be an incentive to desegregate or would be applied for by school districts which are currently resisting integration.[6]

Stans' views, however, did not prevail.

On 5 February 1959, President Eisenhower sent a message to Congress calling for additional civil rights protections. Important parts of that legislation called for a toughened federal obstruction of justice statute and increased investigative authority for the FBI in cases dealing with persons trying to use coercion or violence to block school integration.[7] There was also another side to the administration's new approach. As the president put it:

> I recommend legislation to provide a temporary program of financial and technical aid to State and local agencies to assist them in making the necessary adjustments required by school desegregation decisions. . . . Such assistance should consist of sharing the burdens of transition through grants-in-aid to help meet additional costs directly occasioned by desegregation programs, and also of making technical information and assistance available to State and local educational agencies in preparing and implementing desegregation programs.[8]

The president's new policy was built upon the "carrot and stick" approach. Given his previous moderate approach and his low profile, it represented a significant change of policy regarding the integration question. Its greatest flaw lay not in the approach he developed, but in his tardiness in the face of long-standing segregationist intransigence.

The overly optimistic belief that the opponents of desegregation would comply more readily with court-ordered implementation plans than those reinforced with executive threats to withhold funds rested on two assumptions, neither of which proved true. First, that the judicial approach to desegregation would be more gradual and thus more acceptable to its opponents. Second, that the Court's interpretation of the law would be accepted as final. By 1959, experience had disproven both.

Despite the new approach which the administration was forced to develop against the opponents of school segregation in the 1957–1960 period, it never shifted from its original insistence that classroom construction and desegregation be treated separately. Evidence that it was determined to adhere to its basic policy appeared in its response to telegrams that three members of the administration received from Adam Clayton Powell on 20 May 1960.[9] Powell's telegrams were sent the day after the House Rules Committee by a seven to five vote had cleared a Democratic-sponsored federal aid to education bill for debate, which authorized a federal contribution of $325 million for three years of school construction. Powell's message was straightforward:

> Once again the federal aid to education bill looms before the Congress. Once again I am pleading with you to announce that you will use the power which you have and not allow any federal funds available under the forthcoming bill to be channeled to any school area in defiance of the 1954 Supreme Court decision. If you will so advise me I will not offer the Powell Amendment during the forthcoming consideration of the federal aid to education bill.[10]

The message led to hurried consultation between the president's staff and the attorney general's office and the decision that Gerald Morgan, the president's deputy assistant, would respond for all three of the officials whom Powell had telegrammed.

On 24 May 1960, Morgan sent a letter to Powell. He began it by pointing out that the question raised in Powell's telegram was "very similar" to the one considered in correspondence which the president's staff had carried on with members of Congress in 1956 and that: "The conclusions reached by the

White House in that correspondence still reflect the Administration's position."[11]

His next assertion that it was the federal judiciary which determines good faith compliance to the Supreme Court's school desegregation decision was one stated often previously. What followed, however, was not: "It is the policy of the Executive Branch of the Government to give full and vigorous support to the orders of the Federal Judiciary."[12] The experience gained at Little Rock, in Virginia, and at other confrontations in Tennessee, Mississippi, and Alabama had shattered the administration's earlier confidence that it could build acceptance for desegregation by creating a climate of reason and moderation based on as little executive pressure as possible.

Yet, Morgan's two concluding points indicated that the administration still felt that school construction and desegregation were two separate issues and that the means available for executive support of the latter were very limited. He argued:

> That judicial implementation of the Supreme Court decision, in the manner charted by the Court in its decree, and the meeting of the urgent, overall educational needs of our Country, can go forward at the same time; and
>
> That it cannot be assumed that it is essential, in order that progress be made in complying with the orders of the Federal Court, to reserve or withold funds necessary to progress in meeting our education needs.[13]

Needless to say, Powell again introduced his amendment.

All of the president's problems were not of the Democratic variety. Opposition to federal aid for classroom construction remained strong in his own party. On 24 June 1960, Senator Jacob Javits of New York, one of the leading advocates of a classroom construction bill, wrote Eisenhower informing him that "every Republican on the Rules Committee of the House has joined with its Chairman and two southern Democrats in denying a rule to the bill for federal aid to education, a different version of which has already passed both Houses."[14] Javits asserted that such behavior could lead to Congress, the administration, and the American people being frustrated by the House Rules Committee, whose proper function was to schedule the timing of legislation moving to the House floor. The senator then urged the president to intervene because:

> It seems to me that here is an entirely necessary role for the President as leader of our party and properly justifies the invocation of the President's prestige. I do hope very much that you will think favorably of taking a hand in convincing the Republican members of the Rules Committee that they are doing the wrong thing for the nation and the party. . . .[15]

Eisenhower did not intervene.

Instead, on 29 June 1960, he responded to Senator Javits by restating his support for sound school legislation. With regard to the situation on the Rules Committee, he told Javits:

> As to the members of the House Rules Committee, each of them knows well, or certainly should, exactly what my convictions are. I want legislation that will help to build classrooms, without impairing local and state responsibility for and control over education; legislation that does not become encumbered with matters unrelated to the classroom shortage, such as teachers' salaries and issues better handled by the Judiciary; legislation that allots Federal funds on a basis that gives a clear recognition to need; and legislation that insures that the Federal classroom dollar is matched by the State classroom dollar.[16]

The president's letter to Javits had no effect on the recalcitrant Republicans on the House Rules Committee.

The president's response is a fitting summation of his unchanging position on the school construction issue and its frustrating effect on him. His emphasis on congressional responsibility for the failure of his efforts, and particularly the actions of the majority Democrats, was the version which found its way into his memoirs.[17] His refusal to directly confront the obstructionist Republicans on the House Rules Committee, despite Senator Javits' plea, suggests, however, that he shared in the responsibility for the lack of leadership in the Congress, which led to the repeated defeats of school construction legislation from 1955 to 1960.

On 21 March 1960, Press Secretary Hagerty addressed a memorandum to Eisenhower as the Republican party entered what proved to be a critical election year. Observing that the image of the GOP was "becoming somewhat diffused and distorted," Hagerty cited the causes of that problem as threefold: remarks by the numerous Democratic presidential contenders, lack of agreement on some issues by members of the cabinet, and

> the voting record of the Republican members of the Congress which gives the impression of a divided and confused stand as a party on almost every issue of the day—certainly on civil rights, immigration, aid to education, agriculture, etc.[18]

Hagerty then suggested how the party's image and thus its hopes to elect a Republican president in the coming election could be improved:

> Consequently, I feel strongly that the time has come for the President to restate clearly, simply and forcefully what the Republican Party stands for in the nation and what the President is going to do to get these beliefs adopted by the Congress. Even if unsuccessful, the record will be restated and can act as a guideline for the party nationally. . . .[19]

Both the Javits letter and the Hagerty memorandum unwittingly testify to the ineffectiveness of Eisenhower's approach to leadership vis-à-vis the congressional wing of the Republican party in the closing years of his presidency. Small wonder that the Republican minority in Congress seemed disorganized and divided. The president's distaste for confrontation worked to mitigate the kinds of leverage that his great personal popularity should have permitted him to bear in Congress—even in those critically controversial areas where he could not expect help from Lyndon Johnson and Sam Rayburn.

Interpretation

One of the standard interpretations characterizes the Eisenhower administration's efforts on behalf of federal aid to education as weak, emphasizing that it was unwilling to take a strong initial stand on that issue and that its subsequent efforts were feeble.[20] Although this may be an accurate assessment of the results of the administration's efforts, it does little to explain the causes which underlay it, particularly the crippling effects caused by the impossibility of keeping that issue separated from the school segregation question. On this issue, like several others, Eisenhower and his advisors found that they had become involved in an already fully developed conflict in which the battle lines were already drawn during the Truman presidency.

When examined in view of President Eisenhower's belief in the importance of leaving the primary responsibility for education to the states and local communities and his desire that the federal government's growing intrusion into the lives of Americans be reversed, the administration's advocacy of limited federal aid appears to be consistent with his philosophy. So likewise when one focuses on the Eisenhower administration's efforts to keep the school segregation issue separate from its proposed school construction program, one can see a pattern of consistency between the president's beliefs and his administration's actions. Eisenhower's conviction that the desegregation issue would require a long-range, moderate approach in which education and conciliation would play major roles was the basis of his desire that it be kept separate from the federal aid issue.

His failure to achieve this goal was the result of more than the combination of a lack of realism on his part and a determination to be philosophically consistent. There were simply too many opportunities for those opposed to federal aid to education and those on both sides of the school desegregation issue to score points with their constituencies by permitting the school segregation issue to be tied to the federal aid question. The president, in short, was confronted with a situation where the principles guiding his behavior were not the same as those of many of the members of Congress.

There was little room for Eisenhower's policy of moderation to operate in such an atmosphere. His gradualist, quiet approach to school desegregation and his limited conception of executive responsibility for its enforcement combined to create an impression of weakness and inactivity on his part. Many of the advocates of integration viewed the president as lagging behind rather than encouraging Americans to support the Supreme Court's implementation decision by lending it the full force of his great personal prestige and the power of the presidency. Segregationists also viewed the president's cautious statements as a sign of weakness and were thus encouraged to move toward defiance of the Court's opinions.

The administration's attempt to take advantage of favorable public opinion regarding federal aid, which resulted from the White House Conference on Education in November 1955 to pressure Congress, did not prove successful because it was not of sufficient strength to overcome the very potent coalition which opposed the administration's efforts for the forestated reasons.[21] So likewise did the public reaction to the Russian space accomplishments beginning with Sputnik I in 1957 which led to the National Defense Education Act of 1958 fail to break the deadlock over federal aid to classroom construction. Nevertheless, the administration maintained its position and all attempts at passage of a classroom construction bill were stalemated while Eisenhower remained in office. They continued to run aground on the shoals created by the Powell

Amendment and the administration's refusal to move away from its position that the desegregation and school construction issues be treated separately.

This attempt to trace a portion of the administration's unsuccessful struggle from its own internal documents and public statements is worthwhile for a number of reasons. In addition to the insights it provides about the process whereby the Eisenhower administration formulated and enunciated its policies, it raises a number of questions.

Why did the administration refuse to alter its position in light of its awareness of the certain defeat of classroom construction bills with the Powell Amendment attached? The evidence suggests that many Republican and Democratic congressmen felt that the president did have the power to break the congressional logjam if he had spoken out.[22] Was the president's position ultimately governed by his "gradualist" approach to desegregation? Were the administration's actions based on the president's philosophical precepts or the political necessity of disassociating himself as much as possible from the Court's desegregation decisions? His response to the school construction issue certainly illustrates how hard he worked to avoid involvement in the desegregation question, even though his efforts made him vulnerable to the charge of failure to exercise presidential leadership.

What role did the president himself play in the formulation of that policy? An accurate answer to that question is difficult to obtain. It should be remembered, though, that the president continued to hold strong reservations about the worth of federal aid to education and the dangers of too much activism in the civil liberties realm throughout his two terms.[23] Turning to the related and critically important question of where the president received his "input," it is possible to state that the president and his staff, at least those upon whom he relied most heavily—Sherman Adams, Bryce Harlow, Gerald Morgan, Lewis Arthur Minnich, and Maxwell Rabb—were cautious, conservative men who agreed with and reinforced the president's attitudes on school construction and the desegregation issue.[24] The president relied more heavily on these men than those sending him advice from HEW and the Department of Justice. There were also noticeable signs of disagreement between his staff and members of these two departments on such issues as the nature and scope of the administration's federal aid to education program and its "low profile" approach to the desegregation issue.[25]

While Eisenhower was certainly a man of conservative principles, neither he nor the advisors who formulated and articulated administration policies were blind ideologues. His decision to try for some kind of federal aid for classroom construction proves that there was room for a policy based in part on principles, a perception of national needs, political motives, and even a dash of expediency. All of these were influenced, however, by Eisenhower's penchant for caution, a trait many mistook for weakness.

Ultimately, the federal aid to education issue, inescapably tied as it was to the desegregation question by the Powell Amendment, required that the Eisenhower administration develop a realistic policy based on acceptance of that fact. Instead, the administration, despite its minority position in Congress and the sharp division of both parties on the school construction and desegregation issues, publicly articulated an uncompromising distinction between the two from a position of weakness. It is easy for a historian examining the events from the perspective of two decades of hindsight to conclude that, given those circumstances, the failure of the administration's efforts to achieve a classroom construction bill was virtually inevitable and that Dwight D. Eisenhower's pursuit of moderation contributed to that result.

Chapter 14

Conclusions

The principal conclusion of this study has been stated many times in the preceding chapters: Dwight D. Eisenhower defined his position vis-à-vis the school desegregation crisis as that of a moderate among extremists. Understanding the president's perception of his position is of fundamental importance for those seeking to assess the short- and long-term impact of the Eisenhower administration's civil rights policies. It explains much about what Eisenhower and those members of his administration charged with formulating those policies did and did not do.

The standard generalizations about the motives behind the Eisenhower administration's civil rights policies tend to become blurred when examined in the context that shaped the president's thoughts and deeds. This underscores the need for careful assessment of the impact of the president's fundamental beliefs on the process of presidential decision making and the nature of his leadership from 1953 to 1960. As the foregoing chapters indicate, that approach reveals complexity and sophistication about a president and an administration hitherto characterized, because of the demands of the times and partisanship, as bordering on the simplistic.

The completion of this volume inevitably raises questions about what insights it adds to Eisenhower's own explanations of his behavior. The late president's memoirs adequately summarize the basic assumptions which he stated publicly were the basis of his administration's civil rights policies (or nonpolicies as his critics have charged). Despite Eisenhower's tendency to overblame his Democratic congressional opposition for the failure of his policies, one finds no examples in his memoirs of blatant deceit or willful distortions of historical facts. What Eisenhower's memoirs do reveal is the consistency of his moderation in all aspects of the school desegregation crisis which enveloped his presidency.

What they do not reveal, however, are the fears, assumptions, and influences he carried within himself, the critical assumptions and input that affected Eisenhower's day-to-day thinking as his philosophy collided with the hard realities of the most explosive domestic issue of his presidency. One such example that comes to mind is the total absence in his memoirs of any reference to his pervasive fear that judicially supervised desegregation would lead to confrontation between his administration and state officials on such a large scale that it could not be controlled. Another example was his omission of his critical attitude toward the advocates of rapid desegregation because of the inflammatory results of their behavior. It is on such points as these that the foregoing chapters present critical insights about the effect of Eisenhower's beliefs on his policies; they underscore the element of uncertainty which haunted his actions.

Another conclusion which emerges from this work is that Eisenhower possessed a far more limited conception of both the scope of his executive power and his responsibilities as a party leader than many presidents before and after him. These realities played a critical role in his response to the school desegregation issue. Though Gary W. Reichard has insisted in his volume, *The Reaffirmation of Republicanism: Eisenhower and the Eighty-third Congress,* that the president was a responsible, effective party leader, that conclusion seems difficult to sustain when the president's efforts on behalf of the legislative parts of his civil rights program are examined.[1]

Though the president liked to blame the failure of administration policies on the partisanship of the Democratic majority which he faced during six of his eight years in office, his behavior in the federal aid to education controversy and the debates over the 1957 and 1960 Civil Rights Acts suggest that his explanation leaves something to be desired. There is considerable evidence that the president could have circumvented the effects of the Powell Amendment had he spoken out in favor of withholding funds from those districts in noncompliance with court desegregation orders. Similarly, many congressmen were convinced that decisive statements on his part could have prevented the inclusion of the jury trial amendment in the 1957 act and the exclusion of the federal aid provisions for desegregating schools in the 1960 act.

Another important conclusion that emerges from this work is that the president was the recipient and, as at Little Rock, sometimes the victim of sharply divided counsel from both inside and outside his administration. Evidence of sharp divisions among his advisors appeared at every critical juncture of the Eisenhower administration's response to the school desegregation crisis. In one important sense, the president's response to the mixed advice was totally consistent with his personal moderation. More often than not, those who, like Attorney General Herbert Brownell, urged Eisenhower to take stronger actions on behalf of school desegregation found themselves frustrated by the president's reliance in most situations on those who, like Sherman Adams, urged caution.

However, the continuing pressure of mixed advice had another effect: it tended to remind the president of the controversial, divisive nature of the school desegregation crisis. In that sense, it contributed to his cautious approach and the aura of indecision and inaction which seemed to surround the administration's policies.

The overall impression that emerges from the study of this critical aspect of the Eisenhower presidency is that he was truly committed and consistent in his beliefs about the proper approach to school desegregation. It is also true, as many of his critics have pointed out, that his consistency greatly inhibited his willingness to take decisive action in a time of growing crisis. That flaw, however, was not the product of devious cunning (translated into willful neglect of the civil rights issue) that Murray Kempton sees at the heart of Eisenhower's political personality.[2] It was more the result, as Richard H. Rovere argues, of Eisenhower's possession of beliefs and values which proved inadequate given the critical challenges posed by the school desegregation crisis.[3] Such an assessment seems particularly germane in view of the dominant role his philosophy of moderation played in shaping his approach.

Perhaps as a gift of hindsight, we are left with increased respect for the wisdom of Eisenhower's view that school desegregation was a tremendously complex issue, one that raised basic questions about the nature of American society and defied rapid solution. The years of trial and tribulation since 1954, with their continuing arguments over such thorny issues as de facto and ad hoc segregation, cross-busing, white flight from the central cities to the suburbs, and sophisticated evasive techniques designed to stymie judicially-ordered desegregation, provide convincing proof of the truth of his basic premise. The attempts to use judicial power to resolve such questions seem, in more recent years, to have run into the complexities of black-white bipolarity and growing intransigence about what is still essentially a racial issue with explosive economic, social, and political overtones.

The foregoing study suggests that the president was neither the muddleheaded incompetent his earlier critics portrayed him to be nor the astute executive pictured by some of his recent defenders. One is left with the distinct impression that the truth is somewhere in between. Undoubtedly, his foresight was great, but the caution he espoused led to inaction at a time when the opponents of desegregation could have been checked. The president's experience proves that complex problems defy simple solutions. They raise critical questions about the assumptions and motives of those who have to deal with them, questions which persist over long periods of time.

Finally, a word about the place of this study in relation to the growing revisionist historiography of the Eisenhower presidency. While this study hardly qualifies as one of the complimentary, sympathetic recent works cited by Vincent P. De Santis in his excellent bibliographic essay, it does seek, just as many of those works do, to closely examine an important aspect of the Eisenhower presidency.[4] As De Santis suggests, many of the scholars currently involved in the reexamination of the Eisenhower presidency have thus far avoided constructing history on the basis of emotions and partisanship. The civil rights policies of the Eisenhower administration and the president's role in shaping and articulating them certainly are of critical enough importance to deserve such treatment.

Maxwell Rabb, in commenting on the civil rights policies of the Eisenhower administration, stated:

I have always felt that President Eisenhower's approach to civil rights problems has not received the attention it deserved. His was a low-key and effective approach. It must be remembered that his program took place at a time when the atmosphere was not as pressurized and bitter as it was in the Kennedy and Johnson periods when events, not men, dictated such progress as materialized. The Eisenhower accomplishments resulted from President Eisenhower's own initiative. What is more, what he did represented essential and important advances in the area of civil rights.[5]

While the evidence examined in this study does not fully support Rabb's favorable assessment, it does indicate that he is certainly correct in urging more attention to that aspect of the Eisenhower presidency.

Notes

Preface

1. Elmo Richardson, "Working on Ike," *Pacific Northwest Quarterly* 68 (July 1977):141.
2. Their works in order are: Albert P. Blaustein and Clarence Clyde Ferguson, Jr., *Desegregation and the Law: The Meaning and Effect of the School Segregation Cases,* 2nd ed. (New York: Vintage Books, 1962); Loren Miller, *The Petitioners: The Story of the Supreme Court of the United States and the Negro* (Cleveland: World, 1966); Jack Greenberg, *Race Relations and American Law* (New York: Columbia University Press, 1959); and Richard Kluger, *Simple Justice: The History of* Brown *v.* Board of Education *and Black America's Struggle for Equality* (New York: Alfred A. Knopf, 1976).
3. Their works in order are: Charles C. Alexander, *Holding the Line: The Eisenhower Era, 1952–1961* (Bloomington: Indiana University Press, 1975); Herbert S. Parmet, *Eisenhower and the American Crusades* (New York: Macmillan, 1972); and Gary W. Reichard, *The Reaffirmation of Republicanism: Eisenhower and the Eighty-third Congress* (Knoxville: University of Tennessee Press, 1975).
4. Archibald Cox, *The Role of the Supreme Court in American*

Government (New York: Oxford University Press, 1976), pp. 89–90; see also, Paul L. Murphy, *The Constitution in Crisis Times* (New York: Harper and Row, 1972), p. 315.

Chapter 1

1. John Hope Franklin, *Reconstruction: After the Civil War* (Chicago: University of Chicago Press, 1961), pp. 38, 46, 52, and 107–14.
2. Vernon Lane Wharton, *The Negro in Mississippi: 1865–1890* (New York: Harper and Row, 1965), pp. 243–55; Carl N. Degler, *Out of Our Past: The Forces That Shaped Modern America* (New York: Harper and Row, 1970), pp. 156–59.
3. Degler, p. 158.
4. *Roberts* v. *City of Boston,* 5 Cush. 198 (1849); Leonard W. Levy, *The Law of the Commonwealth and Chief Justice Shaw* (New York: Harper and Row, 1967), pp. 109–17; Donald M. Jacobs, "The Nineteenth Century Struggle Over Segregated Education in the Boston Schools," *Journal of Negro Education* 39 (Winter 1970):76–85; and "Colored Children in the Boston Public Schools," *Baltimore Sun,* 7 September 1855, p. 2.
5. Argument of Charles Sumner against the constitutionality of separate "colored" schools in the case of *Roberts* v. *City of Boston* before the Supreme Court of Massachusetts on 4 December 1849 (Boston, 1849) as cited in Richard Bardolph, ed., *The Civil Rights Record: Black Americans and the Law, 1849–1970* (New York: Thomas Y. Crowell, 1970), p. 16; see also Levy, pp. 111–13.
6. Leonard W. Levy and Harlan B. Phillips, "The *Roberts* Case: Source of the 'Separate But Equal' Doctrine," *American Historical Review* 56 (April 1951):510–18.
7. See the briefs of the four states and the District of Columbia presented prior to the 1953 arguments in the school segregation cases in United States Supreme Court, *Transcripts of Records and File Copies of Briefs, 1954* (hereafter cited as *Transcripts*), vols. 4–12, passim, United States Supreme Court Law Library, Washington, D.C.

8. Franklin, pp. 152–72; and Kenneth M. Stampp, *The Era of Reconstruction: 1865–1877* (New York: Random House, 1965), pp. 204–5.

9. Franklin, pp. 194–217; C. Vann Woodward, *Reunion and Reaction: The Compromise of 1877 and the End of Reconstruction* (Garden City, N.Y.: Doubleday, 1956), passim; Paul H. Buck, *The Road to Reunion: 1865–1900* (New York: Vintage Books, 1959), passim; Ray Allen Billington, *Westward Expansion: A History of the American Frontier,* 2nd ed. (New York: Macmillan, 1960), pp. 617–744; Samuel P. Hays, *The Response to Industrialism: 1885–1914* (Chicago: University of Chicago Press, 1957), passim; and Harold M. Hyman, ed., *The Radical Republicans and Reconstruction: 1861–1870* (Indianapolis: Bobbs-Merrill, 1967), pp. 521–23.

10. C. Vann Woodward, *The Strange Career of Jim Crow* (New York: Oxford University Press, 1957), pp. 49–95.

11. Ibid.; Stampp, pp. 193–213; Franklin, pp. 200–201 and 223–24; and Rayford W. Logan, *The Betrayal of the Negro: From Rutherford B. Hayes to Woodrow Wilson* (New York: Collier Books, 1965), passim.

12. Bardolph, p. 81; see also, Alfred H. Kelly and Winfred A. Harbison, *The American Constitution: Its Origins and Development,* 4th ed. (New York: W. W. Norton, 1970), p. 462.

13. Blaustein and Ferguson, p. 62.

14. Alfred H. Kelly, "The Congressional Controversy Over School Segregation, 1867–1875," *American Historical Review* 64 (April 1959):537–63.

15. Franklin, pp. 222–24; and Bardolph, pp. 75–98.

16. Franklin, p. 112; Wharton, p. 249; and Harry S. Ashmore, *The Negro and the Schools* (Chapel Hill: University of North Carolina Press, 1954), p. 9.

17. Bardolph, p. 90; see also, Ashmore, p. 7; and Gilbert T. Stephenson, *Race Distinctions in American Law* (New York: Association Press, 1911), passim.

18. Blaustein and Ferguson, pp. 62–64.

19. *Mississippi Laws,* 1878 (Chapter 13, Section 35), p. 103 as cited in Bardolph, p. 82; he also cites on pp. 81–82 *Consti-*

tution of Georgia, 1877 (Article 8 in *Code of Georgia,* 1882), p. 1321; and *Constitution of Alabama,* 1875 (Article 13 in *Code of Alabama,* 1876), p. 147.

20. Buck, p. 295.
21. *State* v. *McCann,* 21 Ohio St. 198 (1871); *Ward* v. *Flood,* 48 Cal. 36 (1874); *Cory* v. *Carter,* 48 Ind. 327 (1874); *Bertonneau* v. *Board of Directors,* Fed. Cas. No. 1, 361 (C.C.D. La., 1878); and *United States* v. *Buntin,* 10 Fed. 730 (S.D. Ohio, 1882).
22. Ashmore, p. 11.
23. Ibid.
24. *Hall* v. *Decuir,* 95 U.S. 485 at 553–54 in Lawyers' Edition (1878).
25. *Ward* v. *Flood,* 48 Cal. 36 (1874).
26. Ibid.
27. *People* v. *Gallagher,* 93 New York 438 (1883); for an interesting study of the response of a border state to the question of school segregation in this era, see Robert R. Bunting, "School Segregation in Kansas: A Study in Constitutional and Political Development" (M.A. thesis, Wichita State University, 1972), pp. 1–22.
28. *People* v. *Gallagher,* 93 New York 438 (1883) as cited in Bardolph, p. 92.
29. Ibid.
30. Miller, pp. 14, 181–82, and 211.
31. Robert G. McCloskey, *The American Supreme Court* (Chicago: University of Chicago Press, 1960), pp. 101–35.
32. Ibid., pp. 119–21.
33. Ibid.; Woodward, *The Strange Career of Jim Crow,* pp. 53–54; and Miller, pp. 101–64.
34. *Santa Clara County* v. *Southern Pacific Railroad,* 118 U.S. 394 (1886); for an excellent, concise discussion of this process, see Kelly and Harbison, pp. 500–24.
35. Robert G. McCloskey, *American Conservatism in the Age of Enterprise, 1865–1910* (New York: Harper and Brothers, 1951), pp. 72–126.
36. Ibid., pp. 122–23.
37. Woodward, *The Strange Career of Jim Crow,* pp. 53–54.

38. *Civil Rights* cases, 109 U.S. 3 (1883); and Alan F. Westin, "The Case of the Prejudiced Doorkeeper," in *Quarrels That Have Shaped the Constitution,* ed. John Garraty (New York: Harper and Row, 1964), pp. 128–44. The first step in this direction was the Court's decision in *United States* v. *Cruikshank,* 92 U.S. 542 (1876).

39. *Plessy* v. *Ferguson,* 163 U.S. 537 (1896); C. Vann Woodward, "The Case of the Louisiana Traveler," in *Quarrels That Have Shaped the Constitution,* ed. John Garraty (New York: Harper and Row, 1964), pp. 145–58; and Miller, pp. 165–80.

40. *Plessy* v. *Ferguson,* 163 U.S. 537 at 258 in Lawyers' Edition (1896).

41. Ashmore, p. 11.

42. *Plessy* v. *Ferguson,* 163 U.S. 537 at 264 in Lawyers' Edition (1896).

43. Ashmore, p. 22.

44. Ibid.; and Kelly and Harbison, p. 496.

45. *Cumming* v. *Richmond County Board of Education,* 175 U.S. 528 (1899).

46. Ibid., at 266 in Lawyers' Edition; see also, Miller, pp. 213–14; and Ashmore, p. 22.

47. Kelly and Harbison, p. 496.

48. *Berea College* v. *Kentucky,* 211 U.S. 45 (1908); Miller, pp. 199–205; Ashmore, p. 22; and Kelly and Harbison, p. 496.

49. *Gong Lum* v. *Rice,* 275 U.S. 78 (1927); and Blaustein and Ferguson, pp. 101–2.

50. Ibid.; and Miller, p. 215.

51. Miller, p. 214.

52. Bardolph, p. 216.

53. Ibid., p. 210.

Chapter 2

1. Mary White Ovington, *The Walls Came Tumbling Down: The Autobiography of Mary White Ovington* (New York: Schocken Books, 1970), pp. 100–46; Alfred H. Kelly, "The School Desegregation Case," in *Quarrels That Have Shaped*

the Constitution, ed. John Garraty (New York: Harper and Row, 1964), pp. 249–50; and Charles Flint Kellogg, *NAACP: A History of the National Association for the Advancement of Colored People,* vol. 1 (Baltimore: Johns Hopkins Press, 1967), pp. 9–65.

2. William English Walling, "Race War in the North," *The Independent* (3 September 1908) as cited in Ovington, p. 100.
3. Bardolph, p. 180.
4. Kellogg, pp. 89–115; and Ovington, pp. 113–14.
5. Kellogg, p. 194.
6. Ibid.; and "Bill to Provide Separate Negro Schools Now Up," *Topeka Journal,* 24 January 1917, p. 15; "Negro Is an Issue," *Topeka Journal,* 24 January 1917, p. 16; "Loyalty and Patriotism Features of Big Meeting," *Topeka Capital,* 15 April 1918, pp. 17–18; and "State Meeting: Kansas Branch of the National Association for the Advancement of Colored People," *Topeka Journal,* 21 February 1919, p. 18, Clippings Collection entitled "Negroes," vol. 7—1915–1952, Kansas State Historical Society, Topeka, Kansas.
7. Kellogg, p. 194; and Ovington, pp. 66–78.
8. *Guinn* v. *United States,* 238 U.S. 347 (1915); and *Buchanan* v. *Warley,* 245 U.S. 60 (1917); see Greenberg, pp. 401–2 for a list of the NAACP's successes before the Supreme Court from 1915–1953.
9. William B. Hixson, Jr., *Moorfield Storey and the Abolitionist Tradition* (New York: Oxford University Press, 1972), pp. 98–145.
10. Kellogg, p. 293.
11. Ibid., pp. 187–89; and Ashmore, pp. 17–18.
12. Kellogg, pp. 193–94.
13. Kelly, "The School Desegregation Case," p. 250; and Ovington, pp. 244–82.
14. Kelly, "The School Desegregation Case," p. 250.
15. Greenberg, p. 34.
16. Kelly, "The School Desegregation Case," pp. 245–46.
17. Ibid., p. 246; see also, Ashmore, pp. 24–39.
18. Kelly, "The School Desegregation Case," p. 247.
19. Ibid.; see also, William E. Leuchtenburg, *Franklin D. Roose-*

velt and the New Deal: 1932–1940 (New York: Harper and Row, 1963), pp. 185–87 and 192; Herbert Hill and Jack Greenberg, *Citizen's Guide to Desegregation: A Study of Social and Legal Change in American Life* (Boston: Beacon Press, 1955), pp. 37–38; and Degler, pp. 396–98.

20. Kelly, "The School Desegregation Case," p. 247. A sense of the growing confidence of American blacks can be seen in the editorials of the NAACP's *Crisis* beginning in the mid-1930s.

21. Kelly, "The School Desegregation Case," p. 247.

22. Leuchtenburg, p. 186.

23. Kelly, "The School Desegregation Case," p. 247; see also, Miller, p. 309; Ashmore, p. 47; and Hill and Greenberg, pp. 39, 48, and 61.

24. Kelly, "The School Desegregation Case," p. 248; for insights into the problems and opportunities World War II created for blacks, see the following: Editorial, "The Riots," *Crisis,* July 1943, pp. 199–200; "Along the N.A.A.C.P. Battlefront: Teacher Salary Cases," *Crisis,* August 1943, p. 249; Editorial, "Our Republican Friends," *Crisis,* November 1943, p. 327; "Politicians Win, Education Loses," *Crisis,* November 1943, p. 333; Editorial, "Supreme Court Rules Out White Primaries," *Crisis,* May 1944, pp. 164–65; and Editorial, "F.D.R.'s Death," *Crisis,* May 1945, p. 129.

25. Kelly, "The School Desegregation Case," p. 248.

26. Ibid.; see also, McCloskey, *The American Supreme Court,* pp. 208–10.

27. Kelly, "The School Desegregation Case," pp. 248–49; and Kelly and Harbison, pp. 859–60; for a discussion of the effects of this changed judicial attitude in cases dealing with black civil rights, see Miller, pp. 277–332.

28. President's Committee on Civil Rights, *To Secure These Rights* (Washington, D.C.: Government Printing Office, 1947), p. 82; see also, William Berman, *The Politics of Civil Rights in the Truman Administration* (Columbus: Ohio State University Press, 1970), passim.

29. Greenberg, p. 35. The papers of the American Fund for Public Service are in the New York Public Library.

30. Greenberg, p. 38.
31. Ibid., p. 36.
32. Ibid., p. 35; and *N.A.A.C.P. Annual Report* (New York: 1934), passim.
33. *Yick Wo* v. *Hopkins,* 118 U.S. 356 (1886).
34. Greenberg, pp. 36–37. He also notes that the *N.A.A.C.P. Annual Reports* during this period discuss the association's efforts to develop a legal strategy.
35. Greenberg, p. 39.
36. Kelly, "The School Desegregation Case," p. 251; Hill and Greenberg, pp. 56–59; and *N.A.A.C.P. Annual Report* (1934), passim.
37. Greenberg, p. 35.
38. Hill and Greenberg, p. 57.

Chapter 3

1. *Pearson* v. *Murray,* 169 Md. 478 (1935).
2. "Exclusion of Negroes from State Supported Professional Schools," *Yale Law Journal* 45 (May 1936):1299.
3. *Missouri ex rel. Gaines* v. *Canada,* 305 U.S. 337 (1938).
4. 2 Mo. Rev. Stat. (1929), Section 9622 as cited in "Equal Protection—Admission of Negro to State University Law School," *University of Pennsylvania Law Review* 87 (February 1939):478–79.
5. "Supreme Court to Review Missouri University Case," *Crisis,* November 1938, pp. 361–67.
6. *Missouri ex rel. Gaines* v. *Canada,* 305 U.S. 337 at vol. 83, 213 in Lawyers' Edition (1938).
7. Ibid.; see also, "University of Missouri Case Won," *Crisis,* January 1939, pp. 10–11.
8. Kelly and Harbison, p. 922.
9. Editorial, "Equal Opportunity in Education," *Crisis,* January 1939, p. 17; see also, Ashmore, pp. 32–33.
10. Hill and Greenberg, p. 60.
11. Ashmore, pp. 50–51; and Kelly and Harbison, p. 922.
12. Kelly, "The School Desegregation Case," p. 251; and Greenberg, p. 37.

13. Kelly, "The School Desegregation Case," p. 251.
14. Hill and Greenberg, p. 60.
15. Ben Kaplan, "The Legal Front: Some Highlights of the Past Year," *Crisis*, July 1940, pp. 206–7 and 210; Editorial, "Victory in Louisville," *Pittsburgh Courier* as cited in "From the Press of the Nation," *Crisis,* March 1941, p. 83; and Hill and Greenberg, p. 64.
16. Kelly, "The School Desegregation Case," p. 252; and Hill and Greenberg, pp. 62–64.
17. Kelly, "The School Desegregation Case," p. 254.
18. Kelly and Harbison, pp. 922–23.
19. *Sipuel* v. *Board of Regents of the University of Oklahoma,* 332 U.S. 631 (1948).
20. (Okla. 1947) 180 P. (2d) 135 as cited in Neal Seegert, "Fourteenth Amendment—Equal Protection of the Laws—Racial Segregation in Public Institutions," *Michigan Law Review* 46 (March 1948):642.
21. *Sipuel* v. *Board of Regents of the University of Oklahoma,* 332 U.S. 631 at vol. 92, 249 in Lawyers' Edition (1948); see also, Editorial, "Another Step Forward," *Crisis,* February 1948, p. 41.
22. Seegert, p. 643, footnote 24; and Hill and Greenberg, pp. 66–67.
23. Kelly and Harbison, p. 923.
24. *Sweatt* v. *Painter,* 339 U.S. 629 (1950); Hill and Greenberg, pp. 67–68; Kelly and Harbison, pp. 923–24; and Edna B. Kerin, "Separate Is Not Equal," *Crisis,* May 1950, pp. 288–92 and 332.
25. Hill and Greenberg, p. 68.
26. Ibid., p. 69; and Kerin, p. 291.
27. Hill and Greenberg, p. 69.
28. Ibid., p. 71.
29. Ibid., pp. 69–71; Kerin, p. 290; and Kelly, "The School Desegregation Case," p. 255.
30. *Sweatt* v. *Painter,* 339 U.S. 629 at vol. 94, 1119 in Lawyers' Edition (1950); see also, Editorial, "Supreme Court Rulings," *Crisis*, July 1950, pp. 442–43.
31. *McLaurin* v. *Oklahoma State Regents,* 339 U.S. 637 (1950).

32. Hill and Greenberg, pp. 72–73.
33. Kelly and Harbison, p. 924.
34. Hill and Greenberg, p. 73.
35. *McLaurin* v. *Oklahoma State Regents,* 339 U.S. 637 at vol. 94, 1154 in Lawyers' Edition (1950); see also, Clifford S. Green, "The Fourteenth Amendment and Racial Segregation in State-Supported Schools," *Temple Law Quarterly* 24 (October 1950):222–25.
36. Seegert, pp. 642–43.
37. Green, p. 225.
38. Kelly, "The School Desegregation Case," p. 256.
39. Kelly and Harbison, p. 924; and Editorial, "Integration in Education," *Crisis,* November 1950, pp. 646–47.
40. Kelly, "The School Desegregation Case," p. 257.
41. Ashmore, pp. 50–51.

Chapter 4

1. Eisenhower to B. G. Chynoweth, 15 July 1954, Whitman File (Name Series), Box 5, Dwight D. Eisenhower Presidential Library, Abilene, Kansas (hereafter cited as E.P.L.); for an earlier example of this view, see Eric F. Goldman, *The Crucial Decade* (New York: Alfred A. Knopf, 1969), pp. 218–19 and 266–69.
2. Eisenhower to William Phillips, 5 June 1953, Whitman File (Name Series), Box 25, E.P.L.
3. See, for example, Eisenhower Diary, 24 July 1953, Whitman File (Diary Series), Box 2, E.P.L.
4. Transcript of presidential press conference, 19 March 1953, Morrow Papers, Box 11, E.P.L.
5. Ibid.
6. See Official File (hereafter cited as O.F.), Box 282, E.P.L., for correspondence regarding District of Columbia's school desegregation. See specifically, Eisenhower to Samuel Spencer, 30 November 1953, on that subject. It is not the intention of this author to develop a comprehensive study of this subject, but rather to illustrate concisely Eisenhower's initial, optimistic views about it.

7. Memorandum from Robert T. Stevens to James C. Hagerty, 20 March 1953, O.F., Box 731, E.P.L.
8. Ibid.
9. Ibid.
10. Memorandum from Roger W. Jones to Bernard M. Shanley, 20 March 1953, O.F., Box 731, E.P.L.
11. Ibid.
12. Memorandum from Eisenhower to Secretary of Defense, 25 March 1953, O.F., Box 731, E.P.L.
13. Ibid.
14. Allan Shivers to Eisenhower, 16 July 1953, O.F., Box 731, E.P.L.
15. Ibid.
16. Eisenhower Diary, 24 July 1953, Whitman File (Diary Series), Box 2, E.P.L.
17. Ibid.
18. Ibid.; see also, Dwight D. Eisenhower, *Waging Peace: 1956–1961* (Garden City, N.Y.: Doubleday, 1965), pp. 682–83, for excerpt of letter to Byrnes.
19. "Memorandum for the Record," Eisenhower Diary, 19 August 1953, Whitman File (Diary Series), Box 2, E.P.L.
20. Ibid.
21. Telephone call, Eisenhower Diary, 5 November 1953, Whitman File (Diary Series), Box 3, E.P.L.
22. Ibid.
23. Contrary to this view, see Eisenhower's somewhat amorphous handling of this point in Eisenhower, *Waging Peace,* p. 150.
24. Telephone call, Eisenhower Diary, 16 November 1953, Whitman File (Diary Series), Box 3, E.P.L.
25. Ibid.
26. Ibid.
27. Transcript of presidential press conference, 18 November 1953, Whitman File (Press Conference Series), Box 1, E.P.L.
28. James F. Byrnes to Eisenhower, 20 November 1953, O.F., Box 731, E.P.L.
29. Ibid.
30. Robert F. Kennon to Eisenhower, 20 November 1953, O.F., Box 731, E.P.L.

31. Ibid.
32. Ibid.
33. Eisenhower to James F. Byrnes, 30 November 1953, O.F., Box 731, E.P.L.; and Eisenhower to Robert F. Kennon, 30 November 1953, O.F., Box 731, E.P.L.
34. Eisenhower to James F. Byrnes, Eisenhower Diary, 1 December 1953, Whitman File (Diary Series), Box 2, E.P.L. When the president called Brownell regarding a paragraph in his 1 December 1953 letter to Byrnes, the attorney general informed him that Chief Justice Warren had stated that the administration's brief in the *Brown* case was excellent. Telephone call, Eisenhower Diary, 2 December 1953, Whitman File (Diary Series), Box 3, E.P.L.
35. Eisenhower to James F. Byrnes, 1 December 1953, Whitman File (Name Series), Box 3, E.P.L.
36. Ibid.
37. Ibid.
38. Ibid.
39. Ibid.
40. "Informal Remarks of the President," 10 March 1954, President's Personal File (hereafter cited as P.P.F.), Box 829, E.P.L.
41. Transcript of presidential press conference, 24 March 1954, Whitman File (Press Conference Series), Box 2, E.P.L.
42. Ibid.
43. Emmet John Hughes, *The Ordeal of Power: A Political Memoir of the Eisenhower Years* (New York: Atheneum, 1963), p. 243.

Chapter 5

1. Republican National Committee Papers, News Clippings—Editorials (hereafter cited as N.C.E.), Box 608, E.P.L.
2. "Equal Rights Are for All," *San Francisco Chronicle,* 18 May 1954, p. 18, N.C.E., Box 608, E.P.L.
3. "A Great Blow," *New York Journal American,* 19 May 1954, N.C.E., Box 608, E.P.L.

4. Mason Rossiter Smith, "South's Editors Answer Supreme Court on Ruling," *Cleveland Plain Dealer,* 31 May 1954, N.C.E., Box 608, E.P.L.

5. Ibid.

6. Ibid.

7. Ibid.

8. "Southern Press Reaction," *Washington Evening Star,* 18 May 1954, sec. A, p. 2, N.C.E., Box 608, E.P.L.

9. Ibid.

10. Ibid.

11. Editorial, "Segregation Decision," *Crisis,* June–July 1954, p. 352; see also, Editorial, "Report on Desegregation," *Crisis,* December 1954, p. 613; and Editorial, "Facing 1955," *Crisis,* January 1955, p. 34.

12. "Segregation Decision," p. 352.

13. Ibid.

14. Ibid., p. 353; see also, Wagner Jackson, "Implementing Desegregation," *Crisis,* January 1955, p. 5.

15. *N.A.A.C.P. Annual Report* (New York: 1954), p. 23.

16. Ibid., p. 25.

17. Ibid., p. 24.

18. Ibid.

19. Ibid., p. 27.

20. Ibid.

21. "Brief for Appellants in Nos. 1, 2, and 3 and for Respondents in No. 5 on Further Reargument," 15 November 1954, vol. 4, *Transcripts,* p. 10.

22. Ibid., p. 11.

23. Ibid., pp. 16–18.

24. Ibid., p. 24.

25. Ibid.

26. Ibid., p. 31.

27. Ibid.; see also, Blaustein and Ferguson, pp. 165–66.

28. "Memorandum Brief for Appellants in Nos. 1, 2, and 3 and for Respondents in No. 5 on Further Reargument with Respect to the Effect of the Court's Decree," 6 May 1955, vol. 4, *Transcripts,* p. 10.

Chapter 6

1. John H. Popham, "Reaction of South," *New York Times,* 18 May 1954, p. 23, N.C.E., Box 608, E.P.L.
2. Ibid.
3. Ibid.
4. Ibid., pp. 1 and 23.
5. Ibid., p. 23; and Georgia Department of Law, "Opinions of Attorney General Eugene Cook," vol. 1 (Atlanta, Georgia: 15 October 1954), pp. 1–4, Attorney General's File on *Brown* v. *Board of Education of Topeka*, Box 851, Kansas State Historical Society.
6. Warren Unna, "Talmadge Defies High Court's Ruling," *Washington Post and Times Herald,* 19 May 1954, Republican National Committee Papers, News Clippings—Miscellaneous Comments (hereafter cited as N.C.M.C.), Box 608, E.P.L.
7. "Most Violent Stand Taken by Talmadge," *Washington Evening Star,* 18 May 1954, sec. A, p. 6, N.C.M.C., Box 608, E.P.L.
8. W. D. Workman, Jr., "Court Ruling Becomes S.C. Political Issue," *Charlotte* (North Carolina) *Observer,* 19 May 1954, N.C.M.C., Box 608, E.P.L.
9. Robert C. Albright, "School Ruling Becomes No. 1 Political Football," *Washington Post and Times Herald,* 19 May 1954, N.C.M.C., Box 608, E.P.L.
10. Philip Dodd, "South May Ignore Ruling on Segregation," *Chicago Tribune,* 23 May 1954, sec. 1, p. 5; see also, Frank Van Der Linden, "Carolina Congressmen Warn Against Violence, Bloodshed," *Charlotte* (North Carolina) *Observer,* 18 May 1954, Robert C. Albright, "Southerners Assail High Court Ruling," *Washington Post and Times Herald,* 18 May 1954, p. 1; and Gerald Griffin, "Dixie Senators Rap Ban on Segregation," *Baltimore Sun,* 19 May 1954, p. 1, N.C.M.C., Box 608, E.P.L.
11. Albright, "Southerners Assail High Court Ruling," p. 1.
12. "Eastland Denounces High Court," *New York Herald Tribune,* 28 May 1954, N.C.M.C., Box 608, E.P.L.

13. Ibid.
14. Ibid.
15. G. Theodore Mitau, *Decade of Decision: The Supreme Court and the Constitutional Revolution, 1954–1964* (New York: Charles Scribner's Sons, 1967), pp. 3–8.
16. "Most of the South Looks for an Out," *Washington Daily News,* 18 May 1954, p. 3, N.C.M.C., Box 608, E.P.L.
17. Ibid.; see also, "Gov. Stanley to Call Va. Conference," *Washington Post and Times Herald,* 18 May 1954, N.C.M.C., Box 608, E.P.L.
18. Ibid.; and Popham, p. 23.
19. "Supplemental Brief for the Board of Education of Topeka, Kansas on Questions 4 and 5 Propounded by the Court," 27 September 1954, vol. 4, *Transcripts,* p. 5; and interview with Peter F. Caldwell, Attorney, Topeka, Kansas, 25 June 1970.
20. "Supplemental Brief for the State of Kansas on Questions 4 and 5 Propounded by the Court," 16 November 1954, vol. 4, *Transcripts,* pp. 13–22; and Clippings Collection entitled "Negroes," vol. 8—1953–1967, passim, Kansas State Historical Society.
21. "Supplemental Brief for the State of Kansas on Questions 4 and 5 Propounded by the Court," p. 23.
22. "Brief for Petitioners on the Mandate," 15 November 1954, vol. 10, *Transcripts,* pp. 4–10.
23. Ibid., pp. 19 and 24.
24. "Brief for Respondents on Formulation of Decree," 15 November 1954, vol. 8, *Transcripts,* pp. 1–3; and interview with Milton D. Korman, Superior Court Judge for the District of Columbia, Washington, D.C., 29 March 1972.
25. "Brief for Respondents on Formulation of Decree," p. 4.
26. "Brief for Appellees on Further Reargument," 15 November 1954, vol. 7, *Transcripts,* p. 2; and Blaustein and Ferguson, pp. 164–65.
27. "Brief for Appellees on Further Reargument," p. 2.
28. Ibid., p. 3.
29. Ibid.; see also, "*Amicus Curia* Brief of Attorney General of Florida on Form of Decree," 1 October 1954, vol. 12, *Tran-*

scripts, pp. 1–243; and "Brief of John Ben Shepperd, Attorney General of Texas, Amicus Curiae," 15 November 1954, vol. 12, *Transcripts,* p. 28.

30. "Brief for Appellees on Further Reargument," p. 4.
31. Ibid.
32. Ibid.
33. Ibid.

Chapter 7

1. Gould Lincoln, "Decision Drops Stock of Eisenhower in South," *Washington Evening Star,* 18 May 1954; Frank Van Der Linden, "Sen. Johnston Thinks Jonas Hurt by Ban," *Charlotte* (North Carolina) *Observer,* 19 May 1954; and Charles Lucey, "Political Spot Is on Schools," *Washington Daily News,* 18 May 1954, p. 2, N.C.M.C., Box 608, E.P.L.
2. Lincoln.
3. Hardy A. Sullivan to James C. Hagerty, 5 October 1954, General File (hereafter cited as G.F.), Box 918, E.P.L.
4. Ibid.
5. See, for example, Lincoln; and Lucey.
6. Eisenhower, *Waging Peace,* p. 150. There is ample evidence scattered throughout Eisenhower's personal correspondence and his public statements that proves the president's later position was consistent with that which he took while in office. See, for example, Eisenhower to Charles B. Shuman, 13 January 1959, Eisenhower Papers, Box 24, E.P.L.
7. Their works in order are: Hughes, pp. 241–45; Earl Warren, *The Memoirs of Earl Warren* (Garden City, N.Y.: Doubleday, 1977), p. 291; Kluger, p. 774; and Murphy, p. 315.
8. Hagerty Diary, 18 May 1954, Hagerty Papers, Box 1, E.P.L.
9. Transcript of presidential press conference, Hagerty Diary, 19 May 1954, Hagerty Papers, Box 1, E.P.L.
10. Ibid., pp. 1–2.
11. Transcript of presidential press conference, Hagerty Diary, 16 June 1954, Hagerty Papers, Box 1, E.P.L.
12. Telegram from Eisenhower to Walter White, 29 June 1954, P.P.F., Box 47, E.P.L.; see also, "Memorandum Brief for

Appellants in Nos. 1, 2, and 3 and for Respondents in No. 5 on Further Reargument with Respect to the Effect of the Court's Decree." The contrast between the president's and the NAACP's reaction to the *Brown* case is readily apparent in the editorials of *Crisis* in the initial months after it.

13. Hagerty Diary, 16 June 1954, Hagerty Papers, Box 1, E.P.L.
14. Ibid.
15. Transcript of presidential press conference, Hagerty Diary, 7 July 1954, Hagerty Papers, Box 1, E.P.L.
16. Eisenhower to Swede Hazlett, 23 October 1954, Whitman File (Name Series), Box 18, E.P.L.
17. G.F., Boxes 908–19 and 922 contain the pro and con correspondence which the administration received regarding the 1954 school decision.
18. Maxwell M. Rabb to J. William Barba, 9 June 1954, G.F., Box 916, E.P.L.
19. J. William Barba to Mrs. John P. Hird, 12 July 1954, G.F., Box 918, E.P.L.
20. Maxwell M. Rabb to Reverend L. K. Jackson, 20 July 1954, G.F., Box 911, E.P.L.
21. Telegram from Eisenhower to Walter White, 29 June 1954, P.P.F., Box 47, E.P.L.
22. Ibid.
23. Ibid.
24. Transcript of presidential press conference, 23 November 1954, Morrow Papers, Box 11, E.P.L.
25. Telegram from J. K. Haynes and George Longe to Eisenhower, 25 November 1954, G.F., Box 916, E.P.L.; see also, McCloskey, *The American Supreme Court,* p. 217.
26. "Brief for the United States on the Further Argument of the Question of Relief," 24 November 1954, vol. 11, *Transcripts,* pp. 3–4; see also, Blaustein and Ferguson, pp. 163–64.
27. "Brief for the United States on the Further Argument on the Question of Relief," pp. 6–8.
28. Ibid., p. 27.
29. Ibid., p. 22.
30. "How to End Segregation," *New York Herald Tribune,* 16 November 1954, p. 18, N.C.E., Box 608, E.P.L.

Chapter 8

1. Transcript of presidential press conference, 8 February 1956, O.F., Box 732, E.P.L.

2. Ibid.

3. Ibid.

4. The Eisenhower administration's efforts to create a nonpartisan Civil Rights Commission were motivated to a large degree by such a desire. See, for example, "The Civil Rights Program—Proposed Statement of the Attorney General," 7 March 1956, Whitman File (Cabinet Series), Box 6, E.P.L.; and pre-press conference briefing, 29 February 1956, Whitman File (Press Conference Series), Box 4, E.P.L.

5. Claude O. Vardaman to Eisenhower, 11 February 1956, O.F., Box 732, E.P.L.

6. Bardolph, p. 475.

7. Transcript of presidential press conference, 29 February 1956, Whitman File (Press Conference Series), Box 4, E.P.L.

8. "Racial Tension and Civil Rights," 1 March 1956, Whitman File (Cabinet Series), Box 6, E.P.L.

9. Ibid., p. 4. Hoover repeated his warning in "Hoover Briefing," 6 November 1958, Whitman File (Cabinet Series), Box 12, E.P.L.

10. "The Civil Rights Program—Proposed Statement of the Attorney General," 7 March 1956, Whitman File (Cabinet Series), Box 6, E.P.L.

11. "Personal and Confidential Memorandum for the Attorney General," 9 March 1956, Whitman File (Cabinet Series), Box 6, E.P.L.

12. President's remarks attached to above memorandum, 9 March 1956, Whitman File (Cabinet Series), Box 6, E.P.L.

13. Ibid.

14. For copy of text, see Albert P. Blaustein and Robert L. Zangrando, eds., *Civil Rights and the American Negro: A Documentary History* (New York: Washington Square Press, 1968), pp. 451–53.

15. Transcript of presidential press conference, 14 March 1956, Whitman File (Press Conference Series), Box 4, E.P.L.

16. Ibid.
17. Ibid.; see also, Transcript of presidential press conference, 21 March 1956, Whitman File (Press Conference Series), Box 4, E.P.L.
18. Whitman Diary, 21 March 1956, Whitman File (Diary Series), Box 8, E.P.L.
19. Eisenhower to Billy Graham, 22 March 1956, Whitman File (Name Series), Box 16, E.P.L.
20. Ibid.
21. Ibid.
22. Billy Graham to Eisenhower, 27 March 1956, Whitman File (Name Series), Box 16, E.P.L.
23. Eisenhower to Billy Graham, 30 March 1956, Whitman File (Name Series), Box 16, E.P.L.
24. Ibid.; see also, Transcript of presidential press conference, 1 August 1956, Whitman File (Press Conference Series), Box 5, E.P.L., for his public reiteration of this belief.
25. Billy Graham to Eisenhower, 4 June 1956, Whitman File (Name Series), Box 16, E.P.L.
26. Warren, p. 289.
27. Ibid.; see also, Murphy, p. 315.
28. Transcript of presidential press conference, 14 March 1956, Whitman File (Press Conference Series), Box 4, E.P.L.
29. Telephone call, Eisenhower Diary, 21 March 1956, Whitman File (Diary Series), Box 5, E.P.L.
30. Eisenhower's writings, public and private, and his later oral history interview are punctuated with sharp denials that he had permitted political considerations to interfere with crucial national interest. See, for example, Eisenhower to Edgar Eisenhower, 23 March 1956, Whitman File (Name Series), Box 16, E.P.L.; and Dwight D. Eisenhower interview, Columbia Oral History Project (hereafter cited as C.O.H.P.), pp. 94–95, E.P.L.
31. Transcript of presidential press conference, 8 August 1956, Whitman File (Press Conference Series), Box 5, E.P.L.
32. Ibid.
33. Whitman Diary, 14 August 1956, Whitman File (Diary Series), Box 8, E.P.L.

34. Whitman Diary, 18 August 1956, Whitman File (Diary Series), Box 8, E.P.L.

35. Telephone call, Whitman Diary, 19 August 1956, Whitman File (Diary Series), Box 8, E.P.L.

36. Ibid. Ann Whitman notes that the president finally allowed the words "the Republican Party accepts" school desegregation in place of a statement of strong support in the platform.

37. Transcript of presidential press conference, 31 August 1956, Whitman File (Press Conference Series), Box 5, E.P.L.

38. Thurgood Marshall to Eisenhower, 6 September 1956, G.F., Box 916, E.P.L.

39. Ibid.

40. Ibid., p. 1.

41. Ibid., p. 2.

42. See, for example, William F. Rogers' remarks attached to memorandum from E. Frederic Morrow to James C. Hagerty, 11 September 1956, Hagerty Papers, Box 62, E.P.L.; and telegram from Herbert Brownell to chairman and members of the Anderson County Board of Education, Clinton, Tennessee, 4 December 1956, Staff Research File (Toner and Russell), Box 12, E.P.L.

43. Memorandum from E. Frederic Morrow to James C. Hagerty, 11 September 1956, Hagerty Papers, Box 62, E.P.L.

44. "Pre-press Conference Notes," 11 September 1956, Whitman File (Press Conference Series), Box 5, E.P.L.

45. Transcript of presidential press conference, 5 October 1956, Whitman File (Press Conference Series), Box 5, E.P.L.

46. *Gayle* v. *Browder,* 352 U.S. 903 (1956); for the administration's reaction to this case, see memorandum from Harold H. Healy, Jr. to Andrew Goodpaster, 8 February 1957, Staff Research File (Toner and Russell), Box 12, E.P.L.

47. "Pre-press Conference Briefing," 14 November 1956, Whitman File (Press Conference Series), Box 5, E.P.L.

48. Ibid.

49. See Shanley's summary of what he said, 27 March 1957, Hagerty Papers, Box 62, E.P.L.

50. "Pre-press Conference Briefing," 27 March 1957, Whitman File (Press Conference Series), Box 5, E.P.L.

51. LeRoy Collins to Eisenhower, 6 May 1957, G.F., Box 123, E.P.L.
52. Sherman Adams to LeRoy Collins, 10 May 1957, G.F., Box 123, E.P.L.
53. Memorandum from Maxwell M. Rabb to James C. Hagerty, 3 July 1957, Hagerty Papers, Box 63, E.P.L.
54. Whitman Diary, 19 November 1958, Whitman File (Diary Series), Box 10, E.P.L.
55. Whitman Diary, 10 July 1957, Whitman File (Diary Series), Box 9, E.P.L.
56. Eisenhower to James F. Byrnes, 23 July 1957, O.F., Box 430, E.P.L.
57. Eisenhower to Swede Hazlett, 22 July 1957, Whitman File (Name Series), Box 18, E.P.L.
58. Ibid., p. 5.
59. Ibid.
60. Ibid.
61. Ibid.
62. Ibid.

Chapter 9

1. Hughes, p. 242. Eisenhower condemned the amendment and blamed the emasculation of the civil rights bill on an unholy alliance of Democratic liberals and segregationists. Eisenhower, *Waging Peace,* pp. 148–76.
2. For a full chronology of the events at Little Rock, see *Arkansas Gazette* Editors, *Crisis in the South* (Little Rock: Gazette, 1959), pp. 98–104.
3. Transcript of presidential press conference, 14 March 1956, Whitman File (Press Conference Series), Box 4, E.P.L.; and Eisenhower to Swede Hazlett, 22 July 1957, Whitman File (Name Series), Box 18, E.P.L.
4. Telegram from Herbert Brownell to chairman and members of the Anderson County Board of Education, Clinton, Tennessee, 4 December 1956, Staff Research File (Toner and Russell), Box 12, E.P.L.; and Memorandum from John V. Lindsay to Albert P. Toner, 3 December 1956, Staff Research File (Toner and Russell), Box 12, E.P.L.

5. Eisenhower, C.O.H.P., p. 82; and Eisenhower, *Waging Peace,* p. 175.

6. Sherman Adams, *Firsthand Report* (New York: Harper and Brothers, 1961), p. 355.

7. *Arkansas Gazette* Editors, p. 94; and Eisenhower, *Waging Peace,* pp. 162–75.

8. *Arkansas Gazette* Editors, p. 94.

9. "Pre-press Conference Notes," 3 September 1957, Whitman File (Press Conference Series), Box 6, E.P.L.

10. Telegram from Eisenhower to Orval E. Faubus, 5 September 1957, Staff File (Morgan), Box 6, E.P.L.

11. Telephone call, 11 September 1957, Eisenhower Papers, Box 16, E.P.L.

12. Ibid.

13. Ibid.

14. Ibid.

15. Ibid.

16. Ibid., p. 2.

17. Press Release, 11 September 1957, Staff File (Morgan), Box 6, E.P.L.

18. "Notes Dictated by the President Concerning Visit of Governor Orval Faubus of Arkansas to Little Rock on September 14, 1957," Whitman Diary, 8 October 1957, Whitman File (Diary Series), Box 9, E.P.L.

19. Ibid.

20. Ibid.

21. Ibid.

22. Ibid.

23. Ibid.

24. Hughes, p. 244; and "Statement by the President" and "Statement by the Governor of Arkansas," 14 September 1957, Staff File (Morgan), Box 6, E.P.L.

25. "Statement by the President," 14 September 1957.

26. "Statement by the Governor of Arkansas," 14 September 1957.

27. Whitman Diary, 14 September 1957, Whitman File (Diary Series), Box 9, E.P.L.

28. Memorandum from Andrew Goodpaster to James C. Hagerty, 19 September 1957, Eisenhower Papers, Box 16, E.P.L.

29. Ibid.

30. *Arkansas Gazette* Editors, p. 95.

31. Telephone call, 20 September 1957, Eisenhower Papers, Box 16, E.P.L.

32. Ibid.

33. Ibid.

34. "Statement by the President," 21 September 1957, Staff File (Morgan), Box 6, E.P.L.

35. Presidential Proclamation No. 3204, 23 September 1957, Staff File (Morgan), Box 6, E.P.L.

36. Telephone call, 24 September 1957, Eisenhower Papers, Box 16, E.P.L.

37. Ibid.

38. Telegram from Woodrow Wilson Mann to Eisenhower, 24 September 1957, Hagerty Papers, Box 6, E.P.L.

39. Whitman Diary, 24 September 1957, Whitman File (Diary Series), Box 9, E.P.L.

40. Eisenhower to Alfred M. Gruenther, Whitman Diary, 24 September 1957, Whitman File (Diary Series), Box 9, E.P.L.

41. Ibid.

42. Ibid.

43. Ibid.

44. Whitman Diary, 24 September 1957, Whitman File (Diary Series), Box 9, E.P.L.

45. Eisenhower to Alfred M. Gruenther, Whitman Diary, 24 September 1957, Whitman File (Diary Series), Box 9, E.P.L.

46. Executive Order No. 10730, 24 September 1957, Staff File (Morgan), Box 6, E.P.L.

47. Presidential address on television and radio, 24 September 1957, Staff File (Morgan), Box 6, E.P.L.

48. Ibid.

49. Ibid., p. 2.

50. Ibid., p. 3.

51. Ibid.

52. Ibid., p. 4.

53. Ibid.
54. Whitman Diary, 14–30 September 1957, Whitman File (Diary Series), Box 9, E.P.L.; and Memorandum from Bryce Harlow to Sherman Adams, 1 October 1957, Staff File (Harlow), Box 11, E.P.L.
55. *Arkansas Gazette* Editors, p. 95.
56. Telegram from Richard Russell to Eisenhower, 26 September 1957, Staff File (Harlow), Box 11, E.P.L.
57. Ibid.
58. Telegram from Eisenhower to Richard Russell, 28 September 1957, Staff File (Harlow), Box 11, E.P.L.
59. Ibid.
60. Ibid.
61. Undated draft of letter from Wilbur M. Brucker to Richard Russell, Staff File (Harlow), Box 11, E.P.L.
62. Whitman Diary, 14–30 September 1957, Whitman File (Diary Series), Box 9, E.P.L.
63. Press Release, 1 October 1957, Hagerty Papers, Box 6, E.P.L.
64. Ibid.
65. "Press Conference Notes," 3 October 1957, Eisenhower Papers, Box 16, E.P.L.
66. "Statement by the President," 1 October 1957, Hagerty Papers, Box 6, E.P.L.
67. "Notes on the Legal Principles That Have Guided the President," 3 October 1957, Staff File (McPhee), Box 4, E.P.L.
68. Eisenhower to Walter T. Forbes, 8 October 1957, O.F., Box 732, E.P.L.; and Warren Olney III, "A Government Lawyer Looks at Little Rock," *California Law Review* 45 (October 1957):516–23. For a comprehensive legal justification of the president's actions, see Herbert Brownell, "President's Power to Use Federal Troops to Suppress Resistance to Enforcement of Federal Court Orders—Little Rock, Arkansas," in *Official Opinions of Attorney General,* vol. 41—1949–1960 (Washington, D.C.: Government Printing Office, 1963), pp. 313–32.
69. "Press Conference Notes," 3 October 1957, Eisenhower Papers, Box 16, E.P.L.

70. Ibid., p. 2.
71. Ibid.
72. Ibid., p. 3.
73. *Arkansas Gazette* Editors, p. 95.
74. Memorandum by Andrew Goodpaster, Eisenhower Diary, 15 October 1957, Whitman File (Diary Series), Box 16, E.P.L.
75. Memorandum from Maxwell M. Rabb to Sherman Adams, 16 October 1957, Cabinet Secretariat Papers, Box 25, E.P.L.
76. Telephone call, Eisenhower Diary, 19 October 1957, Whitman File (Diary Series), Box 16, E.P.L.
77. Telephone call, 19 October 1957, Staff File (McPhee), Box 4, E.P.L.
78. Eisenhower, *Waging Peace,* p. 175.
79. *Arkansas Gazette* Editors, p. 96.
80. Ibid.
81. Parmet, p. 513.
82. "Pre-press Conference Notes," 30 October 1957, Whitman File (Press Conference Series), Box 16, E.P.L.
83. *Arkansas Gazette* Editors, p. 96.
84. Eisenhower, *Waging Peace,* p. 175.
85. *Arkansas Gazette* Editors, passim; and Wilson Record and Jane Cassels Record, eds., *Little Rock, U.S.A.: Materials for Analysis* (San Francisco: Chandler, 1960), pp. 170–307.
86. Virgil T. Blossom, *It Has Happened Here* (New York: Harper and Brothers, 1959), pp. 86–87.
87. See Record and Record for a detailed analysis of the various forms of these criticisms, passim.
88. Eisenhower to Ogden R. Reid, 28 September 1957, P.P.F., Box 232, E.P.L.

Chapter 10

1. Eisenhower to I. T. Wyche, 21 October 1957, O.F., Box 732, E.P.L.; see also, Eisenhower to Ralph McGill, 4 November 1957, O.F., Box 732, E.P.L.
2. Memorandum from Maxwell M. Rabb to Sherman Adams, 12 November 1957, Staff File (Morgan), Box 6, E.P.L.

3. Ibid., pp. 1–2.
4. "Confidential Memorandum for the Files," 4 December 1958, Cabinet Secretariat Papers, Box 2, E.P.L.
5. Anthony Lewis, "Negro Leaders Criticize 'Patience' Advice," *New York Times,* 14 May 1957, p. 20; see also, Parmet, p. 553.
6. "Memorandum for the Files," 24 June 1958, O.F., Box 731, E.P.L.
7. Ibid., pp. 1–2.
8. Ibid.
9. Ibid., p. 3.
10. Ibid.
11. Ibid.
12. Ibid.
13. Ibid.
14. Ibid., p. 4.
15. Ibid.
16. Ibid.
17. Ibid.
18. Parmet, p. 512, argues contrary to this author that the conference went smoothly and reflected basic agreement between the president and the leaders.
19. "Pre-press Conference Notes," 6 August 1958, Whitman File (Press Conference Series), Box 7, E.P.L.
20. Ibid.
21. Eisenhower to Ralph McGill, 3 October 1958, O.F., Box 732, E.P.L.
22. "Excerpts from President's Press Conference re Civil Rights," 21 January 1959, Morrow Papers, Box 11, E.P.L.
23. Ibid., p. 3.
24. Ibid., p. 4.
25. Eisenhower to Charles B. Shuman, 13 January 1959, Eisenhower Papers, Box 24, E.P.L.
26. Eisenhower, *Waging Peace,* pp. 161–62.
27. Whitman Diary, 19 November 1958, Whitman File (Diary Series), Box 10, E.P.L.
28. "Memorandum for the President," 28 January 1959, Staff File (McPhee), Box 3, E.P.L.

29. Ibid., p. 2.
30. Ibid., p. 3.
31. Ibid., p. 4.
32. "Notes on Legislative Meeting," 3 February 1959, Whitman File (Legislative Meeting Series), Box 3, E.P.L.
33. Ibid., p. 6.
34. Ibid.
35. Ibid., p. 7.
36. Ibid.
37. Presidential Address to Congress, 5 February 1959, Areeda Papers, Box 7, E.P.L.
38. "Notes on Legislative Meeting," 3 February 1959, Whitman File (Legislative Meeting Series), Box 3, E.P.L.
39. "Notes on Legislative Meeting," 17 February 1959, Whitman File (Legislative Meeting Series), Box 3, E.P.L.
40. Ibid.
41. Ibid., p. 5.
42. Cabinet Minutes, 27 February 1959, Whitman File (Cabinet Series), Box 13, E.P.L.; and Memorandum from Robert Gray to John Hannah, 3 March 1959, Whitman File (Cabinet Series), Box 13, E.P.L.
43. Cabinet Minutes, 27 February 1959, Whitman File (Cabinet Series), Box 13, E.P.L.
44. "Notes on Legislative Meeting," 2 June 1959, Whitman File (Legislative Meeting Series), Box 3, E.P.L.
45. "Notes on Legislative Meeting," 11 August 1959, Whitman File (Legislative Meeting Series), Box 3, E.P.L.; see also, "Notes on Legislative Meeting," 8 September 1959, Whitman File (Legislative Meeting Series), Box 3, E.P.L.
46. Pending Civil Rights Proposals, 3 February 1960, Staff File (McPhee), Box 4, E.P.L.
47. Staff Notes, 20 January 1960, Eisenhower Papers, Box 30, E.P.L.
48. "Notes on Legislative Meeting," 2 February 1960, Whitman File (Legislative Meeting Series), Box 3, E.P.L.
49. Ibid., p. 3.
50. "Notes on Legislative Meeting," 8 March 1960, Whitman File (Legislative Meeting Series), Box 3, E.P.L.

51. Ibid., p. 8.
52. "Excerpt from President's Press Conference," 16 March 1960, Morrow Papers, Box 10, E.P.L.
53. Civil Rights Act, 74 Stat. 86 (1960).
54. Blaustein and Zangrando, p. 477.
55. "Notes on Legislative Meeting," 26 April 1960, Whitman File (Legislative Meeting Series), Box 3, E.P.L.
56. Notes on Legislative Meeting," 16 August 1960, Whitman File (Legislative Meeting Series), Box 3, E.P.L.
57. Telegram from Jacob K. Javits to Eisenhower, 1 December 1960, O.F., Box 732, E.P.L.
58. Ibid.
59. Eisenhower to Jacob K. Javits, 1 December 1960, O.F., Box 732, E.P.L.

Chapter 11

1. Dwight D. Eisenhower, *Mandate for Change: 1953–1956* (New York: Signet Books, 1963), p. 595, describes the size of the classroom shortage; see also, Ralph F. DeBedts, *Recent American History,* vol. 2: *1945 to Present* (Homewood, Ill.: Dorsey Press, 1973), p. 116. Some idea of the intensity of the arguments which surrounded the federal aid issue can be obtained by scanning the articles on the subject which were cited in the *New York Times Index* under the topic listing "Federal Aid to Education" from 1954 to 1960. For a graphic illustration of the nature of the classroom shortage, see the diagrams in Arthur S. Link, *American Epoch,* vol. 3: *1938–1966* (New York: Alfred A. Knopf, 1963), pp. 653–57.
2. DeBedts, p. 62. Harry S. Truman, *Memoirs,* vol. 1: *Year of Decisions* (New York: Signet Books, 1955), p. 534, cites federal aid to education as high on a list of "Fair Deal" priorities. Goldman, pp. 56 and 95, gives some idea of the mood of Congress which led to the frustration of attempts to pass federal aid to education legislation in the Truman years.
3. See, for example, the following articles in the *New York Times*: "United States Chamber of Commerce Opposes Aid," 29 April 1954, p. 26; "Ford Foundation Division Report

Finds Southerners Lag Behind Rest of United States Despite Proportionately Higher Spending by Region: Suggest Federal Aid," 16 May 1954, p. 78; "Dr. Carr (N.E.A.) Urges More," 4 June 1954, p. 21; "H. C. Hoover Warns Against Seeking More Aid," 12 August 1954, p. 23; "American Teachers Federation Maps Legislative Drive for More," 20 August 1954, p. 9; "Tax Foundation Opposes Aid," 4 October 1954, p. 27; and "Megel Sees Showdown in Next Congress under Demo: Charges Eisenhower Administration Stalls on Issue," 29 December 1954, p. 29.

4. Eisenhower, *Mandate for Change,* p. 595; see also, "President Eisenhower Asks Limited Aid, But Warns Against Control, Filmed Speech to White House Education Conference," *New York Times,* 29 November 1955, p. 1; and transcript of press conference of HEW Secretary Oveta Culp Hobby, 14 October 1954, Hobby Papers, Box 49, E.P.L. Marion B. Folsom interview, C.O.H.P., pp. 22–23, E.P.L., notes opposition to the school construction bill among conservative Republican congressmen because of fear of federal control and among southern Democrats because of fear of integration. Ann Whitman notes that President Eisenhower "asserted that education teaching paternalism is not education; it is destroying citizenship, and he took strong exception to the pressure for centralizing and controlling education." "Supplemental Notes on Schools and Education," 8 February 1955, Whitman File (Legislative Meeting Series), Box 1, E.P.L.

5. Memorandum from secretary to Joseph M. Dodge attached to covering memorandum from N.A.R. to secretary, 15 February 1954, Hobby Papers, Box 19, E.P.L.

6. Ibid., p. 2.

7. Ibid.

8. Memorandum from Joseph M. Dodge to Oveta Culp Hobby, 8 January 1954, p. 1, Hobby Papers, Box 19, E.P.L.

9. See footnote 4 of this chapter. "Excerpt of Cabinet Discussion," 16 January 1959, Whitman File (Cabinet Series), Box 12, E.P.L., contains proof of Eisenhower's continued reservations about the wisdom of federal aid to education.

10. Eisenhower, *Mandate for Change,* p. 596.

11. Ibid.; DeBedts, p. 116; and Eisenhower, *Waging Peace,* pp. 216–17; see also, Hobby Papers, Box 44, E.P.L., for a variety of materials reflecting this position as HEW worked with the White House staff to develop the administration's legislative program.

12. Transcript of press conference of HEW Secretary Oveta Culp Hobby, 14 October 1954, p. 15, Hobby Papers, Box 49, E.P.L.

13. Ibid., pp. 15–16. Such a position was completely consistent with Eisenhower's decision at the beginning of his presidency to defer action on the development of a detailed civil rights program until the courts had decided key issues dealing with the national segregation problem. Maxwell M. Rabb interview, C.O.H.P., pp. 11–13, E.P.L.; and Eisenhower, *Mandate for Change,* pp. 292–94.

14. See Eisenhower, *Mandate for Change,* p. 596, for a brief summary of the plan.

15. Roy Wilkins to Sherman Adams, 4 February 1955, G.F., Box 127, E.P.L.

16. Hagerty Diary, 9 February 1955, Hagerty Papers, Box 1, E.P.L.

17. Transcript of press conference of HEW Secretary Oveta Culp Hobby, 10 February 1955, p. 43, Hobby Papers, Box 49, E.P.L.

18. Herbert Zelenko to Eisenhower, 30 March 1955, O.F., Box 731, E.P.L.

19. U.S., Congress, House, Committee on Education and Labor, *Proposed Legislation for Federal Assistance to States for School-Construction Purposes,* 84th Cong., 1st sess., 3–24 May 1955, Part 3, p. 824.

20. Memorandum from Bryce N. Harlow to Oveta Culp Hobby, 2 April 1955, O.F., Box 731, E.P.L.

21. Memorandum from Roswell B. Perkins to Bryce N. Harlow and attached draft, 18 April 1955, O.F., Box 731, E.P.L.; see also, "Press Conference Notes," 29 March 1955, Hobby Papers, Box 57, E.P.L., for a statement of HEW's rationale for keeping the school construction and school desegregation issues separate.

22. Bryce N. Harlow to Herbert Zelenko, 21 April 1955, Staff File (Morgan), Box 6, E.P.L.

23. Ibid.

24. Ibid.

25. "Statement on School Construction," 22 April 1955, Hobby Papers, Box 44, E.P.L.

26. Ibid., p. 12.

27. Ibid., p. 13.

28. Ibid., p. 14.

29. Ibid., p. 15.

30. Transcript of presidential press conference, 8 June 1955, p. 5, Whitman File (Press Conference Series), Box 3, E.P.L.

31. "Excerpt from July 7, 1955, *New York Times,* p. 16, President's Press Conference," O.F., Box 544, E.P.L.

32. Ibid. Secretary Hobby also reaffirmed the administration's faith in gradual court-directed implementation of desegregation in a 20 July 1955 letter to Congressman Emanual Celler, chairman of the House Judiciary Committee, during hearings on proposed civil rights legislation. Hobby Papers, Box 19, E.P.L.

33. Transcript of presidential press conference, 25 January 1956, p. 1, Whitman File (Press Conference Series), Box 4, E.P.L.

34. Ibid., p. 2.

35. "Supplemental Notes by L. A. Minnich on January 10, 1956," Whitman File (Legislative Meeting Series), Box 2, E.P.L.

36. Ibid.

37. Memorandum from L. A. Minnich to Rowland R. Hughes, 24 January 1956, Whitman File (Legislative Meeting Series), Box 2, E.P.L.

38. "War and Peace in Ike's Favor," *Washington Post,* 7 August 1955, O.F., Box 731, E.P.L.

39. Maxwell M. Rabb to Howard Pyle, 8 August 1955, O.F., Box 731, E.P.L. For an interesting discussion of how Rabb came to handle race relations problems in the administration and the approach that he developed to them, see Rabb, C.O.H.P., pp. 2–6.

40. Memorandum from Maxwell M. Rabb to Howard Pyle, 8 August 1955, O.F., Box 731, E.P.L.

41. Memorandum from Joseph H. Douglass to Maxwell M. Rabb, 22 December 1955, Morrow Papers, Box 11, E.P.L.
42. Ibid., pp. 1–3.
43. Ibid., p. 3.

Chapter 12

1. "Conference Adopts Report Prepared by Supt. Wanamaker, Dr. Fuller Backing Aid to Finance Operations," *New York Times,* 2 December 1955, p. 22.
2. Eisenhower, *Mandate for Change,* p. 596. Secretary Hobby emphasized that questions about the desegregation issue caused sharp divisions and should be left for local solution and not discussed at the conference. "Draft of Suggested Homework for Participants," n.d., pp. 1–7, Hobby Papers, Box 21, E.P.L.
3. Eisenhower, *Mandate for Change,* p. 654.
4. Ibid.
5. "Excerpts from Editorials on the President's Education Message," O.F., Box 544, E.P.L.
6. Ibid., p. 1.
7. Eisenhower, *Mandate for Change,* p. 654; and Eisenhower, *Waging Peace,* p. 140. In 1956, the House voted against school construction with the Powell Amendment attached by a 224 to 194 margin and the following year by a 208 to 203 margin.
8. Thomas Ludlow Ashley, Charles A. Boyle, Frank M. Clark, Edith Green, Don Hayworth, James M. Quigley, Henry S. Reuss, and George M. Rhodes to Eisenhower, 10 February 1956, O.F., Box 546, E.P.L.
9. Ibid., p. 1.
10. Ibid.
11. Ibid.
12. Ibid., p. 2.
13. Ibid.
14. Ibid.
15. Ibid.
16. Ibid.

17. Ibid., p. 3.
18. Ibid.
19. Memorandum from Bryce N. Harlow to J. Lee Rankin, 13 February 1956, O.F., Box 546, E.P.L.
20. Memorandum from J. Lee Rankin to Bryce N. Harlow, 21 February 1956, O.F., Box 546, E.P.L.
21. See, for example, Bryce N. Harlow to Don Hayworth, 1 March 1956, O.F., Box 546, E.P.L.
22. Ibid., p. 2.
23. Ibid.
24. Ashley, Boyle, Clark, Green, Hayworth, Quigley, Ruess, and Rhodes to Eisenhower, 6 March 1956, O.F., Box 546, E.P.L.
25. Ibid., p. 1.
26. Ibid.
27. Ibid., p. 2.
28. Ibid.
29. Bryce N. Harlow to Gerald D. Morgan, 8 March 1956, O.F., Box 546, E.P.L.
30. See, for example, Gerald D. Morgan to George M. Rhodes, 15 March 1956, O.F., Box 546, E.P.L.
31. Ibid.
32. Memorandum from attorney general to Murray Snyder, 6 March 1956, Hagerty Papers, Box 61, E.P.L.
33. Transcript of presidential press conference, 14 March 1956, Whitman File (Press Conference Series), Box 4, E.P.L.
34. Transcript of presidential press conference, 21 March 1956, Whitman File (Press Conference Series), Box 4, E.P.L.
35. Eisenhower, *Mandate for Change,* p. 654; and Eisenhower, *Waging Peace,* p. 140.
36. Memorandum from Russell I. Thackrey to Samuel M. Brownell, 10 February 1956, O.F., Box 548, E.P.L.
37. Ibid.
38. Ibid., p. 2. Samuel M. Brownell notes that after the 1954 decision, Assistant HEW Secretary Roswell Perkins studied the situation and recommended cutting off funds if there was no desegregation of land-grant schools. When HEW sought advice from the Justice Department concerning that position, Assistant Attorney General J. Lee Rankin asserted that though

it was a matter for HEW to decide, the Justice Department would not support a fund cutoff. Its position was that there should be no meeting with land-grant college administrators and no fund cutoff for the time being. The result, according to Brownell, was that an opportunity was missed to bring college officials together to initiate positive steps toward desegregation at the university level. Samuel M. Brownell interview, C.O.H.P., pp. 76–78, E.P.L.

39. Memorandum from Maxwell M. Rabb to Bryce N. Harlow, 27 March 1956, Staff File (Harlow), Box 8, E.P.L.

40. U.S. Congress, House, 26 March 1956, *Congressional Record,* p. 5008.

41. John Dingell to Eisenhower, 27 January 1956, G.F., Box 2, E.P.L.

42. Gerald D. Morgan to John Dingell, 15 March 1956, G.F., Box 2, E.P.L.

43. John Dingell to Eisenhower, 27 January 1956, p. 2, G.F., Box 2, E.P.L.

44. Memorandum from Maxwell M. Rabb to Bryce N. Harlow, 27 March 1956, Staff File (Harlow), Box 8, E.P.L.

45. Memorandum from Val Peterson to Maxwell M. Rabb, 3 February 1954, Whitman File (Cabinet Series), Box 4, E.P.L.

46. "Remarks by Rep. Stewart L. Udall on Introducing Federal Aid Bill to Implement the School Integration Decision of the United States Supreme Court," G.F., Box 127, E.P.L.

47. Stewart L. Udall to Eisenhower, 15 June 1955, G.F., Box 127, E.P.L.

48. Bryce N. Harlow to Stewart L. Udall, 17 June 1955, G.F., Box 127, E.P.L.

49. Harold C. Hunt to Graham A. Barden, 27 March 1956, O.F., Box 544, E.P.L.

50. Ibid., p. 2.

51. Ibid.

52. Folsom speech draft, 27 April 1956, Staff File (Harlow), Box 21, E.P.L.

53. Memorandum and attached letter draft from Marion B. Folsom to Sherman Adams, 6 May 1956, O.F., Box 113, E.P.L.

54. Memorandum and attached letter draft, Marion B. Folsom to Sherman Adams, 6 May 1956, O.F., Box 113, E.P.L.
55. Folsom speech draft attached to memorandum from Bryce N. Harlow to Sherman Adams, 20 May 1956, O.F., Box 732, E.P.L.
56. Memorandum from Bryce N. Harlow to Sherman Adams, 20 May 1956, O.F., Box 732, E.P.L.
57. "Draft Statement for the President," 5 June 1956, Hagerty Papers, Box 59, E.P.L.
58. Ibid.
59. Ibid.
60. Ibid.
61. Ibid.
62. L. E. McConnell to secretary of the president, 2 October 1956, O.F., Box 549, E.P.L.
63. Lewis Arthur Minnich note on file card, n.d., O.F., Box 549, E.P.L.
64. Maxwell M. Rabb to L. E. McConnell, 31 October 1956, O.F., Box 549, E.P.L.
65. Carbon of secretary's notes, 10 May 1957, Whitman File (Cabinet Series), Box 9, E.P.L.
66. Ibid., p. 1.
67. Ibid., p. 2.
68. Ibid.
69. Ibid.
70. Eisenhower, *Waging Peace,* pp. 138–40. Charles S. Gubser, a moderate Republican California congressman, favored the school aid bill even with the Powell Amendment attached in 1956 and 1957. He provides an apt description of the confused parliamentary maneuvering which took place when the 1957 classroom bill came up for a vote. He emphasized that although the segregation issues played a role, despite Democratic charges that Eisenhower did not provide leadership, they also had to share blame because they waited until the last minute to support the president's proposal for limited school aid. Memorandum for the record, n.d., Gubser Papers, Box 219, Wichita State University Special Collections, Wichita, Kansas. HEW Secretary Marion B. Folsom explained the

bill's defeat as "due to the combination of the conservative Republicans, who didn't follow the President's wish, and the Southern Democrats who were against it because of integration." Folsom, C.O.H.P., p. 73.

Chapter 13

1. DeBedts, pp. 153–54.
2. "$887-Million, 4-Year Emergency Bill Signed," *New York Times,* 3 September 1958, p. 22. Southern congressmen's fears about desegregation caused many of them to oppose the NDEA of 1958. As Lyndon Johnson advised Folsom prior to the bill's passage: "They don't want to do anything for education. It's going to be a tough job to get that restored. I think you've got a good program and I'll do the best I can for you, but I don't know what I can do or how I can do it." Johnson did get the money for education restored. Folsom, C.O.H.P., p. 102; see also "Coverage of the Administration's Education Proposals," 2 January 1958, Staff Research File (Toner and Russell), Box 10, E.P.L.
3. Public Law 685-864, 2 September 1958, 2 Stat. 1580.
4. Presidential Address to Congress, 5 February 1959, p. 2, Hagerty Papers, Box 6, E.P.L. Evidence of the tough side of the administration's approach appears in a summation of ways to tighten enforcement of desegregation presented by HEW and Justice Department personnel in 1958. President's notes on White House stationery, Staff File (McPhee), Box 4, E.P.L.
5. Memorandum from Maurice H. Stans to Gen. Wilton B. Persons, 28 January 1959, Staff File (Morgan), Box 6, E.P.L.
6. Ibid., p. 2.
7. Presidential Address to Congress, 5 February 1959, pp. 1–2, Hagerty Papers, Box 6, E.P.L.
8. Ibid., p. 2.
9. Telegram from Adam Clayton Powell to Eisenhower, 20 May 1960, O.F., Box 549, E.P.L.
10. Ibid.

11. Gerald D. Morgan to Adam Clayton Powell, 24 May 1960, O.F., Box 549, E.P.L.
12. Ibid.
13. Ibid.
14. Jacob K. Javits to Eisenhower, 24 June 1960, O.F., Box 549, E.P.L.
15. Ibid.
16. Eisenhower to Jacob K. Javits, 29 June 1960, O.F., Box 549, E.P.L.
17. See, for example, Eisenhower's remarks in *Mandate for Change,* p. 654; and *Waging Peace,* p. 140.
18. Memorandum from James C. Hagerty to Eisenhower, 21 March 1960, Hagerty Papers, Box 9, E.P.L.
19. Ibid.
20. DeBedts, p. 116.
21. Eisenhower, *Mandate for Change,* p. 596. Folsom summarized the reasons for the failure of the administration's 1955 and 1956 attempts to secure school construction legislation. He emphasized two causes: the Powell Amendment and the failure of the Democratic congressional leadership to support a classroom construction bill. "Notes of Cabinet Meeting," 10 May 1957, Whitman File (Cabinet Series), Box 9, E.P.L.
22. See, for example, Ashley, Boyle, Clark, Green, Hayworth, Quigley, Reuss, and Rhodes to Eisenhower, 10 February 1956, O.F., Box 546, E.P.L.
23. See footnote 4 of chapter 11; Eisenhower, *Waging Peace,* p. 149; for Eisenhower's reservations about federal aid to education, see "Excerpt of Cabinet Discussion," 16 January 1959, Whitman File (Cabinet Series), Box 12, E.P.L.; see this author's edited version of it in " 'A Good Growl': The Eisenhower Cabinet's January 16, 1959 Discussion of Federal Aid to Education," *Presidential Studies Quarterly* 8 (Fall 1978): 434–44; for Eisenhower's reservations about the uses of the law to improve race relations, see Eisenhower Diary, 24 July 1953, Whitman File (Diary Series), Box 2, E.P.L.
24. See the biographical sketches of these advisors in Republican

National Committee, *White House Staff Book: 1953–1961* (Washington, D.C.: 1961), copy in E.P.L. Though very sympathetic to Eisenhower's approach, Maxwell M. Rabb admitted that he did feel that he preferred more forthright, vigorous action in some instances. Rabb, C.O.H.P., p. 19.

25. See, for example, memorandum from Bryce N. Harlow to Gerald D. Morgan, 8 March 1955, O.F., Box 546, E.P.L. Here, Harlow asserted that he and General Wilton B. Persons were leery of referring a letter from several congressmen regarding the school construction bill to the Justice Department for answer.

Chapter 14

1. Reichard, pp. ix and 237.
2. Murray Kempton, "The Underestimation of Dwight D. Eisenhower," in *America Since 1945,* eds. Robert D. Marcus and David Burner (New York: St. Martin's Press, 1972), pp. 107–14.
3. Richard H. Rovere, "Eisenhower Revisited—A Political Genius? A Brilliant Man?," in *America Since 1945,* eds. Robert D. Marcus and David Burner (New York: St. Martin's Press, 1972), pp. 115–24; see also, Arthur Larson, *Eisenhower: The President Nobody Knew* (New York: Charles Scribner's Sons, 1968), pp. 124–33.
4. Vincent P. De Santis, "Eisenhower Revisionism," *Journal of Politics* 38 (September 1976):190–207.
5. Maxwell M. Rabb to author, 25 April 1978.

Bibliography

**Dwight D. Eisenhower Presidential Library
Abilene, Kansas**

Phillip E. Areeda Papers
Cabinet Secretariat Papers
Dwight D. Eisenhower Papers
General File
James C. Hagerty Papers
Oveta Culp Hobby Papers
E. Frederic Morrow Papers
Official File
President's Personal File
Republican National Committee Papers (News Clippings—Editorials and Miscellaneous Comments)
Staff File (Bryce N. Harlow, Henry Roemer McPhee, Jr., and Gerald D. Morgan)
Staff Research File (Albert P. Toner and Christopher Harvey Russell)
Ann Whitman File (Cabinet, Diary, Legislative Meeting, Name, and Press Conference Series)

Kansas State Historical Society, Topeka, Kansas

Attorney General's File on *Brown* v. *Board of Education*
Clippings Collection entitled "Negroes." Vol. 7—1915–1952 and
vol. 8—1953–1967

Wichita State University Special Collections, Wichita, Kansas

Charles S. Gubser Papers

Columbia Oral History Project, Columbia University, New York

Brownell, Samuel M.
Bush, Prescott
Davis, John William
Eisenhower, Dwight D.
Folsom, Marion B.
Frankfurter, Felix
Granger, Lester
Krock, Arthur
Rabb, Maxwell M.
Waring, Julius Waties
Wilkins, Roy

Interviews

Caldwell, Peter F. Attorney, Topeka, Kansas. 25 June 1970.
Clark, Tom. United States Supreme Court Justice, Washington,
    D.C. 28 March 1972.
Katcher, Leo. Author, Wichita, Kansas. Spring 1971.
Kelly, Alfred H. Professor of History, Wayne State University,
    Detroit, Michigan. 22 July 1970.
Korman, Milton D. Superior Court Judge for the District of Co-
    lumbia, Washington, D.C. 29 March 1972.
Scott, Charles. Attorney, Topeka, Kansas. 25 June 1970.

Wilson, Paul E. Professor of Law, University of Kansas, Lawrence, Kansas. 19 June 1970.

Correspondence

Maxwell M. Rabb to author. 25 April 1978.

Government Documents

Brownell, Herbert. "President's Power to Use Federal Court Orders —Little Rock, Arkansas." *Official Opinions of Attorney General.* Vol. 41—1949–1960. Washington, D.C.: Government Printing Office, 1963, pp. 313–32.

President's Committee on Civil Rights. *To Secure These Rights.* Washington, D.C.: Government Printing Office, 1947.

Transcripts of Records and File Copies of Briefs, 1954. Vols. 4–12. United States Supreme Court Law Library, Washington, D.C.

U.S. Congress. House. Committee on Education and Labor. *Proposed Legislation for Federal Assistance to States for School-Construction Purposes,* 84th Cong., 1st sess., 3-24 May 1955.

U.S. Congress. House. 26 March 1956. *Congressional Record.*

Books

Adams, Sherman. *Firsthand Report.* New York: Harper and Brothers, 1961.

Alexander, Charles C. *Holding the Line: The Eisenhower Era, 1952–1961.* Bloomington: Indiana University Press, 1975.

Arkansas Gazette Editors. *Crisis in the South.* Little Rock (Ark.): Gazette, 1959.

Ashmore, Harry S. *The Negro and the Schools.* Chapel Hill: University of North Carolina Press, 1954.

Bardolph, Richard, ed. *The Civil Rights Record: Black Americans and the Law, 1849–1970.* New York: Thomas Y. Crowell, 1970.

Berman, William. *The Politics of Civil Rights in the Truman Administration.* Columbus: Ohio State University Press, 1970.

Billington, Ray Allen. *Westward Expansion: A History of the American Frontier.* 2nd ed. New York: Macmillan, 1960.

Blaustein, Albert P., and Ferguson, Clarence Clyde, Jr. *Desegregation and the Law: The Meaning and Effect of the School Segregation Cases.* 2nd ed. New York: Vintage Books, 1962.

Blaustein, Albert P., and Zangrando, Robert L., eds. *Civil Rights and the American Negro: A Documentary History.* New York: Washington Square Press, 1968.

Blossom, Virgil T. *It Has Happened Here.* New York: Harper and Brothers, 1959.

Buck, Paul H. *The Road to Reunion: 1865–1900.* New York: Vintage Books, 1959.

Cox, Archibald. *The Role of the Supreme Court in American Government.* New York: Oxford University Press, 1976.

DeBedts, Ralph F. *Recent American History.* Vol. 2: *1945 to Present.* Homewood, Ill.: Dorsey Press, 1973.

Degler, Carl N. *Out of Our Past: The Forces that Shaped Modern America.* New York: Harper and Row, 1970.

Eisenhower, Dwight D. *Mandate for Change: 1953–1956.* New York: Signet Books, 1963.

———. *Waging Peace: 1956–1961.* Garden City, N.Y.: Doubleday, 1965.

Franklin, John Hope. *Reconstruction: After the Civil War.* Chicago: University of Chicago Press, 1961.

Goldman, Eric F. *The Crucial Decade.* New York: Alfred A. Knopf, 1969.

Greenberg, Jack. *Race Relations and American Law.* New York: Columbia University Press, 1959.

Hays, Samuel P. *The Response to Industrialism: 1885–1914.* Chicago: University of Chicago Press, 1957.

Hill, Herbert, and Greenberg, Jack. *Citizen's Guide to Desegregation: A Study of Social and Legal Change in American Life.* Boston: Beacon Press, 1955.

Hixson, William B., Jr. *Moorfield Storey and the Abolitionist Tradition.* New York: Oxford University Press, 1972.

Hughes, Emmet John. *The Ordeal of Power: A Political Memoir of the Eisenhower Years.* New York: Atheneum, 1963.

Hyman, Harold M., ed. *The Radical Republicans and Reconstruction: 1861–1870.* Indianapolis, Ind.: Bobbs-Merrill, 1967.

Kellogg, Charles Flint. *NAACP: A History of the National Asso-*

ciation for the Advancement of Colored People. Vol. 1. Baltimore, Md.: Johns Hopkins Press, 1967.

Kelly, Alfred H. "The School Desegregation Case." In *Quarrels That Have Shaped the Constitution,* pp. 243–69. Edited by John Garraty. New York: Harper and Row, 1964.

Kelly, Alfred H., and Harbison, Winfred A. *The American Constitution: Its Origins and Development.* 4th ed. New York: W. W. Norton, 1970.

Kempton, Murray. "The Underestimation of Dwight D. Eisenhower." In *America Since 1945,* pp. 107–14. Edited by Robert D. Marcus and David Burner. New York: St. Martin's Press, 1972.

Kluger, Richard. *Simple Justice: The History of* Brown *v.* Board of Education *and Black America's Struggle for Equality.* New York: Alfred A. Knopf, 1976.

Larson, Arthur. *Eisenhower: The President Nobody Knew.* New York: Charles Scribner's Sons, 1968.

Leuchtenburg, William E. *Franklin D. Roosevelt and the New Deal: 1932–1940.* New York: Harper and Row, 1963.

Levy, Leonard W. *The Law of the Commonwealth and Chief Justice Shaw.* New York: Harper and Row, 1967.

Link, Arthur S. *American Epoch.* Vol. 3: *1938–1966.* New York: Alfred A. Knopf, 1963.

Logan, Rayford W. *The Betrayal of the Negro: From Rutherford B. Hayes to Woodrow Wilson.* New York: Collier Books, 1965.

McCloskey, Robert G. *American Conservatism in the Age of Enterprise, 1865–1910.* New York: Harper and Brothers, 1951.

———. *The American Supreme Court.* Chicago: University of Chicago Press, 1960.

Miller, Loren. *The Petitioners: The Story of the Supreme Court of the United States and the Negro.* Cleveland: World, 1966.

Mitau, G. Theodore. *Decade of Decision: The Supreme Court and the Constitutional Revolution, 1954–1964.* New York: Charles Scribner's Sons, 1967.

Murphy, Paul L. *The Constitution in Crisis Times.* New York: Harper and Row, 1972.

N.A.A.C.P. Annual Report. New York: 1934, 1954, and 1955.

Ovington, Mary White. *The Walls Came Tumbling Down: The Autobiography of Mary White Ovington.* New York: Schocken Books, 1970.

Parmet, Herbert S. *Eisenhower and the American Crusades.* New York: Macmillan, 1972.

Record, Wilson, and Record, Jane Cassels, eds. *Little Rock, U.S.A.: Materials for Analysis.* San Francisco: Chandler, 1960.

Reichard, Gary W. *The Reaffirmation of Republicanism: Eisenhower and the Eighty-third Congress.* Knoxville: University of Tennessee Press, 1975.

Republican National Committee. *White House Staff Book: 1953–1961.* Washington, D.C.: 1961.

Rovere, Richard H. "Eisenhower Revisited—A Political Genius? A Brilliant Man?" In *America Since 1945,* pp. 115–24. Edited by Robert D. Marcus and David Burner. New York: St. Martin's Press, 1972.

Stampp, Kenneth M. *The Era of Reconstruction: 1865–1877.* New York: Random House, 1965.

Stephenson, Gilbert T. *Race Distinctions in American Law.* New York: Association Press, 1911.

Truman, Harry S. *Memoirs.* Vol. 1: *Year of Decisions.* New York: Signet Books, 1955.

Warren, Earl. *The Memoirs of Earl Warren.* Garden City, N.Y.: Doubleday, 1977.

Westin, Alan F. "The Case of the Prejudiced Doorkeeper." In *Quarrels That Have Shaped the Constitution,* pp. 128–44. Edited by John Garraty. New York: Harper and Row, 1964.

Wharton, Vernon Lane. *The Negro in Mississippi: 1865–1890.* New York: Harper and Row, 1970.

Woodward, C. Vann. "The Case of the Louisiana Traveler." In *Quarrels That Have Shaped the Constitution,* pp. 145–58. Edited by John Garraty. New York: Harper and Row, 1964.

———. *Reunion and Reaction: The Compromise of 1877 and the End of Reconstruction.* Garden City, N.Y.: Doubleday, 1956.

———. *The Strange Career of Jim Crow.* New York: Oxford University Press, 1957.

Articles

Crisis, 1926–1960.

De Santis, Vincent P. "Eisenhower Revisionism." *Journal of Politics* 38 (September 1976):190–207.

Duram, James C. " 'A Good Growl': The Eisenhower Cabinet's January 16, 1959 Discussion of Federal Aid to Education." *Presidential Studies Quarterly* 8 (Fall 1978):434–44.

"Equal Protection—Admission of Negro to State University Law School." *University of Pennsylvania Law Review* 87 (February 1939):478–80.

"Exclusion of Negroes from State Supported Professional Schools." *Yale Law Journal* 45 (May 1936):1296–1301.

Green, Clifford S. "The Fourteenth Amendment and Racial Segregation in State-Supported Schools." *Temple Law Quarterly* 24 (October 1950):222–25.

Jacobs, Donald M. "The Nineteenth Century Struggle Over Segregated Education in the Boston Schools." *Journal of Negro Education* 39 (Winter 1970):76–85.

Kelly, Alfred H. "The Congressional Controversy over School Segregation, 1867–1875." *American Historical Review* 64 (April 1959):537–63.

Levy, Leonard W., and Phillips, Harlan B. "The *Roberts* Case: Source of the 'Separate But Equal' Doctrine." *American Historical Review* 56 (April 1951):510–18.

Olney, Warren III. "A Government Lawyer Looks at Little Rock." *California Law Review* 45 (October 1957):516–23.

Richardson, Elmo. "Working on Ike." *Pacific Northwest Quarterly* 68 (July 1977):141–42.

Seegert, Neal. "Fourteenth Amendment—Equal Protection of the Laws—Racial Segregation in Public Institution." *Michigan Law Review* 46 (March 1948):639–45.

Newspapers

"Colored Children in the Boston Public Schools." *Baltimore Sun,* 7 September 1855, p. 2.

New York Times, 1950–1960.

Unpublished Material

Bunting, Robert R. "School Segregation in Kansas: A Study in Constitutional and Political Development." M.A. thesis, Wichita State University, 1972.

Index